Melanie Moll, Maria Hehle-Fritsch (eds.)

Intercultural Management
Dimensions of the Modern Workplace

"This collection offers valuable insights into the complexities of intercultural management, providing practical examples from various industries that underscore the importance of cultural intelligence in the global workplace. The diverse range of topics explored in these chapters emphasizes the importance of cultural intelligence in fostering leadership, ethical decision-making, and effective global collaboration."

Dr Colleen O'Brien Cherry, Associate Director of Foundation Relations Anthropologist, University of Georgia, Athens, GA

"In today's globally interconnected world, intercultural awareness is more crucial than ever, especially in the workplace. As businesses expand across borders and teams become increasingly diverse, navigating cultural differences becomes key to success. The insights presented in this book offer valuable strategies for improving cooperation and understanding in the workplace—benefiting not only businesses but society at large, especially in a time of global crises and rising nationalism."

Viola Stoehr, co-founder and intercultural trainer, s.cope – team für interkulturelle kompetenz, Stuttgart, Germany

Melanie Moll, Maria Hehle-Fritsch (eds.)

INTERCULTURAL MANAGEMENT

Dimensions of the Modern Workplace

Bibliografische Information der Deutschen Nationalbibliothek
Die Deutsche Nationalbibliothek verzeichnet diese Publikation in der Deutschen Nationalbibliografie; detaillierte bibliografische Daten sind im Internet über http://dnb.d-nb.de abrufbar.

Bibliographic information published by the Deutsche Nationalbibliothek
The Deutsche Nationalbibliothek lists this publication in the Deutsche Nationalbibliografie; detailed bibliographic data are available on the Internet at http://dnb.d-nb.de.

Cover picture: ID 93921529 © Boarding1now | Dreamstime.com

ISBN (Print): 978-3-8382-2004-8
ISBN (E-Book [PDF]): 978-3-8382-8004-2
© *ibidem*-Verlag, Hannover • Stuttgart 2025

Leuschnerstraße 40
30457 Hannover
Germany / Deutschland
info@ibidem.eu

Alle Rechte vorbehalten

Das Werk einschließlich aller seiner Teile ist urheberrechtlich geschützt. Jede Verwertung außerhalb der engen Grenzen des Urheberrechtsgesetzes ist ohne Zustimmung des Verlages unzulässig und strafbar. Dies gilt insbesondere für Vervielfältigungen, Übersetzungen, Mikroverfilmungen und elektronische Speicherformen sowie die Einspeicherung und Verarbeitung in elektronischen Systemen.

All rights reserved. No part of this publication may be reproduced, stored in or introduced into a retrieval system, or transmitted, in any form, or by any means (electronic, mechanical, photocopying, recording or otherwise) without the prior written permission of the publisher. Any person who commits any unauthorized act in relation to this publication may be liable to criminal prosecution and civil claims for damages.

Printed in the EU

Foreword

When I met with my students to begin working on their thesis, we never anticipated that we would be writing a book!

Interacting with students in the Intercultural Management program at the Europäische Fernhochschule Hamburg began with exploring the many intercultural business experiences around us. These ranged from chain supplies in China to recruiting international workers for local companies. As the students moved into thesis writing, their topics arose from curiosity and the desire to better understand the workplace. Some examples were: How can the work in my organization be improved? How do recent global developments (e.g. pandemics, regional conflicts) affect or change my own working context?

We took those ideas and transformed them into critically relevant research questions. At times, designing the research process was more challenging as we looked at topics which had not been previously studied. Good communication between the student and supervisor was a necessity as we put together a methodology piece by piece. As a lecturer in the program, my anticipation grew until I saw the results in the completed thesis. Relating the findings back into the workplace was, and still is, informative and insightful.

Those of us who lead the Intercultural Management program recognized the importance of sharing the topics and findings to others outside our circle. Our objective in this first volume is to showcase the results of hard work and skill sets that our students display. While most students are non-native English speakers, they succeeded in crafting important, relevant works in English that further our understanding of intercultural interaction in the workplace, wherever that may be.

In short, we began by asking questions, and in the process, we wrote a book!

Congratulations to each student represented here, and to all readers of this volume, enjoy the reading journey.

Ruth Beck, Ph.D.
Lecturer, Intercultural Management (M.A.)
Europäische Fernhochschule Hamburg

Table of contents

Introduction 9
Prof. Dr. Melanie Moll

How Client Culture Affects B2B Service Providers 13
Dana Bieck

The Merck Schistosomiasis Elimination Program – From Philanthropy to Sustainable Investment in Global Health 51
Antonia Asche

Internationalization in Germany: How to Attract International, Intercultural Researchers to Work at Hamburg University of Technology (TUHH) 87
Anja Bernhardt

Communication patterns in a digital context 125
Anna Carolin Uhlig

Impact of cultural dimensions on airline booking behavior: A quantitative analysis of structure-seeking behavior of a multinational airline group 165
Daniel Thal

A disabler of cultural diversity: Unconscious bias in recruiting – How ethnicity affects the selection of applicants 199
Christiane Engler

The impact of culture on identity as evidenced through communication: A case study on expat women 239
Maria Hehle-Fritsch

Introduction

Today, we live in an environment that is made up of multiple cultures. People are consistently influenced by one another, and very few people are members of only a single cultural group. While multiculturalism has been criticized for various political reasons, the fact remains that most geographical regions are made up of mixed groups of people. This includes not only regional ethnicities and nationalities, but also differing age groups, religious groups, gender groups, and so forth. No one has just one identity, for example French, or Indonesian, or South African, or a woman, or a Catholic, and so on. People are made up of multiple, dynamic identities, and these identities themselves are often changing or adapting. It is in this sense that we can say we live in a multicultural world.

Because of this, all our interactions with one another must take multiculturalism into account. Being successful in a global market requires being aware of various preferences. True efficiency in business (or any global interaction) requires an attention to the norms and expectations of others. This, in our view, is the core of what we are presenting in this book. Successful **intercultural management** is the ability to act and interact with others in ways that lead to effective and positive outcomes or achievement of objectives.

While many of us have had at least some intercultural experiences, we may not realize the extent to which people need to understand one another. In other words, we might not be aware of how critical it is that we know what real intercultural competence means. Acting in a global context is much more than simply speaking the target language or even the lingua franca. We need to be aware of how we can best interact with others – through speech, but also through our actions, decisions, and so forth. If you wish to be effective in your own interactions, you will need to be equipped to deal with behavior that does not always match your own expectations. It is in this sense that we strongly urge global managers to be informed in intercultural matters. Being a successful intercultural manager in a global corporation involves getting along with coworkers of various cultural backgrounds; this sought-after quality helps people avoid serious misunderstandings and the building of invisible barriers. Companies are looking for people who have an understanding and awareness of cultural variables, and who know how to make sense of the world around them.

If you do a simple google search with the term 'intercultural management' you will find definitions which mostly include terms such as awareness, respect, norms, values, and so on. One important aspect of this construct is that it is a skill – this means that it can be learned! Some people might be more natural learners, but all of us can improve our cultural awareness skills. Having a strong ability to interact in a global environment is what is known as intercultural competence.

In this book, we strive to help you understand the wide range of interactions that are tightly tied to intercultural competence. This involves more than just communicating with language. It includes making decisions, displaying attitudes, understanding the many forms of scheduling, dealing with space issues, and the list goes on. Many intercultural management scholars reference the well-known iceberg model which represents both visible and invisible factors that influence behaviors. True intercultural management is aware of constructs *beneath* the surface of the water, in order to best adapt to and act on those elements *above* the surface of the water.

Our book pulls together a range of studies that examine the notion of intercultural management in differing fields. The studies are culled from theses in a master's program at the Europäische Fernhochschule Hamburg. Students in the program investigate various facets of business and the workplace in order to determine how intercultural factors influence individual behavior, what we can learn from it, and where future research efforts could be invested.

Our objective is to showcase some of the research being done in our program, as well as to assist you, the intercultural manager, be able to recognize patterns and apply your understanding of the data to your own intercultural interactions. In this way, you receive valuable practice in heightening your own awareness of how people make sense of the world around them, whether it is through attitudes towards time, space, gender, hierarchy, or worldviews.

The chapters presented in this book differ widely in what they investigate. From airline booking behavior to bias in recruiting, the chapters offer an insight into important sectors and the challenges they face in a global environment. Furthermore, since the data we include here comes from real-life, business conversations or interactions, the findings should be relevant for many walks of business life. You should be able to recognize some of the examples or issues and compare them to your own experiences.

Chapter 1 deals with client relations and service providers, especially with regard to building an effective service culture in B2B business endeavors. Chapter 2 is a detailed examination of global health issues, specifically the notion of sustainable development when it comes to neglected tropical diseases. Chapter 3 delves into the world of academic research and the issues faced by international researchers when relocating to a foreign environment. Chapter 4 deals with the intricacies of intercultural communication in a virtual setting, especially when dealing with tasks such as negotiation. Chapter 5 examines strategy optimization when it comes to customer booking behavior, specifically using a construct of uncertainty avoidance and regional cultural approaches to time. Chapter 6 covers the idea of cultural diversity in recruiting, and the conscious or unconscious bias faced by applicants based on their ethnicity. And finally, to round things out, Chapter 7 is a thorough treatment of the construction of identity in expats as they struggle to build their intercultural and communicative competence in a new cultural environment.

In summary, we hope that the contents of this book will provide useful insights to you as you observe and investigate the world in which we live, and how the intersectionality of multiple cultural identities affect both the product and the process of our everyday interactions.

Prof. Dr. Melanie Moll

How Client Culture Affects B2B Service Providers

Dana Bieck

Abstract

This work was inspired through personal experience in the single-client service environment. One major challenge represented in this field of work is that service providers must walk a fine line between representing their employer to the client and their client to their colleagues.

Few studies, however, have been published on the subject of how clients influence service providers. In contrast, several studies have been published on the matter of defining service culture, how best to serve the client and how the attitude of service providers affects customer relations.

Using qualitative and quantitative methods, I compare several organizations and their service departments to identify commonalities in service culture through surveys. Next, I use semi-structured interviews to examine both client and provider attitudes towards service culture. Specific behavioral patterns can be observed in different service teams, depending on the client they serve. Some of these patterns will be demonstrated in this paper to support the hypothesis that clients and their client cultures have a direct effect on B2B service providers.

The aim of this analysis will be to lead to new insights within the scope of service provision. This knowledge can then be applied across the scope of service provision, from employee training to client consultancy.

Introduction

This thesis offers insight into the world of B2B service culture. Many expressions and clichés are associated with service culture, such as "do unto others as you would have them do to you" or "the customer is always right". The background of service culture is presented in this work, and the paper presents the hypothesis that B2B service companies are affected by their clients' cultures and values and that clients affect the way services are rendered.

Furthermore, this work offers insight into corporate culture, describing the various attitudes that are found within the parameters of business practice. Very few studies have been published on the subject of how clients influence service providers. In contrast, several studies have been published on the matter of defining service culture, how best to serve the client and how the attitude of service providers affects customer relations. This work extracts examples from the data collected to demonstrate how B2B companies are influenced by their clients.

Research Questions

There is a trend in business to focus on customer experience (CX), a rising demand for better working conditions, more flexibility and a better working atmosphere, and the employee experience movement (EX). However, while much focus has been how employers affect their employees experience and even more attention has been given to how service providers affect their clients, very little work has gone into showing how clients themselves affect service providers.

The service sector makes up 65.03% of the GDP in 2017 ("Share of economic sectors in the global gross domestic product (GDP) from 2007 to 2017 | Statista", 2020), and has become a crucial sector for corporate growth. Companies are increasingly dependent on learning about both CX and EX to meet potential expansion goals.

Several studies indicate that the CX und EX are intricately intertwined. Kramer (2018) demonstrates that companies that engage their employees culturally see profit margins that are up to four times higher than those of their competitors. Walton (1993) confirmed this long before the terms CX and EX were trending buzzwords, insisting that taking care of employees leads to employees taking care of customers.

By defining service culture and examining different corporate cultures across different industries, this paper aims to examine the following questions:

- How do corporate service cultures differ from each other?
- How do clients affect their service providers?
- How does this influence the service industry?

This thesis will have laid groundwork to enable companies across the B2B spectrum to understand how their clients influence their culture and service delivery. This knowledge can empower companies to better engage their clients and employees, encouraging stronger relationships and promoting an understanding for a better working atmosphere for service teams.

It is important to evaluate examples of service culture in order to understand what motivates service companies. A brief illustration of the roles of clients and service providers are provided, and the role of corporate cultures are examined. The background is then tied into the qualitative and quantitative data collected in a series of interviews and a survey of service providers. Finally, the paper discusses findings and limitations and concludes this study, suggesting how B2B service providers can utilize this information to their advantage.

Literature Review

Service culture is defined by examining both business examples and academic sources. One point should be addressed when analyzing the definition of service culture; this definition will encompass mostly western examples of service culture and thus may slightly differ from other approaches or understanding of service.

While researching the term "service culture" and its meaning, several different statements surfaced, showing that there is no consensus in defining service culture. Therefore, to provide an appropriate meaning to service culture, several statements are examined for the purposes of this study.

A website offering consulting services with an aim to improve CX provides this definition: "A culture of service is an organizational culture that prioritizes customer service in all goals, decisions, actions, and everyday operations" ("Service Culture", 2015). According to this definition, a service culture sets the needs of the customer at the center of operations and prioritizes them, perhaps above all other organizational needs.

An academic definition comes from Bruce (2020), who suggests that "to create a service culture, organizations must measure customers' satisfaction as a routine way of doing business and make sure that everyone in the organization knows the results" (Para. 2). Again, the focus is on the customer's needs and experience. Bruce argues that a company who wishes to create a service culture must ensure that all employees in the company are aware of the results of customer satisfaction. Communication and information flow appear essential to creating a successful service culture. Bruce states, "In addition, the organization must clarify the standards of customer service that employees are expected to deliver and explain why customer service is vital to the organization's success" (Para. 2). Bruce emphasizes the importance of communication and that certain standards must be set up for employees to follow.

Kayako.com (2020) states that "Your customer service culture is the set of shared beliefs and priorities that are ideally held by everyone in the company." ("Kayako live chat software helpdesk software and customer success solutions", Para. 1). Such a definition emphasizes shared values. Not only should a business focus on customer needs and communicate customer satisfaction rates (or communicate in general) and set standards for employee behavior, it is also important that employees share a set of values for a service culture to exist. This probably isn't surprising for any student of culture, since culture can be defined as a system of shared values and behaviors.

Consolidating these three interpretations, service culture can be defined as **a shared system of values built upon the principle of putting customer needs first.** Within the parameters of this work, this definition will serve as the basis for understanding service culture and should be kept in mind while reading further.

The Client Relationship

Vargo and Lusch (2008) comment on the importance of customer relationships in their essay "Why Service?", which offers several insightful ideas on the subject: *"Service implies doing this with and for someone. It implies relieving and enabling them in the joint process of value creation. Thus, the service perspective compels the firm to consider the relational approach" (p. 10).* The authors stress a mutual participation in the value creation process. The client, in extending their patronage to the company, is therefore creating value for the company. In the modern world, companies do not only vie for financial gain through singular sales, but also for data. This may be in the form of references, reviews or contact information. A happy client is more likely to remain loyal and more willing to share their experiences about a company with others. This means that a customer relationship is a vital asset, and possibly the key to a successful business.

This holds true in the B2B service world as well. Ostrom, Bitner, Brown, & Burkhard (2010) suggest that companies who operate solely in services and do not provide goods tend to form a closer relationship with their customers, which generally leads to higher customer satisfaction and loyalty. Doheny (2020) states that "the more powerful brands connect more on an emotional level with their customers by invoking feelings such as pride and accomplishment, thus challenging the value paradigm in that customers are often seeking more than functional and rational benefits" (Para.3) Thus, the aim of service culture is not only to create customer satisfaction but also to build relationships, adding to the value chain.

Corporate Culture

While service culture relates to how companies deal with customer relations, corporate culture exemplifies the culture employees experience within a company. The literature is filled with discussions on corporate culture, with each corporation seeming to have their own perspective. A simple definition is that corporate culture refers to shared values, attitudes, standards and beliefs which embody members within an organization (Corporate Culture, 2020). This definition does not really differ from a sociological standpoint. However, whereas a student of culture within a broader scope would see culture as an organic, living phenomenon which derives itself from the actions and practices of the people acting within its bounds, some would argue that corporate culture is set up by company leadership, and then carried out within the ranks of a company. It is entirely possible that reality lies between the two definitions and that corporate culture is both organic and directed by leadership.

Reinforcing the idea that leaders set corporate culture norms, a Harvard Business Review article stated "Founders and influential leaders often set new cultures in motion and imprint values and assumptions that persist for decades" (Groysberg, B., Lee, J., Price,

J., & Cheng, J., 2018). Corporate cultures may be seen, instead of a sociological phenomenon built by persons within an organization, as parameters set up to motivate employees or to guide them into behavior favored by the company.

In other words, despite the idea that values are top-down decisions made by employers and imposed upon employees, one may argue that they are also organic and change with time and influence. Individuals within organizations also have great influence in forming the ideals within a company (Deal & Kennedy, 2000). Accordingly, it becomes evident that corporate cultures can be influenced by individuals anywhere in a company.

This work contents that it is also possible for clients to influence their service provider's culture. Dan (2018) suggests not in positing good or bad agencies, but rather an incompetence of clients, which is why the same agency can do well for one client and terribly for another. Dan's statement supports the idea that clients have an effect on the way services are carried out.

Customer Influence on B2B Companies

Sureshchander et al, Hoang, Hill and Lu (2010) suggest that due to the intangible, heterogenous, inseparable and perishable nature of services, the measurement of service quality is more difficult than that of product quality. In the same way, the cultural influence of a client on service providers proves itself intangible and subjective. Some might argue that client relationships and culture are intangible, and therefore lean heavily on intuition for guidance to answers of how this phenomenon works.

As seen from the literature on the client – service culture relationship, the relationship to a client is an asset for a service provider. There is always a balance of power in relationships. It has already been established in the previous analysis that clients are often perceived to be the more powerful party in a business relationship. However, what gives them this power and why would it have ability to mold the way service teams define service orientation? Following French and Raven's 5 sources of power as laid out in Senior and Swailes (2010), which power may be assigned to the client, and which power the service provider (team) wields will be suggested here.

The first power source, positional (legitimate) power, is difficult to gauge. This sort of power depends on one party's hierarchical position. The client has a perceived power, but is that power legitimate? To answer this question in the B2B context, this work will assume that the client, who controls the revenue within the relationship, holds this power.

Another way this power may be handed to the client is through fear of losing the client (loss aversion). In an article on B2Bs being at risk of losing their clients, Kamins and Vuong (2016) laid out a general distrust of business services providers in clients and suggested that customers care more about services and products than the actual brands of their service providers. This line of thinking supports the idea that the client's wishes and behavior influence the service industry's culture. Client engagement depends on the service provider's ability to induce empathy in the relationship. The service provider will likely have to adapt their behavior or way of communication in order to accommodate the client.

The next two types of power French and Raven outline (in Senior and Swailes, 2010) are expert power and referent power. Expert power refers to power extracted from skills and knowledge and referent power is derived from charisma. These types of power can be associated with the service provider.

Knowledge power for B2B service providers lies in knowing how their products and services are beneficial to the client. In a blog entry about knowledge as a service, Pudnyk (2019) suggests that the need for businesses to access expertise is increasing. Because of this need, services are valuable to clients, making knowledge a strong bargaining chip for service providers. This power is vital for service providers and the way they use it can have an effect on the business relationship. Hippolyte (2007) underscores this idea by referring to knowledge as a resource held by organizations which can be utilized to create sustained value for themselves. By applying knowledge, service providers may therefore be able to exercise expert power.

In business, charisma may be one of the most underrated powers. The finishing statement in Varghese's (2010) article on the power of charisma is "charisma effectively deployed can have electrifying results". As charisma is a personality trait, it is altogether possible that a client is charismatic as well. The reason that this power is allotted to the service provider is that this is a tool that they will need to wield to be successful, whereas a client is not dependent on influence through likability.

However, it may be that charisma does prove useful for curating a long-term relationship, resulting in a stronger negotiation position for the client, if they choose to use collaborative negotiation tactics.

In the world of B2B services, the next two power sources can be seen as client sources. Reward and coercive power can both be used by clients to convince service providers to comply with their wishes. Reward power uses recompense to convince a party to act a certain way, whereas coercive power uses force. The power of reward is straightforward and needs little clarification. The use of coercion to achieve goals is generally considered illegal in many cultures around the world, so it will not be entertained as a legitimate way for a company to influence their service providers within this paper.

Identity Theory

An important and influential factor in the client-service provider relationship is found within the construct of identity theory (Spears, 2012). Spears notes that group identification is a process of learning the group's position, and suggests that within the scope of group identities, it is possible that influence on a group can be internal and willing. However, he mentions that when compliance is external and forced then it is not a reflection of social influence but rather power and compliance. Spears then adds that in categorizing themselves with a social group or category, people learn to infer norms and attributes associated with that group or category.

Service providers serving on single client accounts are, in ways, forced to interact and interject themselves into social settings with their clients. In this way, the client is able to dictate norms and the service provider team's identity is not a reflection of natural social influence but rather power and compliance. This is one possible way that the client is able to affect the identity of the service provider and ultimately influence their perception of service culture.

Virtue identity springs from Virtue Ethics (Dutton, J., Roberts, L., & Bednar, J., 2010), which may be identified as an ethical code that emphasizes virtues or moral character (Hursthouse & Pettigrove, 2016). Dutton et al. cite the virtue perspective, suggesting that work related identity is positive when the identity is pervaded by virtuous qualities that meet the criteria for values that are defined as fundamentally good. This is to say that one's identity at work is positive when one carries out tasks that can be associated with "good".

One way of interpreting this is that if a service team feels that what their client is doing can be characterized as "good", then they will identify with their tasks, potentially causing a rise in productivity. However, if they are unable to identify with what they are doing or who they are doing it for, the service team may show less motivation in carrying out services.

Adaptive identity is an identity approach that proposes individuals should systematically change the content of their identity to achieve a better fit with internal or external standards (Dutton et al., 2010). Whereas virtue identity allows people to find identity in the virtue of what they do, adaptive identity allows people to change their identity to fit the standards of their environment.

In the case of service providers, this may be used to adapt from the ideals of their employer to the expectations of their client. Dutton et. Al. (2010) confirm this idea: "role transitions present professionals with an opportunity to change their identity, and they winnow provisional selves to achieve an appropriate fit with internal (employer) and external (client) perceptions and standards" (p. 8).

In Rothbard's (2020) study conducted with salespersons who represented more than one brand, it was found that workers who reported high levels of identity conflict (between the brands they sold) were less successful in sales. However, workers who found more complementarity between brands had above average sales. Based on these findings, it is reasonable to assume that the same phenomenon could be observed in situations where service providers are caught between their clients and employers. Those who have clients who align with the values of their employers may find performance better than those who cannot find cultural congruency between their employers and clients.

Now that group identity, value identity and adaptive identity have been exemplified, one begins to understand how a client behaves or what a client does can have an effect the EX. Furthermore, from Rothbard's research it is apparent that how a worker identifies with a client has a direct impact on that worker's performance.

The literature gathered in this section, as well as the previous sections offers the reader a basis for understanding how service providers are affected by their clients. The next section will show what approach was taken to examine the dynamics of this hypothesis.

Methodology

For the purposes of this thesis, service culture is defined as a shared system of values built upon the principle of putting customer needs first. To examine this thoroughly, this work refers to biographies surrounding 3 successful, modern, western business models (specifically, Amazon, Walmart and Zappos). The definition of service culture is considered while analyzing the service philosophies of these organizations. Next, examples of corporate cultures within different industries are demonstrated. Company cultures advertised to potential employees from top brand employers in several different industries are examined. The purpose of this practice is to create a cultural scale on which we can measure different companies and industries.

Interviews were conducted within the scope of this work, the results of which are analyzed here. The names of the interviewees have been changed to protect their identities. The interviews were administered during a two-week time frame, and each interview lasted approximately thirty minutes. The answers to the questions are analyzed for similarities between persons working for each perspective industry. Later, the analysis of the interviews is tied into how service culture and corporate culture relate to employee identity in the B2B service field. The interviews were translated from the German language into English. Here are the specific questions which were discussed in the interviews:

1. Discuss the statement: "I identify with my employer's values and culture" (Yes or no, and why or why not?).
2. Are you proud of the client you serve?
3. Would you say that your empathy for the client sometimes leads to a conflict of interests?
4. Is it your goal to find the best solution for your client? Even to your employer's detriment?
5. Define "Service Orientation" in your own words.

These questions were designed to indirectly ascertain the individual's identity and stance towards their employer and the client. Participants were encouraged to speak candidly. The interviews were not transcribed verbatim. The answers were consolidated after the interview, and reread to the interviewees, who were given the option to reiterate what they meant before agreeing to the final transcript.

A further source of data referenced is a survey distributed on German professional social media platforms (Linked-in and Xing) This survey was focused on the subject of service provider identity and was open to any service provider in a B2B situation who managed up to and no more than three accounts (including on-site logistics teams, telecommunications providers, inhouse HR services, production lines or any other line of work that serves/delivers to one client).

Results will be presented below. While very little literature has examined the relationship of client culture on the identity and performance of the service provider, several very important observations have been made by business moguls and academics alike. This work therefore takes a holistic approach to examining this phenomenon, extracting information from business blogs, autobiographies and biographies of well-established tycoons, sociological research, as well as psychological identity theory and organizational culture. A concerted effort will be made to draw connections between the different subjects in order to show the seldom explored, other side of the client-service provider relationship.

Analysis

Understanding service culture is relevant to finding out how B2B cultures are influenced by their clients. This understanding allows for recognition of the service provider mindset. Figure 1 illustrates the role of organizations and relationships between service providers and their clients.

Figure 1.1: Relationship between the Client and Service Provider

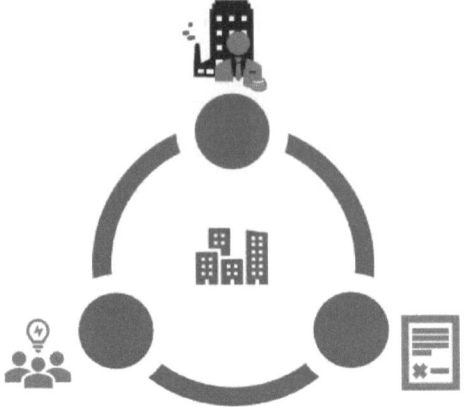

(Author's representation)

At the core of the image above are organizations. These can be any kind of company and may represent a product or service provider. One could view organizations like mini countries, governing their own employees, regulating their own input and output and protecting their own interests while bartering with partners.

Although the relationship is represented by equal input, the client is displayed at the top of the diagram, displaying their position in a relationship. The client is representative of the company holding the financial means in the relationship. The value a client brings is often monetary or at least something of monetary value, like data or referencing.

Next comes the contract. This is typically agreed on by both parties. A contract is usually a written agreement signed by both parties and generally considered legally binding. However, a contract, in the broader sense, can also represent an oral agreement or even unspoken norms within a national culture, a corporate culture or even within the client/ service relationship itself.

The third constituent in this relationship is the service provider. The service provider generally owns intellectual property or resources that the client cannot provide for themselves. This is the value that a service provider brings to the relationship. However, service providers who seek contracts with clients are subject to competition, which makes their position in the relationship slightly more volatile than that of the client.

Now that the relationship basis and assigned roles within the client and service provider relationships have been established, examples of service culture will be shown. These will help better understand this relationship and offer a solid basis for the discussion of how clients influence their B2B service providers.

Industry examples of service culture

Later in the paper, the focus will be solely on B2B customer relationships. However, this section will show examples of B2C interactions. An observance of B2C relations will allow for solidification of the understanding of service culture. This industry is prolific with examples and philosophies of how to live out service culture.

In order to demonstrate industry examples, three very successful businesses are represented and the service culture strategies of three very high-profile entrepreneurs are exemplified. These examples make the data shown here tangible, relatable and understandable to the reader, especially as they are representative of cultural idealisms in western customer service. For this purpose, the autobiographies of Sam Walton and Tony Hseih, as well as a biography about Jeff Bezos have been analyzed to identify patterns in their customer service philosophy. Comparisons are drawn from the literature mentioned in our literature review.

Keeping the established definition of service culture in mind, (a system of shared values based on putting customer needs first) examples of how companies may implement that definition are shown. In understanding how companies feel customers should be treated, one can appreciate the impact of how service culture and employee identity is impacted by customers themselves.

One aspect of customer service that has been established in western cultures is instant gratification. The idea that customers should wait a certain amount of time to have a problem solved or receive a product is unheard of in many companies. Sam Walton (1993) describes his time working on the retail floor at J.C. Penny: "I couldn't stand to leave a new customer waiting while I fiddled with paperwork on a sale I'd already made" (p.23).

Documentation of revenue is necessary for most companies, but Walton's preference for serving the customer over adhering to bureaucratic processes demonstrates both the significance of service culture and an interesting example of how customers affect a company's employees. Knowing that the paperwork was part of his job but feeling agitated by it when he could be serving a customer demonstrates the dynamic between customer and service provider. The customer's presence has a direct impact on the emotional and reactionary state of the employee.

Walton isn't the only example displaying the need to placate the customer's desire for instant gratification. Stone (2013) says of Amazon founder and CEO Jeff Bezos that he "became absorbed with the challenge of delivering products immediately after customers placed their orders" (p. 82).

Amazon's successful Prime program displays the fruits of Bezos's absorption. His drive to fill customer wants and needs as fast as possible, even though Amazon customers are not physically present, further displays the influence customers have on companies. Although the obvious reason for this would be that customers are the source of income for any company offering goods and services, the need for a relationship with the customer often exceeds all other interests.

Customer Relationship as the Key Asset

Amazon and Walmart have demonstrated that the customer relationship does not simply serve short term needs. Both companies have chosen competitive pricing strategies and have proven to be willing to lose money in order to curry favor with customers.

Walton's (1993) insistence that good deals be passed on to the customer and one glaring example of Bezos (in Stone, 2013), taking pre-orders from an in-demand best seller, and then sold it 40% under retail value, with free shipping, both examples of this customer driven behavior. A similar practice, focusing on customer centric culture can be seen with Zappos. Tony Hsieh (2010) exemplified this behavior when he recounted Zappos's practice of upgrading shipping on orders to "surprise" customers. Here, he notes that the company has even gone as far as to suggest competitors if they are not currently carrying a product, thus ensuring that the client receives exactly what they want. This behavior exemplifies how valuable customer relationships really are to service providers and are a telling sign of how much power clients have in that relationship.

Now the importance of a client relationship has been demonstrated and examined at the B2C level, demonstrating how clients in general are in a position of power, one begins to understand how B2B service providers are influenced by their clients.

Moving on from the analysis of service provision in a B2C context, this work will now turn to corporate culture. Not only do employers influence service providing employees culturally, but so do their clients, as most service providers are aware of the values and practices of their customers. Examples of specific companies will be shown in order to demonstrate how culture can differ within specific industries. The information in this step will tie into the analysis of service culture later in this work.

Corporate Culture Images and Ideals

Corporate culture can be observed from the outside of an organization, by observing their self-projections. Companies often convey the lifestyle, values and list of goals they wish to be associated with, especially when attempting to attract new employees.

In the next step of this work, several companies' websites across four business sectors are briefly examined. The businesses examined are in the pharmaceutical, industrial (production), banking and telecommunications industries. This research seeks to ascertain what values each company promotes and how they represent themselves to the outside world.

The analysis will only take into consideration the "cover page" for job seekers (referred to from here on as career page), as this is often an applicant's first impression of the company's values. This analysis aids in identifying industry norms that will help understand the views of the service provider serving these industries, particularly where culture and values are concerned.

This is in no way a full encompassing cultural analysis of each company but rather an evaluation of what first impression these companies make on perspective employees.

Verizon

Verizon is a prominent name in the telecommunications business, especially in North America. According to their website, their highest priories are diversity and sustainability ("Work Culture: Diversity, and Company Social Responsibility", 2020). Their page displays men and women of all ages and races, working together, appearing to collaborate effortlessly. "Our difference is our Strength" ("Work Culture: Diversity, and Company Social Responsibility" 2020). They stress empowerment and social responsibility. They even boast commitment to protecting the planet for future generations. Verizon displays themselves as having strong social and ecological values.

Vodafone

Like their competitor, Vodafone seeks to attract employees with diversity and an interest in the world of the future. "We want you to be as you are" ("Deine Karriere bei Vodafone", 2020), is a statement under the header "Diversity" on their jobs site for Germany.

In contrast to Verizon, Vodafone does not specify any efforts or idealism towards environmental sustainability on their career cover page. Their brand seems to focus instead on working culture and work-life balance for employees.

Bank of America (BOA)
The careers page at BOA is clean cut, organized and precise, much as one may expect when thinking of a bank. They stress the employee's power to make a difference in the world of finance ("Bank of America Careers Site – Apply at Bank of America", 2020). Their focus for potential employees stresses more the benefits of being part of their company, although they do stress that they support diversity and women's issues. They make a point of stressing parental leave in the USA.

HSBC
Here again one can find similarities with the competitor. Although the website is less "clean cut" than that of BOA, and they do not put as much emphasis on the influence of the individual on the banking world, they do convey to the applicant that one can achieve a lot with them and express their commitment to developing their employees' careers. "We are committed to helping you build your personal and professional skills during your career with us" ("Careers | HSBC Holdings plc", 2020). Employees are given extra opportunities to volunteer working hours for charity and the company also makes great effort to emphasize their size and global presence. They stress that life at HSBC encourages inclusiveness, regardless of an employee's background.

Thyssenkrupp
"Why Thyssenkrupp?" asks the website of the industrial giant. ("thyssenkrupp: Career Worldwide", 2020). The company emphasizes diversity, fascinating technology, and an interest in employee development. Overall ThyssenKrupp conveys a sense of progress and innovation. At the top of the page is the slogan "engineering.

tomorrow. together." Thyssenkrupp is mainly in the steel production industry.

Siemens
"Change the future every day" jumps out at the applicant when clicking on Siemen's (2020) global career page. ("Siemens Jobs & Careers" Para.1). The global mammoth also places value on human intelligence stating that it is not companies but rather people that move the world forward and refer to their employees as "innovators". Their site is very future oriented, and no direct mention is made of diversity, but they do mention being present in over 200 countries and the employees depicted on their site represent a wide range of ethnicities and females are also strongly represented.

Glaxo Smith Klein (GSK)
Glaxo Smith Klein (2020) is possibly one of the world's most prestigious and prolific pharmaceutical companies. Their career cover page represents them as being an employer who offers interesting challenges ("Careers | GSK"). "Are you ready to help people do more, feel better and live longer?" the page asks. The company presents themselves as a global healthcare supplier. One employee at GSK (2020) is cited as saying that she "always feels reassured by the fact that she is part of the team". (Para.5) The company places great emphasis on teamwork.

Merck
"Invent with us" invites Merck (2020), an international pharmaceutical company ("Careers at Merck | Merck Job Opportunities",). The company boasts around 69k employees globally (in more than 140 countries) and $42.3 billion in revenue as well as A $9.8 billion budget for research and development. The page in this link is their US page, where they offer more information on diversity and inclusion, benefits and how they work with (military) veterans. They also offer opportunities for students according to their career cover page. Upon scrolling down, one is presented a scrolling banner

which names lists and awards from several publications surrounding the quality of the Merck employer brand. These include recognitions for sustainability and best employer lists for various groups. The company seems to exude pride regarding their diversity and their global position.

Evaluation by Branch

As can be seen, many companies display themselves as being virtuous in order to appeal to candidates. According to Deal and Kennedy (2000), values are the bedrock of any corporate culture. This is a rather strong statement. The idea is that a company's foundation is set and built on its values. Later Deal and Kennedy (2000) suggest that companies with strong cultures acknowledge the importance of their values and their employees and constantly project this ideal. This certainly seems to be reflected in the projections of the companies displayed above.

In order to compare the companies and their perspectives, key themes are derived from the data above and sorted by company or social orientation. Then a scale model to describe distance is used (O'Brien Cherry, 2018). Individual (company) interest and social interest is be measured. The scale is more fluid, like that employed by Moll to measure direct and indirect requests (Moll, 2012). Each company is placed on the scale, using the information gathered from the first page of their career pages as listed above. Individual/company interests will be measured by what a company does for their employees.

This will demonstrate what companies in different industries advertise to job seekers, which is relevant, as people working in single client atmospheres are often so involved in their client companies and have much to do with their clients' employees. The scale is an attempt to measure if these companies measure up to what they advertise in the eyes of their service providers, or if the data is incongruent.

Table 1.1: Key Words Evaluation

Company	Company Interest	Social Interest
Siemens	Global presence Employees as innovators Change the future	Future People-centric
Thyssenkrupp	Innovation Fascinating Technologies Employee Development	Tomorrow (Future oriented) Diversity Progress
HSBC	Employee development Global presence	Employees Volunteer Inclusive
B.o.A	Influence world of Finance	Diversity Women's Issues
Merck	Good Employer Global High Revenue Budget for R&D	Diversity Sustainability
GSK	Interesting Challenges Global presence Teamwork	Help people
Verizon		Diversity Sustainabilit Future oriented
Vodafone	Working Culturee Work Life Balance	Diversity Future Oriented

Figure 1.2: Sliding Scale

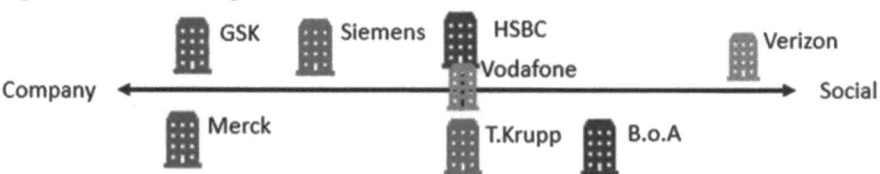

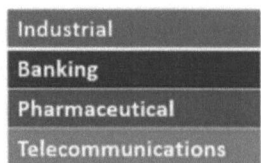

(Adapted from Moll's 2012 model, own representation)

It should be noted that simply because a company is depicted on this scale as being more company (goal) oriented or being more social oriented, does not mean that either company neglects the other spectrum. This scale simply shows where the company stands based on their outward portrayal, as observed on their websites.

Now that the companies are arranged on a visual scale, they can be compared. Verizon has projected itself as being a company that is very interested in general welfare, whereas their competitor Vodafone has placed themselves evenly between social values and employee wellbeing/company interests. GSK and Merck were very similar in their placements, advertising a very employee oriented and goal-oriented image. Siemens and Thyssenkrupp are not very far apart from each other on this scale, although Thyssenkrupp does show more interest in social issues. The banking companies were also comparable culturally, although the BOA did show a slightly higher social interest than HSBC, who showed more employee orientation.

As can be seen from this scale, there does seem to be some congruity between companies who operate in the same business sectors. Of course, each company has an individual philosophy but none of them can be found on different sides of the spectrum to their competitors. This is important when identifying the influence of clients on service providers, as it shows that each industry already sets standards. A service provider may be expected to contribute to the overall goals of their clients. Since this is the case, the client's expectations may mold the scope of service provided.

However, what a company projects and how a company acts may be very different altogether. Furthermore, some individuals may not perceive the values the company advertises to be the true corporate values of their employer. Hofstede, Hofstede and Minkov (2010) relate this sentiment suggesting that different persons within the same company may not answer the same when asked questions about how they see their organization's practices. In order to examine what is meant, and how it relates to this context, it is necessary to look at this from the perspective of the service provider.

Interviews

In this section, sets of interviews are reviewed of service providers (employees of a B2B Service company) serving each of the above-referenced branches: Telecommunications, Banking, Industrial, and Pharmaceutical. All persons interviewed were employed at the same company but rendered services to different clients.

The following texts contain short analysis of charts containing a consolidation of interviews of B2B service providers who work for the same company but on different accounts in different branches. The following questions were asked:
1. Discuss the statement: "I identify with my employer's values and culture" (Yes or no, and why or why not?).
2. Are you proud of the client you serve?
3. Would you say that your empathy for the client sometimes leads to a conflict of interests?
4. Is it your goal to find the best solution for your client? Even to your employer's detriment?
5. Define "Service Orientation" in your own words.

The telecommunications service team's is examined first. Consider the following:

Table 1.2: Interview responses Telecommunications

Branch:	Question1	Question2	Question3	Question4	Question5
Telecommunications					
Isabelle	young dynamic culture	Yes, cleint is employee friendly, loyal and fair to service provider	Feels conflict of intrest	Serves client as long as does not hurt employer	Optimize processes, have open ear, work in solutions, be partner to client
Nicole	Values I can live privately	No, company cares about numbers, not suppliers	One must choose between lying or telling truth, financial intrest is in focus	No, is financially driven, a client is just a client, loyal to employer	Predefined services to mutual benefit of both client and service provider
Louisa	Treatment of employees agreeable	Not proud but feels loyalty to client	No conflict of intrest, only feels obligation to employer	Would do anything for client within reason, acting against employer is not within reason	Anticipate client needs, deliver best solution
Anna	There are a few things I don't identify with	Feels conflicted about changing client atmosphere	Feels desire to serve client, even when employer is not on board	Seeks to represent employer intrests, is willing to compromise on smaller things, not if it hurts employer	Best possible solution in given circumstances within the scope of contract
Katja	Values are self evident	Not proud, no emotional attachment to client	Sees this as an act of balancing between desire to serve client and desire to earn money	No, one should always protect intrests of employer	Quick, reliable results. Offer solutions.

The team in table 2 showed a strong identification with their employer's values and most of them were not proud of their client. Although they answered very individually in comparison to the other teams, most of them reported feeling very conflicted or caught up between their loyalty for their employer and their loyalty to their client, but did not feel so loyal to their client that it would cause them to be detrimental to their employer. Some of the answers suggest that this team would see their client relationship as a means to an end and that their primary drive for serving the client is purely financial. They tended to see themselves as a partner to their client, and their service style was to seek solutions within the ramifications of the contract.

In table 3 are the answers from the banking teams. These teams sat both on and off the client sites. As only two of the participants were located offsite, here it is not differentiated between the two teams, to preserve anonymity.

Table 1.3: Interview responses Banking

Branch:	Q1	Q2	Q3	Q4	Q5
Banking					
Nina	Identifies with readiness to change	Proud of work, proud to be involved in project	Sometimes feels she is between a rock and hard place	Always tries to make everything possible for client, feels that his helps him obtain information from client.	Availability, quick reactions, empathize with client, forget one's own viewpoint. Offer best service
Sarah	Identifies with values/culture. These are very important for her	Finds client and branch very interesting	Tendency to see things from client's view can cause conflict with colleagues	No, the client should be king but it all has to be comertially sustainable	Advisory role, managing expectations availability
Emily	Identifies with her team, feels sense of community is spurned on by "us and them" relationship with client	conflicted by client's big name and bad reputation in press.	Sometimes feels unnessesarily pressured	Discusses descisions with her manager before acting	Exceed expectations, offer client value in things they haven't thought of themselves
Jessica	Identifies with employer values, not client values. Feels employer values are intrinsic	Not proud of client, but was once proud to be involved in a big project	Does not feel she has a choice, has to serve client	Tries to act economically, consults with management	Deliver services in a win-win fashion. Service orientation is based on equality.
Estrella	Identifies with idea that everyone is equal, readiness to change.	Definately not proud of client, grateful for opertunity to learn about branch	Sometimes difficult to allighn employer and client intrests, client forgets we have another employer	Is her goal to find best solution without hurting anyone.	Listening, act as an advisory, guide client in ways they haven't thought of.
Marlene	Feels the employer values are worth aspiring to	not proud of client reputation but grateful for opertunity to learn about branch	Feels conflict with personal values rather than employer values. Cites finger pointing	Would check with employer before making decisions that would be detrimental	Offer best services, act with empathy, friendliness
Heike	young dynamic culture	Not proud of client but proud to have been chosen for project	Doesn't see conflict of intrest, sees it as her job to put client first	Wants to avoid actions being a burdon to employer	Satisfying client on principles of a paternship
Svenja	Likes company atmosphere	Client looks good on a resumé but not proud of them	Doesn't see conflict of intrest	One should act after consulting with employer	Reliability, fast, diligent handling. Availability.

There was no conflict in answers concerning the values and culture of the employer for banking service team members. Everyone identified to some extent with their employer. The values cited by the team members were very dependent on their own team, and this was reflected throughout the survey. The banking teams were very proud of what they did, their own attributions and capabilities, but this did not generally extend to their client. While many found the branch itself interesting and were glad to be included in such a high-profile project, several were negatively influenced by their client's reputation in the media.

This group's answers sometimes reflected a deep-seated distrust of their client or dislike for their client's general behavior. As a rule, they did not identify with their client's culture. The conflict of interest was particularly strong for this client, and although some did not cite feeling a conflict of interest, most felt pressure in their role between client and employer.

The banking teams were goal and solutions oriented but most were not prepared to make decisions without the go-ahead from their manager or employer, and thus were very loyal towards their employer and not just their team. Their service orientation was focused on mutual gain, and they saw themselves as advisors and partners to their client. Some team members even stressed that they were not seen as assistants or servants.

Next, the industrial teams' responses are reviewed (Table 4). All these participants sit offsite at an employer site. Interviewees in this category felt very in tune with the values of their employer but did not identify with their clients culturally, although the general consensus was that their clients' big names and innovative products were interesting.

These participants were not in agreement about whether a conflict of interests was present, but when one was cited then it was generally due to the question of whether the client was profitable or not. Financial concerns were not unimportant to these service providers.

As with the banking team, this team was not prepared to act to the detriment of their employer to placate the client and consulted within their team or manager. Again, profitability was taken under consideration.

These teams stressed the contractual terms; it was important for them to fulfill the terms of their respective agreements. They also tended to see themselves in a more subservient position, citing it important to anticipate the client's needs and to communicate with them.

In Table 4, the last group is examined, the pharmaceutical service team. This team sits onsite with their client.

Table 1.4: Interview responses Pharmaceutical

Pharmaceutical					
Ellen	Values are standard values, self evident	Liked responsibilities, was not proud of client	Wouldn't say there was a conflict of intrests, often had to justify herself to client	Would talk to superiors before making decision to detriment of employer	Act as partner, try to make everything possibe and act friendly in the process, try to find solutions, availability, respectful in communication
Clara	Values in tune with personal attitude	Proud of renowned, successful company	Sees conflict of intrest in that she can't share all information	Employer should alway be at forefront, service does not extend to the detriment of employer	Go above expected, offer encompassing support. Advisory role.
Hannah	Is happy, feels that confirms the values are lived out	Proud of renowned, employee friendly company	Feels she can not serve client due to faulty processes and inadaquite technology	Yes, the client bought (our services) for this purpose	Ensure that the entire organization does right client, be friendly, helpful, ready with advice. Go above and beyond.
Eric	Values great on paper, not lived out	Proud of cleint's smooth, honest communication	Sees no conflict of intrest in being service oriented	Always tries to make everything possible for client, feels that this helps him obtain information from client.	Maximal customer satisfaction, mutual understanding, appreciation, quick information exchange, high dependability,
Markus	Identifies with values	not proud, but enjoys working for client, identifies with them	Feels that handling in favor of client can be disadvantagous to employer	Loyalty to employer has priority	Efforts within the defined processes to deliver the best possible service.

Most participants in this team identified with the values prescribed by their employer, although one individual felt that they were superficial. This team also generally identified with their client.

They were not in agreement about whether there was a conflict of interest that they felt between client and employer, and indeed some showed themselves to relate more with the client than the employer while others were inclined to name loyalty to their employer as a priority. This team, like their industrial service team colleagues, was focused on friendly, anticipative service with a focus on communication style.

Evaluation of Service Provider Survey

The following data are derived from a survey of service professionals, spanning across several industries and carrying out diverse services. 20% of the participants were on-site at their client while 80% were off-site. Most questions were asked along the Likert scale. Most participants were German speakers, as the survey was predominantly shared in German social media networks.

The first data set of evidence shows a strong employer identification index. The rate of identification with one's employer values and culture were high in this survey. Although this is not surprising, if findings from the qualitative study are regarded, since employees identify with their immediate teams, associating company culture and values with their direct colleagues.

An overwhelming majority cited that their job was to protect the interests of their employer, with 77% either agreeing or strongly agreeing to this statement and 72% reported that their employer's financial success was their own personal success. 58% indicated that they were informed about the goings-on at their employer headquarters. The lowest indicator was the identification with a manager's directives. Only 54% of those surveyed signaled that their managers' instructions were more important than client requests.

This last number is very telling, as in most scenarios, even in companies with flat hierarchies, the direct manager is responsible for personal career development and financial compensation. Yet nearly half of the participants agreed that client requests were nearly just as important if not more important than manager directives.

In the second set of data, a consistent trend towards employer identification is still visible. The first two statements were met with strong disagreement, with 45% strongly disagreeing or disagreeing that their client's needs are more important than those of their employer and 49% taking a neutral stance. In contrast, the next questions demonstrate more client friendly tendencies. The overwhelming majority at 86% reported a personal sense of fulfillment in meeting a client's needs. While the majority at 66% took a neutral stance on their client's values and 63% were neutral towards their client's culture, 43% felt that it was their primary task to act according to the needs of their client.

All in all, these data are consistent with the findings of the qualitative interviews. Service provider employees were found to identify with their employer values more than those of their clients. However, they found both fulfillment in their tasks which they carried out for their client and desired to act in favor of their client's needs.

It should be noted here that service providers who sat on-site, as in directly on a client premises, scored slightly higher on the Likert scale for client orientation. Answers were averaged per participant and then sorted according to onsite and offsite. On average, on-site colleagues tended to agree (scaling at 3,1 on a scale from 1-5, where offsite scaled at 2,7). This serves to supports the notion that service providers sitting on-site empathize more with their clients than do those who sit off-site.

The data shown in this section demonstrate two sides of corporate culture; how a company projects their culture and how service providers perceive their employers' and clients' corporate cultures. In the next section, these data are tied together and discussed within the context of this work's definition of service culture. This discussion argues that the culture lived out by a client influences their service providers and how they carry out their services.

Discussion

This work defines service culture as a system of values built upon the principle of putting customer needs first. Such a definition is crucial to investigate how a client can affect their service providers culturally. By defining service culture, it becomes clear that the very existence of a service provider hinges on serving the client's needs, making the client's interests their own.

The relevance of the definition of service culture ties into the analysis of corporate culture. Ideals and actions laid out by Walton (1993), Bezos (in Stone, 2013) and Hseih (2010), illustrated the definition of service culture. These B2C examples also made it possible to visualize how clients affect their service providers in a very palpable way. But how does this translate to the work of B2B service provision? This becomes a little more difficult, as it has been established that the customer – service provider relationship is often intangible, save perhaps a contract which defines business parameters. In order to supplement our literature review on service culture and B2B client influence, identity theory was briefly examined (Spears, 2012).

First, there is the aspect of group identification. When considering the interviews, a very clear identity with the employer values and culture is seen. Spears (2012) has suggested that compliance with group identity can be both willing and internal as well as external and forced, and that people categorizing themselves in groups often adapt to norms associated with that group. Here we propose that service providers are forced to interject themselves into social settings with their clients and that because of this, the client is able to dictate norms to a service provider team.

This could be seen in the interviews, although more prominently in some than others. While most of the interviewees identified with their employer's values, clear differences could be drawn across teams in respect to their definitions of service orientation. For example, while the telecommunications and banking service teams saw themselves as partners and advisors, the pharmaceutical team had a more conventional view of their role in service to the client. Although it cannot be said from the study whether this is a forced behavior due to circumstance or if it is voluntary group identity, it can be hypothesized that a group identity is forming within these teams.

Virtue identity (Hursthouse & Pettigrove, 2016) also comes into play and is displayed in the interviews. It was particularly apparent in the banking service team. This team's identity with what they did, and being selected to work on an important, prominent project was a source of pride for them. However, the opposite emotion was emitted in correlation with their client, whom they felt to be disreputable.

Adaptive identity proposed that individuals change the content of their identity to align with internal or external standards (Dutton et al., 2010). Participants across the board struggled with this idea, and indeed this did not seem to be successful in most cases. However, the data from the quantitative survey did seem to show conflicting data with that of the interviews. While most of the interviewed stated that they would tend to confer with their employer or manager before making a decision that may be detrimental to their employer, over half of the participants in the interview were still inclined to see their client's wishes to be just as important or more important as their manager's directives.

This may indicate a propensity for adaptive identity (Dutton et Al., 2010), and further study into the matter would be necessary to make a decided judgement. Nevertheless, as Rothbard's (2020) study would indicate, service providers who align with their client's values may be more successful in cultivating a stronger relationship with their client. Of course, this is dependent on how well the client's values align with the employer's values.

Another aspect examined was corporate culture. Certain claims were made on different company websites, across the same branches to those the interviewed service teams served. The first interesting point is that cultural congruity was in how the companies portrayed themselves to potential candidates. How did this translate to service providers, who in a sense "work for" their clients?

Congruence could be found in the pharmaceutical branch, where some of the interview participants defined their client as a good and fair employer. This was in line with the findings on the branch in the analysis of the websites in that business sector.

Such comparisons suggest that the influence of clients on their service providers, although it may be subtle, is still influential enough to influence how a service provider identifies with their clients. Based on the results of Rothbard's (2020) study of sales professionals, this may have an effect on service provider motivation and performance. Furthermore, if Dan (2018) is correct, then clients are directly responsible for the service they receive.

Limitations and Directions for Future Research

Thus far, customer service research has been geared towards finding out how service providers influence clients. Due to the limited amount of pre-existing material, there are many opportunities for more research. More studies should be conducted which creatively explore the effects clients have on their service providers. Furthermore, service culture and corporate culture are subject to interpretation. This work is not an exhaustive study on either subject. As such it is possible that while piecing together the puzzle that is the client influence on B2B EX, that some perspectives have not been considered.

Conclusion

This paper aimed to answer the question of the cultural influence clients have over B2B service providers. Service culture has been defined and it has been shown how corporate cultures differ from each other. As this paper has shown, the experience customers have is intricately tied to the experience service teams have with their clients. As the world gets smaller, and business cultures become more imbedded in one another, further research will undoubtedly be made into service cultures and how clients influence them.

References

Bank of America. (2020).

Bank of America Careers Site – Apply at Bank of America

Retrieved from: https://careers.bankofamerica.com/en-us.

Bruce, O. (2020).

Enotes. Retrieved from https://www.enotes.com/homework-help/what-term-service-culture-mean-how-companies-131437.

Corporate Culture. Inc.com. (2020).

Retrieved from https://www.inc.com/encyclopedia/corporate-culture.html.

Dan, A. (2018).

Clients Get The Agency They Deserve. Forbes. Retrieved 5 April 2020, from: https://www.forbes.com/sites/avidan/2018/07/16/clients-get-the-agency-they-deserve/#1741cb0668cd.

Deal, T., & Kennedy, A. (2000).

Corporate cultures (2nd ed., p. 25). Basic Books.

Doheny, J. (2020).

B2B Customer Experience: 6 steps for success | B2B International. B2B International. Retrieved 29 March 2020, from: https://www.b2binternational.com/publications/six-steps-to-b2b-customer-experience-excellence/.

Dutton, J., Roberts, L., & Bednar, J. (2010).

Pathways for Positive Identity Construction at Work: Four Types of Positive Identity and the Building of Social Resources Retrieved from: http://webuser.bus.umich.edu/janedut/POS/Pathways_for_Positive_Identity.pdf.

Glaxo, Smith, Klein. (2020).

Careers | GSK. Gsk.com. Retrieved from: https://www.gsk.com/en-gb/careers/.

Groysberg, B., Lee, J., Price, J., & Cheng, J. (2018).

The Culture Factor. Harvard Business Review. Retrieved, from https://hbr.org/2018/01/the-culture-factor.

Hippolyte MCIArb, A. (2007).

Knowledge Management as a Source of Competitive Advantage [Ebook]. Retrieved from: https://www.academia.edu/42290115/Knowledge_Management_as_a_Source_of_Competitive_Advantage.

Hoang, H., Hill, S., & Lu, V. (2010).

The influence of service culture on customer service quality: Local vs. Foreign service firms in emerging markets [PDF]. Retrieved from: https://www.researchgate.net/publication/320010980_The_influence_of_service_culture_on_customer_service_quality_Local_vs_Foreign_service_firms_in_emerging_markets.

HSBC. (2020)

Careers | HSBC Holdings plc. Retrieved from: https://www.hsbc.com/careers.

Hsieh, T. (2010).

Delivering happiness: A Path to Profits, Passion and Purpose (1st ed.). Grand Central Publishing.

Hursthouse, R., & Pettigrove, G. (2016).

Virtue Ethics (Stanford Encyclopedia of Philosophy). Plato.stanford.edu. Retrieved from: https://plato.stanford.edu/entries/ethics-virtue/.

Kamins, C., & Vuong, A. (2016).

B2Bs at Risk of Losing Customers. Gallup.com. Retrieved from: https://news.gallup.com/businessjournal/194006/b2bs-risk-losing-customers.aspx.

Kayako live chat software helpdesk software and customer success solutions. Kayako. (2020).

Retrieved from: https://www.kayako.com/glossary/customer-service-culture.

Kramer, S. (2018).

Linking Employee Experience to Customer Experience – 10 Stats. Future Of Work. Retrieved from: https://fowmedia.com/stats-linking-employee-experience-to-customer-experience/.

Merck. (2020)

Careers at Merck | Merck Job Opportunities. Retrieved from: https://jobs.merck.com/us/en.

Moll, M. (2012).

The Quintessence of Intercultural Business Communication. Springer Berlin Heidelberg.

Ostrom, A., Bitner, M., Brown, S., & Burkhard, K. (2010).

Moving Forward and Making a Difference: Research Priorities for the Science of Service [Ebook] (p. 7). Journal of Service Research. Retrieved from: https://www.researchgate.net/publication/242686162_Moving_Forward_and_Making_a_Difference_Research_Priorities_for_the_Science_of_Service. Rothbard, N. (2020)

Being of Two Minds (or More): How Multiple Workplace Identities Affect Our Success [Blog] https://ideas.wharton.upenn.edu/research/how-multiple-workplace-identities-affect-success/. Service Culture. Donnellyeffect.com. (2015).

Retrieved, from http://www.donnellyeffect.com/home/solutions/service-culture. Share of economic sectors in the global gross domestic product (GDP) from 2007 to 2017 | Statista. Statista. (2020).

Retrieved from: https://www.statista.com/statistics/256563/share-of-economic-sectors-in-the-global-gross-domestic-product/.

Siemens. (2020).

Siemens Jobs & Careers. siemens.com Global Website. Retrieved from: https://new.siemens.com/global/en/company/jobs.html.

Spears, R. (2012).

Group Identities: The social perspective. In S. Schwarz, K. Luyckx & V. Vignoles, Handbook of Identity Theory and Research (1st ed.). Springer.

Stone, B. (2013).

The Everything Store (pp. 82,111). Back Bay Books, Little, Brown and Company. Thyssenkrupp: Career Worldwide (2020).

Karriere.thyssenkrupp.com.

Retrieved from: https://karriere.thyssenkrupp.com/en.

Vargo, S., & Lusch, R. (2008).

Why "Service" [Ebook] (p. 10). Journal of the Academy of Marketing Science. https://www.researchgate.net/publication/225531719_Why_service.

Varghese, S. (2010).

Forbes.com. https://www.forbes.com/2010/01/25/charisma-speaking-communication-leadership-managing-inspiration.html#47366c12301e.

Verizon.com. (2020).

Work Culture: Diversity, and Company Social Responsibility. https://www.verizon.com/about/careers/work-culture.

Vodafone. (2020).

Deine Karriere bei Vodafone. Retrieved from: https://jobs.vodafone.de/?utm_source=karriereseite&utm_medium=button&utm_campaign=karriere.

Walton, S. (1993).

Made in America (pp. 23,66,164). Bantam Books.

List of Figures

Figure 1.1: Relationship between the Client and Service Provider 26
Figure 1.2: Sliding Scale 34

List of Tables

Table 1.1: Key Words Evaluation..34
Table 1.2: Interview responses Telecommunications..........................37
Table 1.3: Interview responses Banking..38
Table 1.4: Interview responses Pharmaceutical 40

The Merck Schistosomiasis Elimination Program – From Philanthropy to Sustainable Investment in Global Health

Antonia Asche

Abstract

Neglected tropical diseases (NTDs) have existed since ancient times and affect more than one billion people worldwide. Global efforts against NTDs are currently being redirected from morbidity control to elimination. The World Health Organization has recently endorsed a road map that lays out which steps need to be undertaken to achieve this ambitious goal. Global partners are called on to align their strategies accordingly to support the target.

This study focuses on one particular stakeholder, the company Merck and its long-term commitment in the fight against the NTD schistosomiasis. It explores what role Merck should play in driving forward sustainable development in the elimination of schistosomiasis in sub-Saharan African countries. The author consulted scientific literature and conducted semi-structured interviews with key stakeholders inside and outside Merck. A definition of sustainability in the context of NTDs was carved out of this research and three hypotheses were tested against the findings. The study suggests that a multitude of stakeholders as well as a multipronged approach are needed to tackle and eventually eliminate NTDs. Necessary measures include treatments, research and development of new medicines and diagnostics, health education, and hygiene and sanitation measures. The study concludes that Merck has made significant contributions to past achievements in the reduction of disease burden in these areas and will continue to play an important role until the elimination of schistosomiasis as a public health problem.

However, in order to ensure sustainable development, countries affected by NTDs must eventually take the lead. Doing so will have strong positive effects beyond the realm of health and could also support economic development overall.

Introduction

Almost two years after the first reported cases of infections with the new SARS-CoV-2 virus in China, the global COVID-19 (Corona Virus Disease 2019) pandemic continues to have a strong influence on countries worldwide. As a result, there is greater awareness about the major impact that global health challenges have on the health systems and economies of countries. Some global health threats have been around for centuries, including neglected tropical diseases (hereafter NTDs) – a group of 20 diseases affecting one billion people across the globe. As the name implies, these diseases have been largely neglected, mainly because they affect the lives of the poorest and most vulnerable populations. This is why they are also referred to as "diseases of poverty." Thanks to the substantial contributions of a variety of stakeholders, attention to the fight against NTDs has increased during the past two decades. However, the COVID-19 pandemic has led to a serious setback for achievements made in tackling many NTDs. Interventions targeting these diseases have been put on hold and resources redirected to COVID-19 prevention measures. Nevertheless, it is crucial to maintain efforts to fight these diseases in order to promote sustainable development in low- and middle-income countries (hereafter LMICs) hit hardest by NTDs.

The thesis presented here will explore efforts to fight one particular NTD – schistosomiasis (hereafter SCH). This waterborne parasitic disease affects almost 240 million people globally, leading to 200,000 deaths every year. Like with other NTDs, global efforts to control SCH have been intensified in the course of the last 20 years. Under the guidance of the World Health Organization (hereafter WHO), a range of stakeholders including national health authorities, non-governmental organizations (hereafter NGOs), academia, and private sector donors have become involved in addressing the challenges imposed by the disease. This joining of forces has been worthwhile. Today control over the morbidity of SCH and other NTDs has come so far that their elimination appears to be a realistic target. However, reaching this target still remains a challenge and requires commitments from both endemic countries and all global stakeholders.

In the case of SCH, one of the most strongly committed stakeholders is the German company Merck. The science and technology company joined the fight against SCH in 2007 by providing WHO with free dosages of praziquantel (hereafter PZQ), a standard of care treatment against SCH, for the treatment of school-aged children in sub-Saharan Africa. Since then, Merck has extended its commitment substantially to include two additional areas: research and development (hereafter R&D) of drugs and diagnostics as well as support of health education and WASH (water, sanitation and hygiene) initiatives.

Now that the goal of eliminating SCH as a public health problem is in reach, the question arises as to what role a private company such as Merck could and should play in this ambitious endeavor. The research question of this paper is therefore: "How can a company like Merck, in close collaboration with partners, drive forward sustainable development in the elimination of the Neglected Tropical Disease Schistosomiasis in sub-Saharan African countries?"

To answer to this question, after defining NTDs and SCH, this section will examine the general concept of sustainability and its implications for businesses such as Merck. Next, NTDs and SCH will be examined in the context of sustainability. Following this conceptual framework, the evolution of Merck's commitment in the fight against SCH since 2007 will be presented in greater detail. As the title of the paper indicates, the company's commitment has long been mainly of a philanthropic nature. With the demand for more sustainable strategies, Merck needs to reevaluate the nature of its role. The paper will thus ask what the company can do differently in the future. Drawing on the results of interviews with key stakeholders inside and outside of Merck, the author will argue that a private donor company such as Merck will continue to play a crucial role in achieving the ultimate goal of eliminating SCH. While there is evidence that drug donation programs may not be sustainable because of the dependencies they create, in the case of NTDs, they will continue to contribute to sustainable development if complemented with the right set of additional interventions.

Neglected Tropical Diseases and the Global Efforts to Tackle Them

In his book 'Forgotten People – Forgotten Diseases', Peter Hotez (2013) writes that the rise of diseases such as HIV/AIDS and severe acute respiratory syndrome (SARS) has created more awareness about health issues in the developing world. In particular, the commitments and investments of organizations and celebrities have fueled advocacy and resource mobilization for health topics in these regions. However, as Hotez argues, while attention was focused strongly on these two specific health crises, another one remained long forgotten – NTDs.

NTDs is a collective term for a group of 20 ancient diseases affecting more than one billion people worldwide. Typically found in tropical and subtropical regions, these diseases hit the most vulnerable and poorest populations especially hard (World Health Organization [WHO], 2021a).[1]

NTDs are chronic conditions since reinfection often occurs. Long-lasting infections result in disability and disfigurement imposing a

---

1   The group of people considered to be very poor live on less than US$ 1.25 per day (Hotez, 2013).

heavy economic burden on communities. Co-endemicity of people with several NTDs is rather common in affected LMICs (Hotez, 2013). Patients infected with one or more diseases struggle due to their poor health condition; they are often unable to work while at the same time confronted with higher medical costs (Fitzpatrick et al., 2017).

As Hotez (2013, p.11) points out, "the NTDs not only occur in the settings of poverty; they also actually promote poverty." He goes on to argue that LMICs will not be able to economically advance as long as this group of tropical diseases continues to exist. Fitzpatrick et al. (2017) agree by saying that funding activities against NTDs are valuable investments not only for their role in preventing death and morbidity. Prevention of these diseases, they argue, also translates to far lower economic and social costs for the communities, thus helping to create more social justice. Hence the benefits far exceed the costs carried by external donors, and financial resources freed up could be reinvested to meet other health challenges.

The burden imposed by NTDs is so high that it equals that of diseases such as HIV/AIDS and malaria (Hotez, 2013). However, since mortality due to NTDs is low, or at least time-delayed, they are often not prioritized on government agendas in endemic countries (Hotez, 2013). NTDs were long overlooked and the interventions to address them were inadequate as high-quality treatments were not available in sufficient amounts. But the fight against NTDs took a new turn in 1987 when the American pharmaceutical company MSD (known as Merck & Co. in US and Canada)[2] pledged to donate their drug Mectizan as long as necessary to eliminate the

---

[2] MSD is not to be confused with the company Merck, which is the focus of this thesis. There are two different companies that call themselves Merck. One is headquartered in the United States and holds the name rights in the US and Canada. The other Merck, headquartered in Darmstadt, Germany, holds the name rights for the rest of the world (Merck, n.d.b).

NTD onchocerciasis – also known as river blindness. (Bradley et al., 2021).

In subsequent years, a number of other pharmaceutical companies followed MSD with similar commitments. Today, 11 companies donate drugs for the treatment of NTDs. Thanks to these donations, mass drug administrations (hereafter MDAs)[3] for these diseases have become possible and, according to the WHO (2021a) have led to a significant reduction of disease burden.

It is clear that far more efforts must be undertaken by the entire NTD community to go beyond merely controlling NTDs to eliminate and eradicate them (WHO, 2021a). To this purpose, WHO has developed a second roadmap in a consultative process with the NTD community. The document was endorsed by the World Health Assembly at the end of 2020 and was officially published in early 2021, marking a decisive year for NTDs. The new WHO NTD roadmap sets new targets in accordance with the United Nations Sustainable Development Goals (hereafter SDGs) for the control and elimination of 20 diseases by 2030 and provides guidance on how to achieve these objectives. It builds on three main strategies: 1) advancing programmatic action, 2) leveraging cross-sector and cross-disease approaches, and 3) facilitating country ownership (WHO, 2021a).

The Case of Schistosomiasis

SCH, also known as bilharzia or snail fever, is one of the 20 NTDs targeted by WHO. It affects 240 million people globally and leads to 200,000 annual deaths as a result of long-term infections (WHO, 2021c). Children are among the most affected groups of this parasitic waterborne disease and the symptoms are severe. An infection with SCH in childhood can lead to anemia, malnutrition, stunted

---

[3] MDA and preventive chemotherapy are the approaches used to treat all people in a given geographical area, e.g., all children in one school, without prior testing for infection (WHO, 2021b).

growth, abdominal swelling and other serious symptoms. Patients suffering from the disease often have blood in the stool or urine as the parasite attacks inner organs such as the liver, kidney and bladder. Left untreated, SCH infections can lead to cancer and death.

Figure 1.1:   The Lifecycle of Schistosomes (From Centers for Disease Control and Prevention)

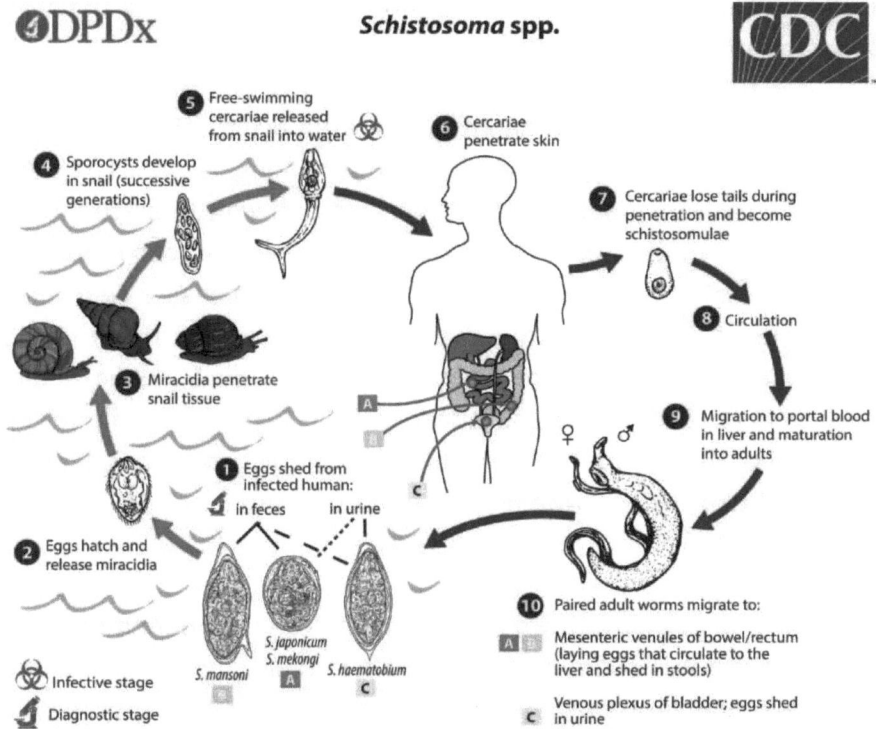

(Retrieved August 10, 2021, from https://www.cdc.gov/dpdx/schistosomiasis/modules/Schistomes_LifeCycle_lg.jpg)

Figure 1.1 shows the life cycle of the schistosoma. There are several different species of the parasite that affect humans including, *Schistosoma japonicum*, *Schistosoma mekongi*, *Schistosoma mansoni*, and *Schistosoma haematobium*. The latter two forms are predominant in Africa. The lifecycle begins when eggs of the parasite are released into waterbodies through feces or urine. When the eggs hatch, they release free-swimming larvae known as miracidia, which swim to enter a snail host. The parasites develop into cercaria in their intermediate host and are again released into water. The cercaria then penetrate the skin of humans as they bathe, wash, or play in contaminated waters. Once inside the body, the parasite matures and travels through different organs, depending on the species. Adult worms mate and lay eggs that are released through urine or feces, and the cycles begins again.

SCH is mainly controlled through preventive chemotherapy. Entire populations in a given geographical area are treated at once in MDAs of the drug PZQ without previous diagnosis. WHO recommends this strategy because PZQ is a safe and well-tolerated medicine (Linazaa et al., 2021). MDAs with PZQ have reduced morbidity of SCH remarkably, making elimination of the disease a reachable target (Hotez, 2013). The disease-specific targets set by the WHO NTD roadmap for SCH foresee its elimination as a public health problem in all 78 affected countries by 2030 (WHO, 2021a). In addition, 25 of these countries should have completely stopped transmission of the disease within the same timeframe.[4]

Sustainability

Although not new, the term 'sustainability' and its definition have gained impressive momentum during the past several years. Initially, sustainability was understood mainly in the environmental sense. In 1987, the United Nations (UN, 1987) Brundtland Commission established the definition of sustainability as humanity ensuring "that it meets the needs of the present without compromising the ability of future generations to meet their own needs" (p16). This definition remains relevant today as climate change becomes

---

[4] WHO differentiates between elimination as a public health problem and elimination as the interruption of transmission. The former refers to a reduction of high-intensity infection below a level of 1%. In the case of the latter, infection no longer occurs in humans as the parasites no longer exist (WHO, 2021a).

increasingly visible in unprecedented extreme climate conditions such as the frequent occurrence of floods, forest fires, and hurricanes. Discussions surrounding environmental sustainability have become an increasingly significant element of the political discourse. The pressure on governments to take bold action is growing and will continue to do so (Intergovernmental Panel on Climate Change, 2021).

Almost a decade after the Brundtland Commission Report, the understanding of sustainability was expanded beyond the environmental to include economic and social aspects. The concept thus shifted to a multiple-system perspective. John Elkington (1999) first formulated the implications of this shift for the private sector. His theory of the Triple Bottom Line argues that companies should consider three categories in their management decisions – people, planet and profits – while taking care to act in an ethical and morally acceptable way.

The full range of stakeholders including shareholders, customers, and employees are paying more and more attention to these additional areas (Buchholz et al., 2020) – a fact that is reflected in the growing number of published corporate social responsibility reports. Companies are increasingly held accountable for conditions amongst their suppliers and sub-suppliers and therefore down the entire supply chain (Buchholz et al., 2020). In order to maintain their long-term license to operate, companies will have to act in a sustainable way.

Following the Brundtland definition of 1987 and the formulation of the Triple Bottom Line in the 1990s, the year 2000 marks the next cornerstone in the development of the concept of sustainability. In this year, the member states of the UN defined eight Millennium Development Goals. In 2015, 17 goals were then extended when the General Assembly of the UN agreed on its 2030 Agenda for Sustainable Development (UN, n.d.).

The UN (n.d.) website refers to SDGs as "an urgent call for action by all countries – developed and developing – in a global partnership" and thus remarks that "2015 was a landmark year for multilateralism and international policy shaping". The UN's SDGs thus expanded sustainability into a 17-dimensional concept.

Sustainability at Merck

Headquartered in Darmstadt, Germany, the science and technology company known as Merck operates globally. It is specialized in developing and providing high-quality products in its three businesses healthcare, life science and electronics. The following statement from the company's website sums up its mission:

> As a sustainable enterprise, we create long-term value through our core business while seeking to balance environmental, social and governance aspects – for us as a business, for our stakeholders and for society at large. In doing so, we are helping tackle the great challenges facing today's world, such as disease, poverty, hunger, and climate change. (Merck, 2021b)

Aspects of the previously introduced concepts of Triple Bottom Line and SDGs are clearly reflected in this statement of company goals. In fact, sustainability aspects have become so important to Merck that in 2020, it changed the name of its reporting tool from Corporate Responsibility Report – published since 2003 – to Sustainability Report. The new name reflects a redefinition of company goals in accordance with the SDGs and the development of a comprehensive sustainability strategy (Merck, n.d.a).

Merck was among the pharmaceutical companies to sign the London Declaration on NTDs in 2012. It made its first substantial commitment to the fight against the NTD SCH in 2007 by signing a Memorandum of Understanding with WHO. Under this agreement, Merck pledged to donate its drug PZQ for the treatment of the disease as long as necessary to eliminate it. Starting with a donation of 25 million tablets in 2008, Merck increased its annual provision of PZQ through the years and now maintains production capacities for providing up to 250 million tablets per year (Merck, 2020). To date, the company has donated more than 1.3 billion tablets to WHO for use in MDAs targeting school-age children in sub-Saharan Africa. This quantity of PZQ has allowed for the treatment of 520 million children (Merck, 2020).

Thanks to this investment, Merck is the largest German investor in NTDs and globally the only donor of PZQ for SCH treatments. The massive scaling-up of available treatments went hand in hand with substantial reductions in the prevalence of SCH. However, to control and eventually eliminate a disease as complex as SCH, additional actions must be undertaken. Elimination will be extremely challenging and cannot be achieved with treatment alone. This life cycle of this vicious parasite needs to be interrupted at different levels simultaneously (Merck, 2020). This realization is one of the reasons why Merck has extended its commitment in the fight against SCH significantly since its initial efforts. As indicated above, increasing production capacities for PZQ was the first crucial step.

Figure 1.2: Infographic on Merck's integrated approach towards SCH elimination

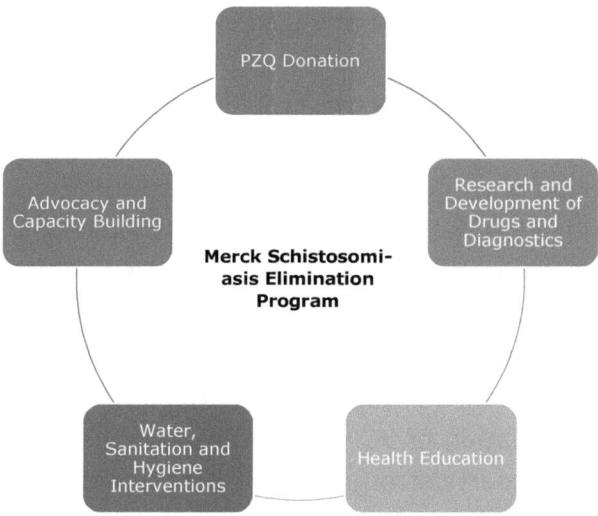

(Figure developed by the author)

Then in 2018, the integrated approach to eliminate SCH in selected countries by 2030, as shown in Figure 5 was introduced. It combines the long-standing tablet donation program with other disease-control activities developed in recent years. All activities are now united in the MSEP. One key element of this program is the Merck's Global Health Institute, which was launched in 2017. This initiative focusses on R&D regarding new treatments, drugs, and diagnostics for infectious diseases such as SCH and malaria (Merck Global Health Institute, n.d.). As a member of the Pediatric Praziquantel Consortium, the Institute is cooperating with ten other partners to develop a new SCH medication for younger children, which is now in the final clinical testing phase. While the current PZQ formulation is only suitable for use with adults and children older than six, the new pediatric medication will make it possible to treat younger children so that all age groups are included in measures to eliminate the disease.

Sustainable Development to Tackle Neglected Tropical Diseases

Ertl et al. (2021) point out that in 2019, more than 30 African countries spent more on the repayment of their debts than on their public health systems. Solving the problem of high indebtedness will therefore be crucial for building resilient health systems. Against the background of limited budgets, a clear strategic and evidenced-based prioritization must occur. The focus should be placed on areas with high multiplying effects for the entire health system.

As mentioned before, in the course of last decade, a paradigm shift has taken place in the NTD community. While previous interventions focused on the control of morbidity, today the ultimate goal is the elimination of SCH as a public health problem (Monnier et al., 2020). Experts strongly agree that although elimination is now seen as a realistic target, interventions will not end once it is achieved. Thuo et al. (2020) as well as Hotez (2013) emphasize that once reduction to a level below 1% is reached – the level used to define elimination of a disease as a public health problem – continued action will be necessary to maintain this level. Thuo et al. (2020) define three phases of NTD elimination programs: first, starting and scaling up the program; second, continuing treatments to reduce morbidity; and third, scaling down interventions and monitoring of the achievements. Fitzpatrick et al. (2017) also stress that intervention efforts cannot be terminated since a large group of people struggling from the consequences of their long-term infections will continue needing support. Hence the authors insist that continued support over a longer term is a responsibility of the health systems and should be included in UHC packages.

There is widespread agreement in the scientific community regarding the definition of sustainability provided by the WHO framework and the strategic areas that require the most attention by all stakeholders as mentioned above. Country ownership is perceived as being the most important element to achieve sustainability. A mobilization of domestic resources and a move away from donor-dependance will support countries in achieving UHC (Bradley et al., 2021). This requires that countries include NTD targets and interventions into their national plans and allocate parts of their domestic funds to these activities (Sodahlon et al. (2020). The heavy dependence on external resources represents a real threat for these countries as a halt of cash-inflow could have dramatic consequences.[5] WHO maintains that dedicating 1% of domestic expenditure on health would suffice to achieve the targets set by the roadmap (WHO, 2021a). Further, the multiplying effect of NTD interventions means that the economy beyond the health sector would profit from these investments due to people's increased productivity.

---

5 Such consequences became obvious when the UK government announced that it would massively cut its financial support of NTD interventions (Filou, 2021).

WHO maintains that cross-sectoral and cross-disease collaborations are key to achieving sustainable progress in NTD elimination (WHO, 2021a). The literature on this topic strongly agrees that integrated approaches are necessary to successfully target and eventually eliminate NTDs. All experts acknowledge that a variety of interventions will be required, but their views on the appropriate areas of emphasis differ slightly from paper to paper. WHO (2021a), Bradley et al. (2021), De Assis et al. (2021), The Economist Intelligence Unit (2020), and Manjang et al. (2021) each recommend an integrated approach including at minimum the following: treatments; health education and WASH; vector control; R&D of new drugs and diagnostics; and improved information systems, for example M&E. Concerted action in all these areas will be fundamental to eventually achieving the elimination of SCH as a public health problem.

Unfortunately, as Linazaa et al. (2021) argue, medicine donations alone will not solve the problem of NTDs. The Economist Intelligence Unit (2020) concurs by pointing out that even if a disease is eliminated as a public health problem, infection rates are likely to increase again after treatment campaigns are concluded. WHO (2021a) cites examples of countries where NTDs could only be eliminated through a set of several interventions. In the case of SCH, the administration of PZQ as provided by Merck is highly efficient in treating the disease, but re-infection rates are still high in endemic areas. This makes it necessary to repeat treatment rounds (Manjang et al., 2021). In high and moderate risk areas, MDA continues to be the most cost-effective approach. In low-risk areas, targeted approaches might be more efficient (Turner et al., 2020). MDAs have proved to successfully control morbidity. However, when moving towards elimination, more customized strategies are needed (The Economist Intelligence Unit, 2020).

Research Question & Methodology

The thesis statement argues that "the healthcare company Merck can drive forward sustainable development in the elimination of schistosomiasis in sub-Saharan Africa." The research question which evolves from this statement asks how Merck could achieve this target. Formulated it reads: "How can a company like Merck, in close collaboration with partners, drive forward sustainable development in the elimination of the neglected tropical disease schistosomiasis in sub-Saharan African countries?"

In order to arrive at a comprehensive answer to this research question, it is first necessary to determine whether the company Merck would be able to achieve sustainable development on its own. If not, what interventions are needed to successfully eliminate SCH. In a final step, the question is what role Merck can play in these interventions. Three hypotheses derive from these considerations:

- The elimination of SCH can be achieved by the efforts of the healthcare company Merck alone.
- The control and eventually elimination of SCH is possible if provision of treatment, health education, WASH measures, and research & development in diagnostics and medicines are combined in a sustainable integrated approach with support of Merck.
- If the combination of multiple strategies is necessary to eliminate a disease like SCH, Merck can play a crucial role by engaging in a number of these activities, such as providing treatments, supporting health education, and addressing supply chain issues.

In order to evaluate these hypotheses, the author chose to carry out qualitative research in the form of a case study focusing on the MSEP. As demonstrated in the previous section, sustainability in the NTD context is an extremely complex topic. The format and scope of this project would not suffice for an in-depth analysis of the entire field, which would have included drug donation programs from other pharmaceutical companies targeting other NTDs. Therefore, the author chose to focus on one particular NTD, that is SCH. Moreover, the author decided to focus on the contribution of only one stakeholder in the global fight against NTDs, Merck.

Two types of data collection are used for this research: a detailed literature review on the state of knowledge in the scientific discussion (as presented in the previous chapter) and data retrieved from key informant interviews. The key messages from the scientific articles as well as the statements from the interviewees were then tested against the research question with regard to whether they support or contradict the hypotheses previously defined.

Because of the qualitative nature of this research, the interviewees at Merck and in the NTD community were carefully chosen. Stakeholders employed by Merck were selected due to their extensive knowledge about sustainability, SCH, and Merck's commitment in both fields. In order to complement the internal view with external perspectives, the author requested interviews from stakeholders in the NTD community. Three interview partners were chosen for this purpose – one from an endemic country, one from an NGO active in an endemic country, and one from WHO.

All interviewees confirmed their willingness to be interviewed and signed a consent form. The author prepared open-ended questions for each interviewee. All interviews except one were held virtually and recorded via Microsoft Teams; the interview with Dr. Manfred Klevesath took place physically in the Merck offices in Darmstadt and was recorded via mobile phone. The legal department and work council of Merck were informed by the author about the interviews with Merck employees and approval was granted.

Presentation of Results

Asked about their personal understanding of sustainability, all Merck internal interviewees replied with statements similar to the Brundtland definition. Waltz emphasizes the interconnectedness of environmental, economic, and social aspects of sustainability. Klevesath expresses similar views and explains that companies like Merck act sustainably if they meet their business objectives while being mindful of environmental and social factors. Buchholz joins Klevesath and Waltz in claiming that business should not only avoid negative impacts of their activities, but also contribute to society positively. He points out that solutions to achieve the SDGs will require investments from businesses and that actions are needed now. He sees environmental challenges as the most obvious changes at the moment but predicts that social inequality and political instability will also have major impacts on millions of people worldwide, causing conflicts and other major challenges. In his view, social, economic, and environmental factors are all intertwined.

Buchholz cites organizational readiness as a key factor for incorporating sustainability at all levels of business. Developing a sustainability strategy starts with defining sustainability within the context of the organization and then integrating this definition into business activities wherever possible. Buchholz points out that a sustainable business strategy in the next phase means that economic factors (such as net present value, return on investment etc.) are taken into account along with sustainability factors when business decisions are made. However, in order to define such sustainability factors, it is necessary to provide them with a certain value so that they can be included and assessed in a business plan. Buchholz notes that the SBV tool developed by Merck provides such a monetary value of a given project for society.

Klevesath agrees that sustainability needs to be quantifiable in order to be taken into consideration in portfolio management and other business decisions. This will require the definition of a universally valid standard and tools like the SBV can be very helpful first steps towards evaluating and rating the different activities. Decision making is becoming more complex as the number of influencing factors increases, sustainability being one of them.

Asked about his understanding of sustainability in NTDs, Garba Djirmay replied that countries should be able to maintain the NTD programs and related activities when external funding ends. Hence countries should be in a position not only to maintain the efforts, but also to go even further to attain the ultimate goal of eliminating NTDs. In the case of SCH, this means that once elimination as a public health problem is achieved, countries should move towards interruption of transmission where possible. Garba Djirmay cites country ownership as a crucial factor for program sustainability, which is why it is also mentioned so prominently in the WHO roadmap. According to Garba Djirmay, this ownership comes with specific responsibilities. Not only should countries take the lead and continue to collaborate with a multitude of partners. They should also integrate NTD-specific targets and strategies into their national health plans. Further, NTD interventions should be included in routine health services at health centers. Garba Djirmay criticizes that due to the external funding of the interventions, even health workers see them as external programs. Since they do not feel responsible, they do not see the necessity to integrate these interventions into their daily work.

In Garba Djirmay's view, country ownership should take place on various levels. This will require both training of health personnel and increasing internal funding of NTD interventions. Garba Djirmay emphasizes that although countries are already funding numerous activities such as salaries, electricity, cars etc., they should also pay directly for drug distribution activities. Additionally, countries should invest in M&E activities as this will help them gain more in-depth understanding of the disease situation within their borders. Asked whether countries are able to fund these additional activities, Garba Djirmay confirmed and clarified that they are not asked to take over the funding of all activities currently underway. Considerable impact has been made in controlling SCH, and the burden of the disease has decreased and will continue to do so. This means that the extent of required activities which countries need to maintain will also decrease.

Tchuem Tchuenté argues along similar lines by maintaining that in a world of disease control, sustainability is the capacity of countries to maintain program intervention and services – especially in public health. After the termination of major financial and technical assistance from external and internal donors, countries must be able to provide ongoing prevention, treatment, and intervention. Hence in the first step towards ownership, countries must have a clear vision. Global targets set by the WHO roadmap should be translated to the country level. The country's vision should be mentioned explicitly in the national plan, which includes a clear definition of the intervention, the role of each of the partners, the timeline, and the funding resources that should be used. As every country has its own unique characteristics, each must define its own national roadmap for achieving its vision.

Tchuem Tchuenté was reporting from Cameroon, where SCH continues to be a serious health problem although significant progress has been achieved in reducing the prevalence of the disease. In 2017, the country decided to move from morbidity control to elimination of SCH and developed a dedicated roadmap laying out key programmatic actions that need to be implemented in order to achieve interruption of transmission. The roadmap defines seven programmatic actions: 1) completion of precision mapping at district level, 2) expansion of treatment to all at-risk groups; 3) strengthening the health systems operational capacity; 4) intensifying multisectoral action (including WASH, snail control etc.); 5) efficient M&E program; 6) advocacy and funding for the new approaches; and 7) encouragement of country and community ownership. The control and eventually elimination of SCH remains a challenging target. Tchuem Tchuenté made it clear that Cameroon will continue to require support from multisectoral partners in order to achieve this goal.

Bruck contributed insights from Ethiopia, another endemic country in sub-Saharan Africa. The NALA Foundation has experienced good governmental support here. Bruck agrees with the other interviewees that commitment from the government is extremely important, but also cites limited available resources as the greater problem. In the region of Bench Maji, where the joint project with Merck was launched, a significant reduction in the prevalence of SCH has been achieved. The NALA Foundation is currently considering applying the project approach in other areas as well. However, Bruck believes that it would not be sustainable for NALA to remain in one area for many years because it would create too much dependency. Like the other interviewees, Bruck strongly advocates for the involvement of the community. In her view, sustainability includes two aspects. First, communities own the projects and maintain or upscale them on their own. Second, approaches such as the one applied by NALA need to be scalable and applicable in different settings by different communities. When asked which steps would be necessary to eliminate SCH in Ethiopia, she named three different levels: (1) awareness: local actors, authorities, communities need to understand how SCH impacts their lives and how they can prevent it; (2) capacity to tackle the disease, e.g., the technical means to carry out prevention measures; and (3) actual realization of prevention.

Waltz defines sustainability in the NTD context as countries taking more responsibility so that external support can be slowly reduced. He draws a strong connection between economic development and the reduction of prevalence of these poverty-related diseases. However, when it comes to the political commitment needed to achieve this sustainable development, Waltz sees huge challenges to overcome. He believes that if political will were combined with the already available resources, then elimination would be easier to attain. At present, the sense of urgency is often lacking, says Waltz.

Zaadnoordijk understands sustainability in the NTD and SCH context as win-win solutions for countries and their partners. Countries should take the lead but should also be held accountable for pushing the sustainability agenda forward. Zaadnoordijk assigns responsibility to the partners who should take the WHO roadmap as a guide and support countries in the best way possible. Like Waltz, she also points to the difficult situation in some countries due to war, political changes, and a lack of transparency. In order for NTD programs to be sustainable, roles and responsibilities must be made much clearer in the future.

Finally, Reinhard-Rupp defines sustainability in the NTD context as breaking the cycle of poverty. She argues that if people can live healthier lives, they can contribute to the economic development of their countries. However, if they are always struggling with disease – including not only SCH but also many other diseases – they cannot escape the vicious cycle on their own and thus need external support. It would therefore be sustainable to eliminate SCH to reduce the burden from the disease as well as to enable economic prosperity.

Merck-Internal Views on the Merck Schistosomiasis Elimination Program

According to Waltz, the MSEP has been very much reduced to the social dimension in the past because of its philanthropic nature. In his view, this remains a weak spot from an economic perspective. On the other hand, he argues, the development towards sustainable models is still quite new, leaving room for considerable progress. In the early days of corporate responsibility, the term mainly referred to "doing good." This also meant that pharmaceutical companies like Merck were limited to philanthropic models. Much has changed in development aid since then, says Waltz. He adds that the term "neglected tropical diseases" did not previously exist, making concerted action against these diseases extremely difficult. For this reason, demands for the donation program to become more sustainable represent a current trend. Waltz thus finds it notable that Merck took a critical decision very early by committing to donate PZQ as long as it takes to eliminate the disease. This distinguishes the company from other donors who only commit on a five-years basis. Merck's pledge secures the global supply of PZQ, and since the populations impacted by NTDs are also the poorest on earth, tablet donations will continue to be the main access strategy to treatments.

The PZQ donation program is perceived by most interviewees as philanthropic activity and therefore not understood as being particularly sustainable. Buchholz, Klevesath, Reinhard-Rupp, Waltz, and Zaadnoordijk expressed this without questioning the value of the program to the population in Africa. Buchholz attributes it with playing an important societal role. He explains that a healthcare company like Merck must meet societal expectations to benefit as many people as possible. Since it is specialized in high-specialty products affordable to only a few people in the world, Merck cannot meet this claim with its business activities alone. This is why the company benefits from a program like the MSEP, which helps a huge number of people who cannot even afford the most basic health services, Klevesath acknowledges. Thanks to this program, Merck can meet its social responsibility, contributing in turn to sustainability. His vision for the next decade would be for Merck to support countries in their elimination efforts so that some countries can reach this goal by 2030. From this point, only a few countries should continue to require support from the company. At the moment, the PZQ donation still comprises the largest share of Merck's commitment, but Klevesath would like to see this amount to gradually being taken over by the countries in the coming years and for the company to develop even more expertise beyond the provision of tablets. For him, a sustainable investment in the MSEP context would include a decrease in purely philanthropic activities and an increase in other activities that serve a useful purpose and create social value but also generate at least some financial return for the company. This transition should go on until Merck can finally end its support due to low SCH prevalence and leave the responsibility with the countries.

In the view of Reinhard-Rupp, a donation program per se is not sustainable, yet there is no other alternative in the global fight against SCH. PZQ treatments enable the reduction of morbidity, which is an extremely important gain, but additional interventions would be necessary to eliminate SCH. Reinhard-Rupp elaborates further that while donations in emergency situations are important for now, they will generate dependencies if they continue for many years. If medicines are dispensed free of charge, there is no incentive for local manufacturers to produce PZQ themselves. The goal should be for Merck to slowly end its donations because on the one hand, the morbidity of SCH is low enough, and on the other hand, countries have economically advanced to a stage where they have enough capacities to procure or produce PZQ themselves. If two to three countries could produce the drug (as well as other NTD drugs) and sell it to other countries, this could represent a way to end dependency on donations. Merck could and would continue to concentrate its activities on the most disadvantaged and poorest countries that still have a long way to go to reach these capacities.

Zaadnoordijk agrees that a donation program is not sustainable in itself. Nonetheless, she points out that countries were able to build capacities through the donation program. Thanks to the MSEP and other comparable programs, supply chain infrastructures have been developed. Through these drug donation programs, most previously unreached remote populations could be reached. Zaadnoordijk adds that the enormous social impact of the MSEP has also been demonstrated in the SBV evaluation of the program. By focusing on eliminating SCH, Merck contributes to healthier lives and in consequence healthier economies. In this way, she says, the MSEP plays an important role in achieving sustainability.

Waltz also agrees on this point. He explains that it is rather unlikely that Merck will invest even more in the provision of tablets. This is not because it is too expensive, but because the existing commitment would be sufficient if used in a more efficient way. Waltz makes clear that the treatments will remain free of charge for patients simply because the group affected by diseases such as SCH belong to the bottom of the socio-economic pyramid. If countries have a clear strategy for the elimination of SCH, the company will definitely support these endeavors within its realm of responsibility. This might also include the provision of tablets for adult treatment. Countries who have made progress in the reduction of SCH prevalence so that they can start aiming at elimination should define clear strategies regarding how to reach this goal. This includes more targeted treatment approaches and will also encompass treatments of all risk groups – including adults – in some high endemic areas.

Waltz argues that if countries are successful at testing and providing treatments in moderate to low-endemic regions, a significant number of tablets will be made available to treat entire populations in high-endemic regions. The current MDA approach focusing on school-aged children has been the right choice thus far as the drug is well tolerated and prevalence rates were still very high. However, the more infection rates decrease, the more people are treated with PZQ in MDAs although they are not infected with the disease. In order to change this, further investments in diagnostics such as rapid diagnostic tests are necessary to identify disease hotspots. Waltz cites efficient M&E as another important aspect of gathering the data needed to provide treatments in a more targeted way. This is why the company is working with an agency on the development of an M&E framework for countries. The next step in the development will be its testing in a few African countries. The project will be finalized as soon as the COVID-19 pandemic allows.

Reinhard-Rupp also places great importance on the development of diagnostics and explains that Merck is currently developing a rapid diagnostic test for SCH. The tool will be ready for the market in approximately two years.

According to Reinhard-Rupp, knowledge transfer is a further important contribution Merck can make to support sustainable development towards SCH elimination as this includes capacity-building in research. She points out several training courses and curricula developed by the Merck Global Health Institute for research students in endemic countries. This not only increases knowledge about the diseases in country, but also encourages young professionals to stay when they see there are projects to work on. Their knowledge-sharing and advocating for action may help these diseases to move up on national agendas. Reinhard-Rupp sees this as a long and slow development, but holds that it can nevertheless have a positive impact. She cites biological vector control as an additional promising field for Merck to explore. This entails finding non-toxic solutions to tackle the parasites in their intermediate hosts. Reinhard-Rupp sees more potential for Merck to make an impact through technology and knowledge transfer than by exercising political influence. The company can advocate for the importance of tackling NTDs, but cannot play an active political role and probably should not. The interviewees agreed that Merck should not overstep boundaries by going beyond its realm of expertise.

All interviewees working on SCH-related projects clearly agree on one point: Merck is very unique in its activities aimed at overcoming one specific disease. Although other companies donate drugs for NTDs, Merck's approach is very special because it does not limit its responsibility for the provision of treatments. Instead, it takes into account all activities necessary to eliminate SCH. If these activities fall within the company's realm of expertise, it carries them out itself. For all other activities it seeks out strong partners. All concur that this attitude is in fact sustainable.

External Views on Merck's Role in the Elimination of Schistosomiasis

When key stakeholders outside of Merck were asked about the role they would ascribe to the company in global SCH elimination efforts, all agreed that Merck should continue providing PZQ for the treatment of school-aged children. Garba Djirmay points out that countries should take more responsibility for fighting NTDs, but that they will still need support. It would be asking too much to expect them to purchase the drugs as well as to invest in NTD intervention and new M&E frameworks. Tchuem Tchuenté agrees on this point. He notes that Merck is the only donor of PZQ globally, and that if countries wish to eliminate SCH, they will need not less, but rather even more PZQ to treat additional groups. At the same time, he also emphasizes that adult treatment should only take place in regions with clear elimination strategies.

R&D of drugs and diagnostics such as rapid diagnostic tests is another area where Merck will play an important role in the vision of Garba Djirmay and Tchuem Tchuenté. Garba Djirmay names additional treatments, diagnostics and maybe even a vaccine against SCH, welcoming the prospect of pharmaceutical companies continuing to invest in these activities. He explains further that the availability of rapid diagnostic tests would support the M&E efforts of countries regarding SCH. Required improvements in operational research are mentioned by both Garba Djirmay and Tchuem Tchuenté.

Another key area in the eyes of the external stakeholders is the transfer of knowledge from Merck to the individual countries. Merck is highly experienced not only in pharmaceutical production, but also in the development of training programs and processes. Garba Djirmay suggests that companies like Merck help countries build capacities, for example for local manufacturing not only of PZQ, but also other medicines. In his view, it would be a very desirable development if countries in sub-Saharan Africa could produce NTD drugs. Moreover, intercontinental trade could potentially be supported by the availability of pharmaceutical production on the continent.

Bruck believes that the strength of a company like Merck lies partially in its appetite for innovation. Private sector companies have the capital to experiment with new ideas and support the development of new concepts. Bruck sees Merck as playing a special role as a leader and providing an example of how companies should act. The company has a very clear agenda and also supports other partners – such as the NALA Foundation in their efforts to address additional components such as WASH and health education.

In sum, the interviews indicate that Merck's contribution in the form of tablet provision will need to continue to sustain the system and reduce morbidity further. Having said this, moving the process forward in terms of both elimination and sustainability will require the affected countries to take the lead. The main challenges identified by most of the interviewees are related to sustainable funding, which should come in part from the countries themselves, depending greatly on political stability and commitment in these countries.

Discussion

This paper began with the thesis statement: "The healthcare company Merck can drive forward sustainable development in the elimination of schistosomiasis in sub-Saharan Africa." Based on the findings from the literature review and the conversations with key informants, the author has reached several conclusions.

NTDs affect the poorest and most vulnerable populations in the world. The countries negatively influenced by these diseases are predominantly ones with low- or middle-income. Therefore, it will be extremely challenging for them to solve the problem of NTDs alone. The question is thus how partners can best support the countries. Many countries are not yet in a position to fully assume NTD interventions; the required capacities must be created within the next several years. This is a difficult task that will require innovative and unique approaches from various stakeholders across sectors and across diseases. The findings in the literature as well as the statements from the interviewees therefore contradict the first hypothesis of the thesis, which states that the elimination of SCH can be achieved by the company Merck alone. This approach is neither possible nor desirable. Sustainability in the NTD context includes not only the elimination of these diseases, but also the independence of countries from external support. Merck and other global stakeholders should assist and encourage countries, but not take the lead.

The second hypothesis of the thesis maintains that the control and eventual elimination of SCH will be possible if the provision of treatments, health education, WASH measures, and R&D in diagnostics and drugs are combined in a sustainable integrated approach. The results from the literature review and the conversations with the interviewees partially confirm the hypothesis in the sense that a sustainable approach definitely requires these activities. The in-depth analysis of the subject has demonstrated that the endeavor to eliminate a disease like SCH requires not only the availability of high-quality treatments and funding for their implementation, but also continued interventions in the areas of health education and WASH. New drugs and diagnostics need to be developed and brought to the market. Supply chain improvements as well as new strategies for vector control must also be on the agenda.

Wherever possible, the treatment campaigns of entire populations in a given geographical area should be taken into consideration and aligned with specific targets. Innovative solutions in various fields that connect several diseases and sectors will be necessary. The global community will need to take a broader perspective beyond NTDs and support countries in strengthening their health systems to eventually achieve UHC. In the judgement of this author, the global fight against NTDs has an enormous potential to act not only as a multiplier of developments beyond the healthcare sector, but also as an indicator of the actual strength of a health care system and of poverty alleviation.

The third hypothesis of the thesis is concerned with the significance of Merck's role in the elimination efforts. Clearly, Merck is in a position to play a crucial role by engaging in a number of activities, such as providing treatments, supporting health education, and addressing supply chain issues. In the case of Merck's PZQ donation, this includes the continued provision of treatment for school-aged children and – where it makes sense – extending it to adults. Merck will continue to align with other pharma donors to optimize processes and increase transparency in the supply chain. One of Merck's core areas of expertise lies in pharmaceutical development and production, and the company will continue to make this knowledge available to countries. This includes the development of a medicine for preschoolers as well as additional drugs. Further support of operational improvements through the establishment of an M&E framework for countries and the development of a rapid diagnostic test could also become valuable contributions.

The research has shown that Merck in fact has played an important role in the fight against SCH and will continue to do so in future. The company committed to providing PZQ tablets until elimination of SCH long before anyone believed that this goal was achievable. Further, Merck not only continued, but also increased it engagement substantially over the past 14 years. This resulted in a shift from a purely philanthropic commitment towards a more complex approach. Although the provision of large amounts of PZQ will most probably continue to be the main element of the company's contribution, it will not be the only one. The integrated approach Merck is taking towards the elimination of SCH has been presented in detail. The author believes that this unique set of strategies will more or less remain the same on the path towards the 2030 WHO targets. However, what each pillar includes will still evolve. The third hypothesis, that Merck can play a crucial role in supporting a broad range of activities contributing to the elimination of SCH, can be considered confirmed.

The current discussion of sustainability and the growing call of all stakeholders for sustainable approaches will help shape the strategies of global partners working to eliminate NTDs. The recent endorsement of the WHO NTD roadmap and the accompanying sustainability framework does not signal the end of the discussion of sustainability, but rather its starting point. WHO has set the strategic framework. Now all other stakeholders will need to decide individually how they want to contribute to the objectives set by the roadmap. The unique characteristics of NTDs in general and SCH in particular will guide these decisions. The German company Merck started having these reflections very early. In the view of the author, the company could be seen as a role model in the way it has shifted from a purely philanthropic donation program toward a more sustainable investment in global health.

It should be emphasized that the research presented in this paper has some limitations. As pointed out, tackling the entire group of NTDs is a very complex endeavor. Consequently, this thesis can only offer a comprehensive but not exhaustive analysis of all factors, stakeholder involvements, and disease peculiarities. Very recent developments could only be mentioned briefly without detailed discussion. This includes for instance the implications of the COVID-19 pandemic for progress made against NTDs. Another major health crisis could have very serious consequences for already weak health systems.

Conclusion

The definition of sustainability in the NTD context is a unique one. It is not only about preserving particular types of resources, but also about enabling additional resources, capabilities, and capacities of countries to make their own choices in the future. The definition of sustainability in relation to NTDs goes beyond the elimination of a group of 20 insidious diseases and the accompanying reduction of a serious health burden. It also involves creating country capacity to maintain elimination. Concerted action from all stakeholders is necessary to support affected countries. The efforts of one specific stakeholder, the science and technology company Merck, was examined in detail. The research question asked what role the company should play in driving forward sustainable development in the elimination of SCH in sub-Saharan African countries.

The author found that eliminating the NTD SCH is such a complex endeavor that it cannot be achieved alone, but rather in cooperation with a variety of partners, which is why the first hypothesis was not supported. Elimination also requires a multipronged approach including cross-sector and cross-disease interventions. The second hypothesis identifying the need for treatments, R&D, WASH and health education was confirmed and extended to include an even broader scope. Finally, the third hypothesis specifying the contribution of one particular partner, namely Merck, was supported. The author demonstrated that Merck has played an important role in reducing the burden of the disease SCH.

The author recommends that the company continue supporting the sustainability agenda as long as it takes to eliminate SCH as a public health problem. With its unique set of expertise in pharmaceuticals, Merck secures the availability of high-quality treatments and provides new medicines and diagnostic tools as well as financial support for additional interventions such as health education and WASH. Both the literature and the interviewed experts concurred that these activities are crucial. Merck's continued commitment is assured because the company has promised to provide PZQ until elimination of SCH is achieved. However, the commitments of other companies are up for renewal every couple of years. This study has shown how fragile the entire system of NTD interventions is. If elimination of NTDs is to be achieved, the contributions of all stakeholders involved need to be sustained.

Global efforts in the fight against NTDs have enabled huge achievements in reducing the burden of these diseases. Nonetheless, they continue to prevent populations in LMICs from living healthy and fulfilled lives. If these diseases remain prevalent, citizens of the affected countries will not be able to lift themselves out of poverty, as their poor health conditions also impact their economic performance. This vicious cycle must be interrupted. The presented study has shown that this will require increased ownership of countries where NTDs are endemic. Only if the entire NTD community encourages countries to take the lead will they be able to eliminate these insidious diseases, improve the health of their populations, and in turn improve their economic development. Healthier people lead to healthier economies and vice versa. By breaking the cycle of poverty, sustainable development is possible. Eliminating NTDs will have a catalyzing effect on these efforts.

References

Bradley, M., Taylor, R., Jacobson, J., Guex, M., Hopkins, A., Jensen, J., Leonard, L., Waltz, J., Kuykens, L., Sow, P. S., Madeja, U., Hida, T., Ole-Moiyoi, K., King, J., Argaw, D., Mohamed, J., Rebollo Polo, M., Yajima, A., & Ottesen, E. (2021, January 16). Medicine donation programmes supporting the global drive to end the burden of neglected tropical diseases. Transactions of the Royal Society of Tropical Medicine and Hygiene, 115, 136–144. https://doi.org/10.1093/trstmh/traa167

Buchholz, H., Eberle, T., Klevesath, M., Jürgens, A., Beal, D., Baic, A., & Radeke, J. (2020, October 13). Forward thinking for sustainable business value: A new method for impact valuation. Sustainability 2020, 12(20), 8420. https://doi.org/10.3390/su12208420

De Assis, T. M., Rabello, A., & Cota, G. (2021, April 23). Economic evaluations addressing diagnosis and treatment strategies for neglected tropical diseases: an overview. Revista do Instituto de Medicina Tropical de São Paulo 2021;63, Article e41. https://doi.org/10.1590/S1678-9946202163041

Economist Intelligence Unit (2020). Breaking the cycle of neglect: Reducing the economic and societal burden of parasitic worms in sub-Saharan Africa. https://wormfreeworld.eiu.com/downloads/report-Complete.pdf

Elkington, J. (1999). Cannibals with Forks: The triple bottom line of 21st century business. Capstone Publishing.

Ertl, V., Kaiser, M., & Weidenbach, S. (2021, February). Gesundheit nachhaltig stärken: EU-AU-Kooperation für resiliente Gesundheitssysteme in Subsahara-Afrika. https://www.kas.de/documents/252038/11055681/Gesundheit+nachhaltig+st%C3%A4rken.pdf/290727e8-a7f1-8ef0-3848-626c82cdcbb0?version=1.0&t=1613480214419

Filou, E. (2021, June 14). UK aid cuts will result in the destruction of millions of doses of life-saving drugs. The Telegraph. Retrieved from https://preview.telegraph.co.uk/global-health/climate-and-people/uk-aid-cuts-will-results-millions-doses-life-saving-drugs-destroyed/

Fitzpatrick, C., Nwankwo, U., Lenk, E., J de Vlas, S., & Bundy, D. A. P. (2017). An Investment Case for Ending Neglected Tropical Diseases. In K. K. Holmes, S. Bertozzi, B. R. Bloom, & P. Jha (Eds.), Disease Control Priorities (3rd ed., pp. 411-431). The World Bank. https://doi.org/10.1596/978-1-4648-0526-4

Global Schistosomiasis Alliance (n.d.). Working Groups and Work Streams. Retrieved October 23, 2021, from https://www.eliminatesc histo.org/working-groups-and-work-streams

Hollingsworth, T. D., Mwinzi, P., Vasconcelos, A., & de Vlas, S. J. (2021, February 11). Evaluating the potential impact of interruptions to neglected tropical disease programmes due to COVID-19. Transactions of the Royal Society of Tropical Medicine and Hygiene 2021, 115, 201–204. https://doi.org/10.1093/trstmh/trab023

Hotez, P. J. (2013). Forgotten people/Forgotten diseases: The neglected tropical diseases and their impact on global health and development (2nd ed.). ASM Press. https://doi.org/10/1128/ISBN978-1-55581-875-3

Intergovernmental Panel on Climate Change (2021, August 9). Climate change widespread, rapid, and intensifying – IPCC. https://www.ipcc.ch/2021/08/09/ar6-wg1-20210809-pr/

Linazaa, R. V., Garnera, T., & Genovezos, C. (2021, April 22). Building supply chain capacity for neglected tropical diseases: experience from the Ascend West and Central Africa programme. Transactions of the Royal Society of Tropical Medicine and Hygiene 2021, 0, 1–6. https://doi.org/10.1093/trstmh/trab068

Manjang, B., Ochola, E. A., & Elliott, S. J. (2021, January 18). The use of non-pharmaceutical interventions for the prevention and control of schistosomiasis in sub-Saharan Africa: A systematic review. Global Public Health. https://doi.org/10.1080/17441692.2020.1869799

Monnier, N., Barth-Jaeggi, T., Knopp, S., & Steinmann, P. (2020, October 30). Core components, concepts and strategies for parasitic and vector-borne disease elimination with a focus on schistosomiasis: A landscape analysis. PLoS Negl Trop Dis 14(10), Article e0008837. https://doi.org/10.1371/journal.pntd.0008837

Merck (2020). Sustainability Report 2020: Focus Programs. Retrieved September 12, 2021, from https://www.merckgroup.com/en/sustainability-report/2020/products/health-for-all/focus-programs.html#accordionSpecial1

Merck (2021a). Storytelling Lab. Retrieved September 23, 2021, from https://www.merckgroup.com/en/sustainability/health-for-all/schistosomiasis/storytelling-lab.html

Merck (2021b). Sustainability. Retrieved September 12, 2021, from https://www.merckgroup.com/en/sustainability.html

Merck (n.d.). Reports & Guidelines. Retrieved September 12, 2021, from https://www.merckgroup.com/en/sustainability/reports-and-guidelines.html

Merck (n.d.). The Name and Brand: Merck. Retrieved October 23, 2021, from https://www.merckgroup.com/en/company/the-name-and-brand-merck.html

Merck Global Health Institute (n.d.). Merck Global Health Institute. Retrieved October 23, 2021, from https://www.merckglobalhealthinstitute.com/en/home.html).

Sodahlon, Y., Ross, D. A., McPhillips-Tangum, C., Lawrence, J., Taylor, R., McFarland, D. A., Krentel, A., Anyaikea, C., Batcho, W. E., Bougouma, C., de Pádua Careli Dantas, A., Dhingra, N., Guambe, M. M., Ibrahim, K., Kargbo-Labour, I. J., Matwale, G. K., Momprevil, F., Monteiro, M. A. A., Nko'Ayissi, G. B., Omondi, W. P., ... Ntuli Malecela, M. (2020, October 8). Building country capacity to sustain NTD programs and progress: A call to action. PLoS Negl Trop Dis 14(10), Article e0008565. https://doi.org/10.1371/journal.pntd.0008565

Thuo, I. W., Ndiaye, K., & Mookherji, S. (2020). Factors influencing the sustainability of neglected tropical disease elimination programs: A multi-case study of the Kenya National Program for elimination of lymphatic filariasis. American Journal of Tropical Medicine and Hygiene 102(5), 1090–1093. https://doi.org/10.4269/ajtmh.19-0261

Turner, H. C., French, M. D., Montresor, A., King, C. H., Rollinson, D., & Toor, J. (2020, August 7). Economic evaluations of human schistosomiasis interventions: a systematic review and identification of associated research needs. Wellcome Open Research. https://doi.org/10.12688/wellcomeopenres.15754.2

United Nations (1987). Report of the World Commission on Environment and Development: Our Common Future. http://www.un-documents.net/our-common-future.pdf

United Nations (n.d.). The 17 Goals. Retrieved August 9, 2021, from https://sdgs.un.org/goals

World Health Organization. (2021, January 28). Ending the neglect to attain the Sustainable Development Goals. A road map for neglected tropical diseases 2021–2030. https://www.who.int/publications/i/item/9789240010352

World Health Organization. (2021, January 28). Ending the neglect to attain the Sustainable Development Goals: a sustainability framework for action against neglected tropical diseases 2021–2030. https://www.who.int/publications/i/item/9789240019027

World Health Organization (2021, May 18). Schistosomiasis. https://www.who.int/news-room/fact-sheets/detail/schistosomiasis

List of Figures

Figure 1.1: The Lifecycle of Schistosomes 57
Figure 1.2: Infographic on Merck's integrated approach 61

Internationalization in Germany: How to Attract International, Intercultural Researchers to Work at Hamburg University of Technology (TUHH)

Anja Bernhardt

Abstract

A globalized world connects societies and internationalization calls for people from all over the world. This also applies to research organizations. However, at least in Germany, universities usually concentrate on international students. The demand for specialists with a technical background and concluding researchers in developed countries such as Germany is high. Respective specialists might be available outside of Germany and even outside the European Union. Nonetheless, there are hurdles to overcome and international researchers from outside the EU face additional legal and administrative challenges. This requires a conscious welcoming culture and an awareness of acculturation processes which involves all participants. In this context, it is important to offer services at a university that facilitate entry barriers and that promote integration.

The results of this work support the hypothesis that to attract international researchers from outside the EU, German universities need to offer services that facilitate entry barriers and that promote integration. Using both qualitative and quantitative methodology, the author argues that it is important to address all stakeholders at a university. With this work, she proposes to broaden the discussion to include the group of international researchers. In particular, it is important to find out what makes universities attractive to this group.

Introduction

The positioning of this thesis is in the research field of intercultural management, while concentrating on internationalization strategies at German universities. This work focuses on the welcoming culture of the organization and specifically, on what is necessary to promote acculturation. In this context, acculturation is understood as a mutual change process (Ward et al., 2001) which affects all stakeholders in an international, intercultural organization. This work aims to broaden the discussion about what makes universities attractive for an intercultural researcher.

The statement of this thesis is that internationalization strategies at German universities must address international students and international researchers alike. Therefore, this thesis seeks to find answers to the question which services universities need to offer if they want to attract international researchers. The author assumes that international researchers could appreciate especially those offers that promote and facilitate their arrival and promote integration. This is suggested by the author's experience with international researchers in her research group.

At least at Hamburg University of Technology (TUHH), internationalization strategies concentrate on international students and ways to increase their annual number. As a result, available support services from TUHH are solely offered to this group. This work aims to extend this focus towards international, intercultural researchers and here especially towards researchers from countries outside the EU. This group of individuals faces additional challenges in contrast to those coming from EU member states.

As their countries of origin and their cultures vary, she understands them as international, intercultural researchers. The same holds true when addressing international researchers in this work. Therefore, to facilitate reading, international, intercultural researchers will be addressed as InRs, and international students as InSs from now on.

The author works at TUHH at a research group where researchers from around the world work and study. For the purpose of this work, in 2020 she conducted interviews with colleagues coming from Jordan, Malaysia, Pakistan, Turkey, Russia, and Ukraine. Conversations with her colleagues confirmed that they all shared similar challenging experiences when relocating to another country and culture. They admitted that there are many hurdles to overcome and that sometimes researchers even regret choosing to move to Germany for work or study.

These conversations are a major reason for proposing this research topic. The author is of the opinion that in the attempt to attract InRs from outside the EU, German universities need to offer services that facilitate entry barriers and that promote integration. This will attract more InRs, and this in turn will promote the internationalization of the university. It will not only serve their interests but will also improve the international reputation of the organization.

Literature and Research Questions

Today, many societies are undergoing change as their populations become more international and intercultural. In Germany this cultural diversity is also evident (Statista, n.d.).

Cultural diversity must also be present in organizations. This will stimulate creativity and innovation and thus, promote business opportunities (R. Bouncken, 2009; R. Bouncken et al., 2016). This is true for universities as well, since their "business" is research and education (Bremer, 2018; Stahl-Rolf et al., 2018). Nevertheless, this creates international competition of and for ideas and talent, resulting in collaboration which eventually promotes innovation (Cabrera & Le Renard, 2015).

Apart from cultural diversity because of societal changes, it can also be a result of targeted internationalization processes. These do not only influence internal cultures and structures of any organization. They open new pathways of global exchange and the connectivity of people and knowledge, which could ultimately improve relations between nations. This results in internationalization, globalization and standardization of higher education. The conclusion is that internationalization brings advantages for the university and should therefore be promoted (Fromm, 2014).

Nevertheless, the current efforts to internationalize universities are not sufficient. Therefore, the Federal Ministry of Education and Research (hereafter BMBF) and the Joint Science Conference (hereafter GWK) request respective improvements at German universities (BMBF, 2016; GWK, 2013). The German Rectors' Conference – The Voice of the Universities in Germany – (hereafter HRK) even offers audits to support German universities in their attempt to create or adjust their internationalization strategy (HRK, n.d.).

Germany is an attractive country for InRs, especially if the focus is on research rather than education (Lepori et al., 2015). Yet, InRs can be empathetic role models for InSs and potentially improve their success rates (Tran, 2020).

Internationalization is best defined as an approach to equally reach out to InSs, staff and researchers (Kehm & Teichler, 2007). Even though one goal of German universities is to attract more InRs, there is little evidence of their presence because German universities have no common system for recording their number (DAAD, 2016). Therefore, internationalization at universities needs to be quantified by numbers and e.g. success rates of InRs as well (Wit, 2009). In addition, internationalization processes need to involve all participants of the university, including those who are already there (Bremer, 2018).

Nonetheless, internationalization at universities is often measured by the number of InSs enrolled, the availability of international study exchange programs, availability of courses taught in English, and the international content of coursework. However, for students and researchers, international recognition and here, international rankings are likewise important. These rankings focus on excellence in education, quality of the faculty and institutional performance, or on an outstanding single researcher (Rust & Kim, 2015).

One major driver of internationalization is mobility. The EU promotes mobility by offering international programs particularly for students and staff (EC, n.d.-b). Third country nationals can participate as well but need to fulfil visa requirements (EC, n.d.-a). On the national level, the Federal Government of Germany funds mobility as well. Due to increasing mobility, they conclude that the current generation of students and researchers consider living and working in intercultural environments to be the norm (TFG, n.d.). This in turn should facilitate integration of InRs when they work in Germany based on a generally valid welcoming culture.

It is important to understand why InRs want to study and/or work abroad. Their reasons for migration and/or mobility seem to follow a different set of rules if compared with those of other professions. Mobility of InRs is organized by themselves in the pursuit of an international reputation and research networks. Three major motivators are (1) the expert status of other researchers at a potential host university, (2) the interest to collaborate with other researchers in their field, and (3) an attractive research infrastructure at the host university (Wegner, 2016).

Prerequisites of mobility include preparation and the search for the "right" university. To understand how InRs search for international universities, it is also important to acknowledge that different cultures might have different approaches on how to search for information on the internet (Hermeking, 2005).

A welcoming culture provides services that are available if desired. So far, much has been done to create programs for InSs at German universities to facilitate their arrival and stay. Nonetheless, there is a lot of potential to do the same for InRs since they also face similar issues when relocating to another country, at least at TUHH. One approach is to establish a welcoming center at the university that bundles services for them prior to the arrival, during the stay and prior to moving back home or to a different country (vbw, 2012; Yan, 2020).

Services for InRs facilitate their arrival, stay, work and education and should include joining family (Beck, 2012). Especially prior to and upon arrival, professional support is needed (Schaer et al., 2017; Suter & Cangià, 2020). Here, it is important that university administrations and the city or government work closely together to facilitate the arrival of InRs (Föbker et al., 2014). One reason is that academic grades are not recognized from all countries and therefore, verification of the Central Office for Foreign Education (hereafter ZAB) is necessary (BiBB, n.d.).

Processes prior to starting a job also require time. This includes visa application processes and overcoming transfer obstacles for accompanying family (EC, n.d.-d; Suter & Cangià, 2020). In addition, for an accompanying working partner/spouse, dual career services should be implemented – either at the same organization or outside of it (Brenner, 2019).

InRs understand a good welcoming culture not as an all-round carefree package. What they need is a contact person in case of need (Wegner, 2016) who is able and willing to help (Pivodic, 2019). A welcoming culture at German universities should include the ability of university faculty and administration staff to communicate in English and to recognize this language as lingua franca in academic environments. They should consider learning and improving this language as a further opportunity that facilitates communication rather than an obstacle (Jenkins, 2014; Mauranen et al., 2010; Smit, 2010). Not only students and researchers, but also administrative and technical staff should be able to at least communicate effectively in English even if their language proficiency is not as good as a native speaker's (Jenkins, 2014).

Acculturalization

Internationalization happens to a large extent when individuals move to a different country. This causes a continuous acculturation process of change and adjustment, stemming from constant interaction between intercultural groups of people from at least two different cultural backgrounds. The traditional interpretation of acculturation tends to focus on groups rather than the impact on the individual level (Redfield et al., 1936).

The contemporary view added the intercultural psychological dimension of the individual to the discussion (Graves, 1967). This individualized approach has been refined. According to Berry (1980, 1997), acculturation of individuals is collaboration between maintaining one's own culture while accessing a new culture. This is an individual process which manifests itself in four different strategies: assimilation, separation, marginalization and integration.

As stated by Berry, assimilation happens when it is not important to the individual to preserve one's own culture and when the individual is eager to learn from or even adopts the other culture. Separation happens when individuals focus on their own cultural identity and avoid others in the attempt to preserve their own culture. Marginalization is an ambivalent strategy of avoidance – in respect of one's own culture as well as of other cultures. Integration is a strategy that does not give up one's own culture while accepting other cultures.

Therefore, one of the most important questions when relocating to a different country is how an individual adjusts and accepts changes in a different cultural environment. Doing this requires an individualistic acculturation strategy to cope with culture stress (Berry, 1997). The level of stress that someone experiences during and after relocation is also dependent on the acculturation strategy an individual chooses (Ward & Kennedy, 1994; Ward & Rana-Deuba, 1999). This in turn will establish an individual degree of cross-cultural competence (Chiu et al., 2013).

The acculturation process is complex because it offers multiple options, e.g., how situations are perceived and how people react. Therefore, acculturation is also relative to the power of individuals or groups in a situational context. Often, acculturation happens between a minority (here, the InR) and a majority (here, the university and the research group) and success or failure depends on personal prerequisites. Therefore, acculturation is perceived as relative to the power of the stronger party (Navas et al., 2005).

In addition, personality is a major driver in acculturation which either leads towards success (challenge) or failure (shock, threat) (van der Zee & van Oudenhoven, 2013). Therefore, success or failure of acculturation depends both on the individual and on the environment. Not every person, not even with the same cultural background, adjusts in the same way and success or failure is situational. This is the challenge to formulating a universally applicable answer to acculturation strategies and processes (Nauck, 2015).

To complicate matters further, the degree of success and failure of acculturation is not only the result of one's own personality, but also dependent on the degree of differences between host and one's own culture (Ward & Kennedy, 1994) and will also depend on the relationship between them (Sam & Berry, 2010).

Then again, acculturation requires the motivation of a visiting InR to explore a new culture of a host country and host institution and also the desire to integrate new aspects revealed to one's own culture (Recker et al., 2018; Ward & Kennedy, 1994). The InR should therefore actively cope with the changes and apply suitable strategies (Ward et al., 2001).

The invisible aspects are more difficult to address and to change because they are hard to identify. Nonetheless, culture is learned behavior and thus, can be at least adjusted when recognized (Hall, 1989; Hofstede, 2001).

Hypothesis and Research Question

The hypothesis developed both from the author's observation of her international research colleagues at a research group at TUHH and from theory compiled in the previous section about internationalization, welcoming culture and acculturation. Both observation and theory led this author to the following hypothesis:

To attract international researchers from outside the EU, German universities need to offer services that facilitate entry barriers and that promote integration.

Two questions accompany the research:
1. Perspective of international researchers: Which services do international researchers need that promote the arrival and integration of a diverse international and intercultural group of researchers, focusing on researchers from outside the EU?
2. Which of these services are already being provided at German universities and which should be introduced or need improving in the attempt to attract InRs?

The following section will introduce the methodology that confirmed the hypothesis and answered the research questions.

Methodology

The framework of this work is a qualitative, exploratory research. The study employs MAXQDA 2020 (VERBI Software, 2020), a software package for qualitative data analysis, to compare the content of the interviews. A thematic analysis (Braun et al., 2019; Guest et al., 2012) was used to identify common themes. Three of the most important themes addressed by the Ips include (1) problems with the language, (2) unclear or no provision of information on TUHH's webpage, and (3) lack of support with legal and administrative issues.

To answer the second research question and to find out if and in what way the needs for these services are already being addressed by universities in the attempt to attract InRs or if there is room for improvement, the author compared major concerns of IPs with the services currently offered by the university. In addition, she compared the findings with those of two other German universities. The researched literature was used to interpret the results and to substantiate and supplement further recommendations.

Perspective of International Researchers

For the purpose of this paper, one-on-one semi-structured interviews with six participants from third countries were conducted. They originate from Jordan, Malaysia, Pakistan, Russia, Turkey, and Ukraine. The participants work and study in miscellaneous disciplines in the fields of sustainable waste and resource management. All of them have a common goal: to complete their academic studies with a PhD in Engineering.

All six participants to participate. Therefore, it was possible to collect and compare primary data. The one-on-one interviews lasted between 29 and 45 minutes. To ensure their privacy, the names of the participants are pseudonymized in this work, but the country names are revealed. Before starting each interview, the author introduced the research project to each participant including its objectives and format of the interviews. Each participant signed a data protection notice and consent form, agreed to audio recording, to transcription and to analysis of data for the purpose of this research (Gibson, B., Hua, Z., 2016). After the interviews, the author transcribed the audio-recordings using a naturalized transcription to preserve the features of oral language (Bucholtz, 2000; Davidson, 2009).

The author wanted to compare major concerns raised by the IPs with the services offered by her own as well as other universities. For this purpose, she approached the international office TUHH and here, the team leader (hereafter TL) for incoming students. The TL is in charge of orientation and integration programs and the author expected to find solutions for the concerns of the InRs that are already available, even if they might not have gotten through to her target group.

In a first icebreaker meeting, the author introduced her ideas about her project. Already then, the TL confirmed that services are only available for InSs who are registered at the university. Nonetheless, the TL is of the opinion that these services should be offered to InRs as well. To promote this approach at the university, the TL asked this author for recommendations for its implementation.

As one IP revealed the importance of international recognition of universities, also online, the author selected the universities according to their worldwide ranking from three renowned international organizations as well: Times Higher Education (THE, n.d.), QS Quacquarelly Symonds Limited (QS, n.d.) and ShanghaiRanking Consultancy (SRC, n.d.). In all rankings, the best two German universities are currently Technical University of Munich, followed by RWTH Aachen University. In addition to international rankings, all universities included in this study have a similar technical specialty as TUHH.

Findings

The statement of this thesis is that internationalization strategies at German universities must address InSs and InRs alike. In the attempt to understand the perspective of InRs, this author wants to know which services they need that promote the arrival and integration of a diverse international and intercultural group of researchers, focusing on researchers from outside the EU.

To find out which services are already available, which should be introduced, or which need improving in the attempt to attract InRs, the TL for InSs at the international office TUHH was consulted, as well as comparisons from two other German universities.

Interviews

Six interviews with IPs from six different third countries were performed. This background shall support the subsequent presentation and discussion of the most important themes that were raised by her IPs.

Recognition of Master's Degrees of Interview Partners

Table 1.1: Recognition of Master's Degrees of Interview Partners

Interview partners	Country of origin	Master completed at home country university	Additional stay at a German university	Master completed at TUHH	Automatic recognition of degree at TUHH for PhD studies
Anastasia	Russia	no	no	yes	yes
Dalir	Pakistan	yes	no	no	no
Ecrim	Turkey	yes	yes (1 year)	no	no
Galyna	Ukraine	yes	yes (2 months)	yes (a second master after completion of home country master)	no (home country master)
Sarah	Jordan	yes	yes (1 year)	no	no
Wang	Malaysia	no	no	yes (double master: TUHH/NIT[1])	yes

---

1 Northern Institute of Technology, NIT

This table also provides an overview of where the participants performed their master's degrees. It shows that four of them completed their master studies at a home country university and two of them at TUHH. Two programs at home country universities even required an additional stay at a German university for a year (Ecrim and Sarah) and Galyna did an internship at a German university for two months. Nonetheless, their degrees were not automatically recognized at TUHH.

Ecrim is a PhD student with a scholarship from a German organization. Her scholarship facilitated the acceptance of her degree at TUHH but it was not automatically recognized. Dalir and Sarah needed recognition of their studies from the ZAB. Galyna's first master would have needed the same. Dalir performed an additional oral test before he was entitled to enroll as a PhD student.

Two participants completed their master's at TUHH (Anastasia and Wang). Wang did a double master's at TUHH and the Northern Institute of Technology, Hamburg (hereafter NIT). After completion of a master's degree at her home country university, Galyna completed a second master at TUHH.

Two of the participants finance their stay with a PhD scholarship (Dalir, Ecrim) while four of them have employment contracts as a research associate. In the research group with German as well as international colleagues, all are treated equally, independent of their own financing (employment contract or scholarship) or nationality.

When asked about what services and support are necessary at TUHH to attract InRs from third countries, the IPs brought up the following three major topics: language issues, provision of clear and visible information online and support in terms of visa and employment.

Problems with Language

When asked about their language of communication at their current position, all the IPs answered that English is the primary language. Therefore, it could be assumed that this language is more important than German. English is considered the lingua franca at international universities (Jenkins, 2014).

Nonetheless, researchers also need to have a good command of German because the level of command of the language spoken in the host country is fundamental to promote a successful interaction between the InR and the host institution (Masgoret & Ward, 2006). As an example, Ecrim confirms that she writes in German to communicate with TUHH's administration or with local companies.

The ability to speak and write the local language is a major facilitator which promotes integration and is an acculturation strategy (Ward et al., 2001; Ward & Kennedy, 1994). This is not only important when communicating with German colleagues but also when applying for research funding where the grant holder is a German organization. Here, a high level of academic writing in German is an essential tool for success. Academic writing (in German) is a toolbox that clearly specifies the use of the language itself (Moll & Thielmann, 2017).

Only one of the IPs (Dalir) hardly speaks any German. He states that he feels excluded in the research group especially when German researchers do not speak English in his presence, or when he tries to communicate with the university administration. Nonetheless, he, too, is of the opinion that to know the local language is a major driver for integration, also for the accompanying family, especially if a partner wants to work. As an example, consider the following statement:

> 'So either they [the university] can help to their family also to at least integrate, um, in this society by the providing some courses or language course or – if any PhD wants to – offer with this facility [at the research group], so it would be so much better' (interview with Dalir).

To know the local language will improve Dalir's overall satisfaction (Smith & Khawaja, 2011) since he communicates in his own language, Pakistani, most of the time.

After the interview, Dalir mentioned that he decided to continue learning German after all, possibly the result of not feeling equal among his peers. Thus, his acculturation in respect to local language ability was initiated by peer pressure, which is the majority culture in regard of the language use (Navas et al., 2005).

The importance of the knowledge of the local language is confirmed in literature (Lopez & Bui, 2014). Language is both a prerequisite and a goal which promotes satisfaction and sociocultural adaptation (Ward, 2001). Therefore, language proficiency is a major facilitator and driver during the acculturation process (Ward & Rana-Deuba, 1999) which in turn improves the overall satisfaction (Berger et al., 2019). This was clearly expressed and confirmed by all IPs.

Consequently, if acculturation is understood as a mutual change process, the university needs to provide language courses that are available for all international groups (Smith & Khawaja, 2011) and not only for InSs which is currently the case at TUHH.

TUHH's Website

In contrast to available support at TUHH for InSs, the support InRs get often stems from their own networks (Smith & Khawaja, 2011). When asked about how they found their current job, health insurance, housing, and support for partners, all of them stated that the university provided neither information nor support. Therefore, assuming that the international office would be the first contact point also for InRs, some of the IPs suggest providing a booklet with relevant information about those topics for upload on the webpage.

In addition, there should be a contact person if more information is needed. Furthermore, in the section "international office TUHH" a link should lead to job advertisements. In respect of the job advertisements, they suggest to provide them in both German and in English – especially if the goal at TUHH is to attract InRs. Moreover, important documents such as employment contracts should be provided in English as well.

The IPs revealed that their major goal was the completion of their academic studies and that they looked for respective opportunities at international universities. Literature confirms that the completion of education is a major driver for migration (Gezentsvey & Ward, 2008).

Most of them found their current position at the research group at TUHH through word of mouth by members of this research group. In other words, a majority found their current position through their own private and/or professional networks (Hajro et al., 2019).

A review of acculturation experiences of InSs revealed that networking is an important factor that facilitates acculturation processes once in the foreign country. This eases stress factors associated with the studies but also helps with the life in a different culture. Here, networks in the home country as well as in the host country provide support (Smith & Khawaja, 2011).

When asked about German and/or home country acquaintances, all of the IPs revealed that respective strong relationships supported them prior to their arrival and during their current stay in Germany. Only Dalir who hardly speaks German has no German friends. Nonetheless, he received support from a local association in Hamburg whose members are mainly from his home country.

Even when strong networks with colleagues, friends and family helped the IPs before and during their arrival in Germany and at TUHH, additional support needs to be offered by the university to facilitate processes (Berger et al., 2019). One example is the provision of relevant information to explain and facilitate administrative matters. To grant information is a major facilitator that promotes acculturation processes. This means easy access for self-research and the possibility to approach staff to receive advice (Smith & Khawaja, 2011).

Support for legal and administrative issues

Five out of the six IPs have a good command of the German language – three of them studied at TUHH and two of them completed their home studies for a year at a German university. The five IPs just mentioned started to learn the language already in their home countries and most of them continued once they arrived in Germany. Nonetheless, at the beginning, all of them had difficulties with the language, and were overwhelmed when being confronted with legal and administrative issues.

As an example, when asked what kind of visa permission she needs for her current job at TUHH, Galyna brought up her experience as a student. After the completion of her master's at her home country university, she completed a second one at TUHH. Her experience at TUHH reveals that not even students get adequate support at the international office TUHH in respect of visa issues.

According to Galyna, back then she had only basic language skills and would have needed the support of the university because at the foreigner's office,

> 'the lady refused to change the language to English, so it was in German. And then she asked questions and I had to translate with my Google translator to-to be able to answer her questions which were beyond being basic, like, what is the purpose of your stay' (interview with Galyna).

Galyna is of the opinion that without the support of her later partner who experienced similar obstacles (he is not a German citizen, either) she would not have been granted the visa. In addition to Galyna, four of the IPs revealed that they had problems with legal and administrative issues concerning their visa and/or employment contract, or visa issues prior to being granted a scholarship.

Sarah provided another example of the urgent need for support from TUHH. When she applied for the job and got accepted, the

German embassy did not want to grant her a working visa because she was not able to show a signed employment contract from TUHH. However, she was not allowed to sign her employment contract at TUHH because she could not provide a working visa. Then again, even when she completed her studies at the German-Jordanian University, her degree was not accepted by TUHH and she needed verification by the ZAB.

She received support from a former colleague from the research group, but not from TUHH. Altogether, it took five months before the issue was solved even when she thinks that the refugee crisis at the time might have had an influence on the duration. Sarah said that she was really depressed after this experience.

The only IP who received support no matter the issue was Wang who registered for a double master at TUHH and at the NIT. Nonetheless, he says that the support he received did not come from TUHH but from NIT.

Wang stated that although international rankings are very important, he decided to study at TUHH even if its ranking was not the best. Wang enrolled for a double master at TUHH and at NIT, the latter a privately financed institute. He was granted a scholarship for the tuition fees from NIT. According to Wang, at NIT, there is a contact person who provides support, no matter the topic.

The way visa obstacles are solved is crucial because this can either promote or hinder the well-being of InSs (Yan, 2020). Therefore, as demanded by the GWK (2013), it is important to facilitate the processes for getting a visa. As revealed during the interviews, this aspect is particularly important for those who did not graduate with a master in Germany. Legal and administrative matters can become complicated and can lead to seemingly unsolvable situations, as revealed by Sarah.

In addition to the findings from the interviews, the author compared which services are already available at universities and which should be introduced or need improving in the attempt to attract

InRs. For this purpose, she approached the TL for incoming students at the international office TUHH. This TL is also the first contact person in respect of integration programs.

Services at Selected Technical Universities in Germany

The interview with Galyna shows that, at least at TUHH, services for InSs are available, but only after registration. This in turn means that support for InS only begins when a visa is already in place. The only available information about visa requirements on TUHH's website is that InSs might need to apply for a visa. No contact person for additional support is provided.

The TL's answers reveal that services are available for InS and that for this group, there are welcome weeks at the beginning of each semester and intercultural activities during the semester such as international gatherings, social events and painting workshops. TUHH's webpage confirms the TL's statements. The international office TUHH provides a culture of welcome for its InSs. "Welcome @ TUHH: You are not alone!" (TUHH, n.d.-g).

However, the TL confirms that no services are offered to InRs. The TL stresses that the services for InSs need to be expanded for InRs as well. When asked about what the process at the university that automatically refers InRs to services of the international office, the TL states that she is not aware of such a process especially because her office does not get any information about the arrival of InRs at all.

According to TUHH's website, an InR who wants to work and/or complete studies at TUHH needs to contact the schools, institutes or research centers directly to find a host and a supervisor. However, no appropriate contact person is named who deals exactly with this topic. In addition, research groups like the one where the author's IPs work are not mentioned here at all. Moreover, IPs complained that two important links are missing here: a link that leads to TUHH's administration to deal with employment contract matters, and job openings and scholarships.

When asked about what the TL and her team need to include personal assistance to InRs as well, she states that the international office TUHH has the expertise and experience to support InRs but that an additional position at her office would be needed.

To complement the information gained from the TL's answers and TUHH's webpage, the author analyzed and compared her findings with the information available online on the homepages of two additional technical universities in Germany, TUM and RWTH.

In this way, she used the outside perspective of her IPs. Like Wang, she considered international rankings. The reason for the latter is that some of the key figures for internationality at a university are worldwide rankings and thus, recognition and the number or percentage of InSs and InRs (Wit, 2009).

If internationalization should likewise be reflected according to its students, researchers and staff (Kehm & Teichler, 2007), it is surprising how difficult it is to find statistical data about InRs and international staff. The following reveals that universities provide few services for InRs.

Services for International Researchers at TUHH, TUM, and RWTH

Table 1.2: Services for International Researchers at TUHH, TUM, and RWTH

University:	TUHH	TUM	RWTH
Office Designation:	International Office TUHH	TUM Global & Alumni Office	Welcome Center for International Researchers
Addressed groups:	International students and guest researchers	International students and international researchers	International students and researchers
Target group:	International students	International students and researchers	International students and researchers

Checklist offered for first overview:	No	yes	yes
Additional support from employees, also in English:	No	yes	yes
Job openings in English:	No	yes	yes
Support with visa formalities:	no	yes	yes
Support with employment contract:	no	yes	yes
German classes are available:	no	yes	yes

(Compiled by this author from university webpages (RWTH, n.d.-a; TUHH, n.d.-b; TUHH, n.d.-d; TUM, n.d.-b, TUM, n.d.-c))

Table 1.2 provides an overview of service units and available support for InRs at TUHH, TUM, and RWTH. The services selected in the table reflect the requirements of the author's IPs for services necessary at TUHH. Again here, it needs to be stressed that there is no common understanding about who is an InR and therefore, the addressed groups might vary even when addressed as "international researchers".

No other entity exists than the international office TUHH (TUHH, n.d.-d) where services are only provided to InSs (TUHH, n.d.-b), but TUM and RWTH provide a range of services to their InRs. They offer a checklist with information about procedures before and during the stay, including information about visa and employment. In addition, personal assistance is accessible and if required, in English. During their stay, InRs can attend German classes in various formats.

Even if the quality of the services of the two other German universities cannot be evaluated from an outside perspective, the first impression the author gets from studying their websites is a positive one. She also found the websites clearly arranged and the sites with collected information and a contact person easy to find. The impression from TUHH's website is different. Some examples in the following will underpin this critique.

The term "international researcher" does not exist on TUHH's webpage. Instead, TUHH uses the term "guest researcher from abroad". For guest researchers, TUHH mainly provides a collection of information in form of Internet addresses (TUHH, n.d.-b). Then again, the section "Visiting International Research Students", sub section "Internships/projects at TUHH", sub section "Erasmus Traineeship" defines a guest researcher: a registered *'student, PhD candidate, Postdoc, Professor'* (TUHH, n.d.-e). This also defines who is eligible to get access to TUHH's infrastructure. However, a professor would probably not look for information in the student's section.

From these examples, it can be seen that the author's IPs are correct when complaining about the lack of clarity. As an example, the following two screenshots of TUHH's website section of the international office TUHH illustrate the lack of clarity.

Selection of Links for Guest Researchers provided by TUHH

Figure 1.1: Selection of Links for Guest Researchers provided by TUHH

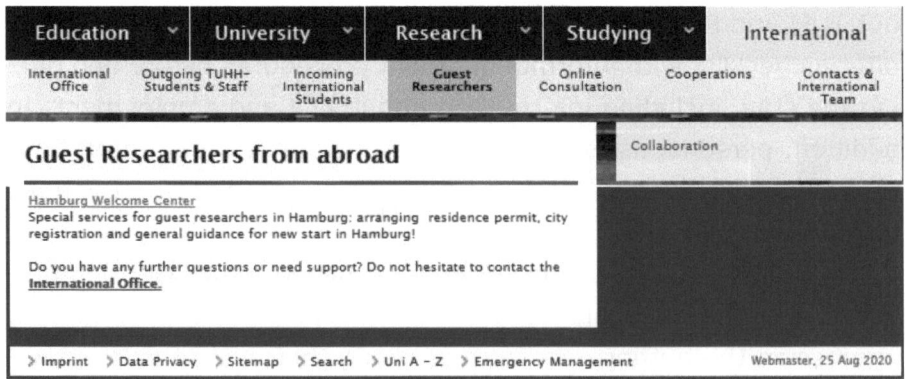

(Extracted by the author from TUHH's webpage (TUHH, n.d.-b)

Figure 1.1 above shows only two links extracted by the author from the website for the purpose of this work, and for a better clarity. One link leads to Hamburg's immigration office, the "Hamburg Welcome Center". According to TUHH's webpage, this link will lead to special services in respect of residence permit, city registration and general guidance for the start in the city.

It can be assumed that the second link will lead to the international office. TUHH's website suggests to contact this office in case of additional questions or need for additional support (TUHH, n.d.-b). From an external perspective, being an InR, this link should lead to a source of assistance. But it does not – in fact, it leads to a site for orientation and integration for incoming students, not for international researchers.

In other words, the services neither address guest researchers nor InRs. Services are intended exclusively for InSs: "general counselling for TUHH international students" (TUHH, n.d.-c). As already stated, this was confirmed by the TL for incoming students.

Discussion

The main focus of this work is that internationalization strategies at German universities must address InRs and students alike. However, at TUHH the focus is on InSs. The hypothesis is that German universities need to offer services that facilitate entry barriers and that promote integration if they want to attract InRs from outside the EU.

The hypothesis was confirmed by the author's IPs, six InRs from six different third countries coming from Jordan, Malaysia, Pakistan, Russia, Turkey, and Ukraine. Their perspective revealed which services InRs need that promote the arrival and integration of a diverse international and intercultural group of researchers, focusing on researchers from outside the EU. The theoretical framework of this work based on research on internationalization.

Internationalization at German universities is a necessary goal. The findings of this work contribute to the understanding that internationalization is a process that needs to embrace and involve all stakeholders at the organization and in the end, not only InSs. This requires services that promote the arrival and integration of a diverse international and intercultural group of researchers and students alike, especially for those arriving from outside the EU. One reason is that non-Europeans face additional challenges in respect to e.g. visa issues.

Even when InRs prepare their arrival to a new environment well, they still might need support before and at least during their stay at TUHH or any other university. In this regard, the most frequent topics and concerns of the IPs were problems with the local language, unclear or no provision of information on TUHH's webpage and a lack of support with legal and administrative issues concerning their master's degree, visa and employment.

When researching online, an InR might get the impression that TUHH's welcoming culture is reserved for InSs only. For its InSs, TUHH provides local language courses and multiple programs that shall facilitate their arrival and stay. Nevertheless, these are often not mandatory events. Therefore, the decision to participate can be interpreted as an acculturation strategy, which in the end will facilitate interaction with locals and provide the opportunity to learn about the new culture and its people.

The term "guest researcher" used at TUHH implies a guest status for researchers. However, both InRs and InSs should be understood as such. They often stay only for a limited time at TUHH or other universities. On this basis alone, a welcoming culture should be more common.

Even when TUHH visibly shows a welcoming culture to its InSs, services are only available after registration. Therefore, as with InRs, no service is available to them in respect of legal and administrative issues such as visa matters or the recognition of previous studies. In the attempt to facilitate entry barriers, all international stakeholders at TUHH should be able to access such service.

According to the IPs, language is the most important issue because it affects all other topics in one way or another even when English is the language InRs use the most in their jobs at TUHH and in addition when writing their PhD thesis. On the other hand, although the knowledge of the local language is a major facilitator in respect of e.g. their arrival, to be fluent in German is not a prerequisite for working and/or studying at TUHH, at least not for an InR.

Nonetheless, InRs should have a good command of the German language. Therefore, tailored one-on-one German language courses should be arranged that fit into the individual schedules of InRs. To know the local language is one important facilitator which eases cultural stress and which promotes cross cultural competencies. To recognize cultural differences and to adjust towards them is an acculturation strategy as well (e.g. Beck, 2012; Chiu et al., 2013). As an example, respective offers would have helped IP Dalir to better integrate.

The acquisition and administration of research grants is a second example of how language is an essential prerequisite for success at a university. Here, German is required when setting budgets for grant applications even when the grant holder is international and solely communicates in English. One reason for this is that national evaluation criteria must still be observed when applying for a grant to purchase scientific equipment. This must already be considered during the application phase for a research grant.

Consequently, regardless of the source of funding, both languages are essential for the successful acquisition and administration of funds. InRs at TUHH therefore either need to be fluent in the local language or can rely on German language support, regardless of the department they approach. One prerequisite for this support is that not only InSs and InRs but also university staff communicate effectively in both German and English.

In addition to good German language skills, the knowledge of local legal issues in respect of employment and PhD studies is important. If InRs do not have this knowledge, they should be able to rely on support offered by the university. One example where support is essential is the recognition of their academic training at home country universities. A recognized master's degree is one prerequisite for an employment contract as a research associate at TUHH. In addition, it is a prerequisite for the completion of academic education. Therefore, the international office TUHH should provide support with legal and administrative issues even already before the arrival of the InR. To facilitate visa issues and the recognition of former degrees, they should closely work together with administrations such as embassies, foreigner's offices and ZAB.

Limitations, Challenges and Outlook for Future Research

The research for this work is limited to six interviews with InRs working at only one university. Investigations at two additional German universities were limited to an outside perspective. Research on internationalization at German universities is mostly limited to the organizational perspective, and on InSs. Therefore, more research on the following issues would provide more insights about the current situation of InRs in Germany, before necessary measurements can be identified that would enhance and improve the attraction and working conditions of InRs in the long run:

1. A clear definition of the term "InR" must be developed to improve the comparability of findings.
2. Certain approaches work better to promote intercultural diversity at universities.
3. Further investigation should find out if or how InRs find an employment at TUHH and other German universities without the support of private or research networks.

4. Moreover, accompanying partners need to be heard as well. During these interviews, the voice of the partners was only communicated through the researchers. Therefore, additional research might reveal a more rounded picture of the situation, e.g. in respect to employment and well-being (Gribble et al., 2019) or satisfaction with new life conditions in a different country (Beck, 2012).

Summary and Conclusion

The preliminary hypothesis is confirmed. Universities need to offer services that facilitate entry barriers and that promote integration, especially if they want to attract InRs from outside the EU.

Some universities in Germany already provide services to its international stakeholders even when TUHH does not. From an outside perspective, the services for InRs at the other two universities (TUM and RWTH) look attractive. Nonetheless, without further research at their organizations, nothing can be stated about the quality.

In the attempt to promote the acculturation process, support should start already before InSs or InRs leave their home countries. For example, information about prerequisites for employment and/or a study program must be provided in advance.

Even when international researchers do understand German, in case of need, English speaking staff should be available to provide legal information and support to facilitate entry barriers and their stay.

If universities want to attract InRs, they should provide information and support. Therefore, this work intends to stimulate the extension of research on internationalization processes at universities towards InRs.

References

Beck, R. E. (2012). Examining the relationship between self-initiated expatriation and cross-cultural adjustment among expatriate spouses within nonprofit organizations: A quantitative causal-comparative study (Publication No. 3499896) [Doctoral dissertation, Capella University]. PQDT Open. https://search.proquest.com/docview/962410783?accountid=14435

Berger, R., Safdar, S., Spieß, E., Bekk, M., & Font, A. (2019). Acculturation of Erasmus students: Using the multidimensional individual difference acculturation model framework. International Journal of Psychology: Journal International De Psychologie, 54(6), 739–749. https://doi.org/10.1002/ijop.12526

Berry, J. W. (1980). Acculturation as varieties of adaptation. In A. M. Padilla (Ed.), Acculturation: Theory, Models and Some New Findings (pp. 9-25). Westview Press.

Berry, J. W. (1997). Immigration, Acculturation, and Adaptation. Applied Psychology, 46(1), 5–34. https://doi.org/10.1111/j.1464-0597.1997.tb01087.x

Bouncken, R. (2009). Creativity in Cross-Cultural Innovation Teams: Diversity and its Implications for Leadership. In P. Meusburger, J. Funke, & E. Wunder (Eds.), Knowledge and Space: Vol. 2. Milieus of Creativity: An Interdisciplinary Approach to Spatiality of Creativity (1st ed., Vol. 2, pp. 189–200). Springer Netherlands.

Bouncken, R., Brem, A., & Kraus, S. (2016). Multi-cultural teams as sources for creativity and innovation: The role of cultural diversity on team performance. International Journal of Innovation Management, 20(1), 1650012-1-34. https://doi.org/10.1142/S1363919616500122

Braun, V., Clarke, V., Hayfield, N., & Terry, G. (2019). Thematic Analysis. In P. Liamputtong (Ed.), Handbook of Research Methods in Health Social Sciences (pp. 843–860). Springer Singapore. https://doi.org/10.1007/978-981-10-5251-4_103

Bremer, U. (2018). Internationalization Strategies of German Universities. Book series of the HHL Leipzig Graduate School of Management. Springer Fachmedien Wiesbaden. https://doi.org/10.1007/978-3-658-22133-1

Brenner. (2019). Dual Career Service. Ein innovatives Instrument zur Personalrekrutierung und Mitarbeiterbindung [Dual Career Service. An innovative instrument for personnel recruitment and employee retention]. Series: Essentials. Springer Gabler Wiesbaden.

Bucholtz, M. (2000). The politics of transcription. Journal of Pragmatics, 32(10), 1439–1465. https://doi.org/10.1016/S0378-2166(99)00094-6

Bundesinstitut für Berufsbildung (Federal Institute for Vocational Education and Training) [BiBB]. (n.d.). Recognition in Germany. Information portal of the German government for the recognition of foreign professional qualifications. Recognition Finder. Would you like to work in your profession in Germany? Federal Institute for Vocational Education and Training. Retrieved on September 19, 2020 from https://www.anerkennung-in-deutschland.de/html/en/skilled-workers.php

Bundesministerium für Wissenschaft und Forschung (Federal Ministry of Education and Research) [BMBF]. (2016). Internationalisation of Education, Science and Research: Strategy of the Federal Government. Federal Ministry of Education and Research (BMBF). https://www.bmbf.de/upload_filestore/pub/Internationalisation_Strategy.pdf

Cabrera, A., & Le Renard, C. (2015). Internationalization, Higher Education, and Competitiveness. In E. Ullberg (Ed.), New perspectives on internationalization and competitiveness: Integrating economics, innovation and higher education (pp. 11–16). Springer International Publishing.

Chiu, C.-Y., Lonner, W. J., Matsumoto, D., & Ward, C. (2013). Cross-Cultural Competence. Journal of Cross-Cultural Psychology, 44(6), 843–848. https://doi.org/10.1177/0022022113493716

Davidson, C. (2009). Transcription: Imperatives for Qualitative Research. International Journal of Qualitative Methods, 35–52. https://doi.org/10.1177/160940690900800206

Deutscher Akademischer Austauschdienst (German Academic Exchange Service) [DAAD]. (2016). Wissenschaft Weltoffen 2016: Daten und Fakten zur Internationalität von Studium und Forschung in Deutschland ; Fokus: Internationale Mobilität von Wissenschaftlern [Wissenschaft Weltoffen 2016: Facts and figures on the internationality of studies and research in Germany; Focus: International mobility of academics and researchers]. W. Bertelsmann Verlag. https://doi.org/10.3278/7004002ow.

Die Bundesregierung, Deutschland (The Federal Government, Germany) [TFG]. (n.d.). International Mobility. Federal Funding Advisory Service for Research and Innovation, The Federal Government (TFG). Retrieved on October 1, 2020 from https://www.foerderinfo.bund.de/en/international-mobility-1821.php

Dual Career Netzwerk Deutschland (Dual Career Network Germany) [DCND]. (n.d.). Our Members. Dual Career Network Germany (DCND). Retrieved on December 6, 2020 from https://www.dcnd.org/en/2-2-our-members/

Eriksen, T. H. (2014). Globalization: The key concepts (2nd ed.). Bloomsbury Academic.

European Commission [EC]. (n.d.-a). Erasmus+ Progamm Guide: Eligible Countries. European Commission (EC). Retrieved on October 1, 2020 from https://ec.europa.eu/programmes/erasmus-plus/programme-guide/part-a/who-can-participate/eligible-countries_en

European Commission [EC]. (n.d.-b). Erasmus+Programme Guide: Mobility project for higher education students and staff. European Commission (EC). Retrieved on October 1, 2020 from https://ec.europa.eu/programmes/erasmus-plus/programme-guide/part-b/three-key-actions/key-action-1/mobility-higher-education-students-staff_en

European Commission [EC]. (n.d.-c). Migration and Home Affairs: Third-country National. European Commission (EC). Retrieved on September 22, 2020 from https://ec.europa.eu/home-affairs/what-we-do/networks/european_migration_network/glossary_search/third-country-national_en

European Commission [EC]. (n.d.-d). Germany. Are you a non-EU citizen whishing to carry out research in Germany? European Commission (EC). Retrieved on October 9, 2020 from https://ec.europa.eu/immigration/country-specific-information/germany/researcher_en

Föbker, S., Temme, D., & Wiegandt, C.-C. (2014). A warm welcome to highly-skilled migrants: how can municipal administrations play their part? Tijdschrift Voor Economische En Sociale Geografie, 105(5), 542–557. https://doi.org/10.1111/tesg.12112

Fromm, N. (2014). Transnational higher education by German universities: Main drivers and components. TranState Working Papers, No. 181, University of Bremen, Collaborative Research Center 597 – Transformations of the State, Bremen. https://www.econstor.eu/bitstream/10419/98404/1/788914383.pdf

Gemeinsame Wissenschaftskonferenz (Joint Science Conference) [GWK]. (2013). Strategie der Wissenschaftsminister/innen von Bund und Ländern für die Internationalisierung der Hochschulen in Deutschland: (Beschluss der 18. Sitzung der Gemeinsamen Wissenschaftskonferenz am 12. April 2013 in Berlin) [Strategy of the Federal and State Science Ministers for the Internationalization of Higher Education in Germany (Resolution of the 18th Session of the Joint Science Conference on April 12, 2013 in Berlin)]. https://www.bmbf.de/files/aaaInternationalisierungsstrategie_GWK-Beschluss_12_04_13.pdf

Gezentsvey, M., & Ward, C. (2008). Unveiling Agency: A Motivational Perspective on Acculturation and Adaptation. In R. M. Sorrentino & S. Yamaguchi (Eds.), Handbook of motivation and cognition across cultures (1st ed., pp. 213–235). Academic Press.

Gibson, B., & Hua, Z. (2016). Interviews. In H. Zhu (Ed.), Guides to research methods in language and linguistics: Vol. 8. Research methods in intercultural communication: A practical guide (pp. 181–195). Wiley-Blackwell.

Gill, A. (n.d.). Equity, Diversity & Inclusion: Definitions. Research Services Office, University of Toronto. Retrieved on October 28, 2020 from https://research.utoronto.ca/equity-diversity-inclusion/equity-diversity-inclusion

Graves, T. D. (1967). Psychological acculturation in a tri-ethnic community. Southwestern Journal of Anthropology. - Albuquerque Vol. 23(4), 337-350. http://www.jstor.org/stable/3629450

Gribble, R., Goodwin, L., Oram, S., & Fear, N. T. (2019). 'it's nice to just be you': The influence of the employment experiences of UK military spouses during accompanied postings on well-being. Health Psychology Open, 6(1), 1-10. https://journals.sagepub.com/doi/pdf/10.1177/2055102919838909

Guest, G., MacQueen, K. M., & Namey, E. E. (2012). Applied thematic analysis. SAGE Publications.

Hajro, A., Stahl, G. K., Clegg, C. C., & Lazarova, M. B. (2019). Acculturation, coping, and integration success of international skilled migrants: An integrative review and multilevel framework. Human Resource Management Journal, 29(3), 328–352. https://doi.org/10.1111/1748-8583.12233

Hall, E. T. (1989). Beyond culture. Anchor Books/Doubleday.

Hermeking, M. (2005). Culture and Internet Consumption: Contributions from Cross-Cultural Marketing and Advertising Research. Journal of Computer-Mediated Communication, 11(1), 192–216. https://doi.org/10.1111/j.1083-6101.2006.tb00310.x

Hochschulrektorenkonferenz (German Rectors' Conference) [HRK]. (n.d.). Audit "Internationalisation of Universities". HRK German Rectors' Conference. Retrieved on October 6, 2020 from https://www.hrk.de/activities/audit-internationalisation-of-universities/

Hofstede, G. H. (2001). Culture's consequences: Comparing values, behaviors, institutions, and organizations across nations / Geert Hofstede (2nd ed.). Sage Publications.

Jenkins, J. (2014). English as a Lingua Franca in the International University: The politics of academic English language policy. Routledge.

Kehm, B. M., & Teichler, U. (2007). Research on Internationalisation in Higher Education. Journal of Studies in International Education, 11(3-4), 260–273. https://doi.org/10.1177/1028315307303534

Lazarus, R. S., & Folkman, S. (1987). Transactional theory and research on emotions and coping. European Journal of Personality, 1(3), 141–169. https://doi.org/10.1002/per.2410010304

Lepori, B., Seeber, M., & Bonaccorsi, A. (2015). Competition for talent. Country and organizational-level effects in the internationalization of European higher education institutions. Research Policy, 44(3), 789–802. https://doi.org/10.1016/j.respol.2014.11.004

Lopez, I. Y., & Bui, N.H. (2014). Acculturation and Linguistic Factors on International Students' Self-Esteem and Language Confidence. Journal of International Students, 4(4), 314–329. https://www.ojed.org/index.php/jis/article/view/451

Masgoret, A.-M., & Ward, C. (2006). Culture learning approach to acculturation. In D. L. Sam, J. W. Berry, D. L. Sam, & J. W. Berry (Eds.), The Cambridge Handbook of Acculturation Psychology (pp. 58–77). Cambridge University Press. https://doi.org/10.1017/CBO9780511489891.008

Mauranen, A., Hynninen, N., & Ranta, E. (2010). English as an Academic Lingua Franca: The ELFA project. English for Specific Purposes, 29(3), 183–190. https://doi.org/10.35360/njes.108

Moll, M., & Thielmann, W. (2017). Wissenschaftliches Deutsch: Wie es geht und worauf es dabei ankommt. Serie: Studieren, aber richtig: Vol. 4650 [Academic German: How it works and what is important. Series: Study, but do it right: Vol. 4650]. UVK Verlagsgesellschaft mbH; UVK/Lucius.

Nauck, B. (2015). Acculturation. In F. J. R. van de Vijver, D. A. van Hemert, & Y. H. Poortinga (Eds.), Multilevel Analysis of Individuals and Cultures (2nd ed., pp 379-410). Taylor and Francis.

Navas, M., García, M. C., Sánchez, J., Rojas, A. J., Pumares, P., & Fernández, J.S. (2005). Relative Acculturation Extended Model (RAEM): New contributions with regard to the study of acculturation. International Journal of Intercultural Relations, 29(1), 21–37. https://doi.org/10.1016/j.ijintrel.2005.04.001

Pivodic, L. (2019). How to welcome a new international researcher into your team. Nature, 576(7785), 169–170. https://doi.org/10.1038/d41586-019-03231-x

QS Quacquarelly Symonds Limited [QS]. (n.d.). QS World University Rankings 2021. QS Quacquarelly Symonds Limited. Retrieved on September 19, 2020 from https://www.topuniversities.com/university-rankings/world-university-rankings/2021

Recker, C., Milfont, T. L., & Ward, C. (2018). A Dual-Process Motivational Model of Acculturation Behaviors and Adaptation Outcomes. Universitas Psychologica, 16(5), 1–15. https://doi.org/10.11144/Javeriana.upsy16-5.dmma

Redfield, R., Linton, R., & Herskovits, M. J. (1936). Memorandum for the Study of Acculturation. American Anthropologist, 38(1), 149–152. https://doi.org/10.1525/aa.1936.38.1.02a00330

Rust, V. D., & Kim, S. (2015). Globalization and Global University Rankings. In J. Zajda (Ed.), Second International Handbook on Globalisation, Education and Policy Research (pp. 167–180). Springer Netherlands. https://doi.org/10.1007/978-94-017-9493-0_11

RWTH Aachen Universität (RWTH Aachen University) [RWTH]. (n.d.-a). Services for International Researchers. Welcome Center, RWTH Aachen University (RWTH). Retrieved on October 3, 2020 from https://www.rwth-aachen.de/cms/root/Forschung/Angebote-fuer-Forschende/Die-RWTH-heisst-Sie-willkommen/~hcijf/Services-fuer-internationale-Forschende/lidx/1/

RWTH Aachen Universität (RWTH Aachen University) [RWTH]. (n.d.-b). Welcome Center for International Researchers. Welcome Center, RWTH Aachen University (RWTH). Retrieved on October 3, 2020 from https://www.rwth-aachen.de/cms/root/Zielgruppenportale/~hcbpq/Welcome-Center-fuer-internationale-Forsc/lidx/1/

Sam, D. L., & Berry, J. W. (2010). Acculturation: When Individuals and Groups of Different Cultural Backgrounds Meet. Perspectives on Psychological Science : A Journal of the Association for Psychological Science, 5(4), 472–481. https://doi.org/10.1177/1745691610373075

Schaer, M., Dahinden, J., & Toader, A. (2017). Transnational mobility among early-career academics: gendered aspects of negotiations and arrangements within heterosexual couples. Journal of Ethnic and Migration Studies, 43(8), 1292–1307. https://doi.org/10.1080/1369183X.2017.1300254

Searle, W., & Ward, C. (1990). The prediction of psychological and sociocultural adjustment during cross-cultural transitions. International Journal of Intercultural Relations, 14(4), 449–464. https://doi.org/10.1016/0147-1767(90)90030-Z

Shafaei, A., & Razak, N. A. (2016). Internationalisation of higher education: Conceptualising the antecedents and outcomes of cross-cultural adaptation. Policy Futures in Education, 14(6), 701–720. https://doi.org/10.1177/1478210316645017

ShanghaiRanking Consultancy [SRC]. (n.d.). Academic Ranking of World Universities (ARWU) 2020. ShanghaiRanking Consultancy (SRC). Retrieved on September 21, 2020 from http://shanghairanking.com/ARWU2020.html

Smit, U. (2010). English as a lingua franca in higher education: A longitudinal study of classroom discourse. Trends in applied linguistics: Vol. 2. Mouton De Gruyter. https://doi.org/10.1515/9783110215519

Smith, R. A., & Khawaja, N. G. (2011). A review of the acculturation experiences of international students. International Journal of Intercultural Relations, 35(6), 699–713. https://doi.org/10.1016/j.ijintrel.2011.08.004

Stahl-Rolf, S., Hotmannspötter, D., Hutapea, L., Mecks, E., Pfaff, D., Proff, von S., & Reuß, K. (2018). The Diversity Factor. How Cultural Diversity Impacts Innovations in GermanyFaktor Vielfalt: Die Rolle kultureller Vielfalt für Innovationen in Deutschland. Bertelsmann Stiftung.

Statista GmbH [Statista]. (n.d.). Anzahl der Ausländer in Deutschland nach Herkunftsland von 2017 bis 2019 [Foreigners in Germany based on their country of origin between 2017 and 2019]. Research Department Statista. Statista GmbH. Retrieved on September 30, 2020 from https://de.statista.com/statistik/daten/studie/1221/umfrage/anzahl-der-auslaender-in-deutschland-nach-herkunftsland/

Suter, B., & Cangià, F. (2020). Time and family on the move: 'Accompanying partners' in geographical mobility. Time & Society, 29(3), 813–835. https://doi.org/10.1177/0961463X19897431

Technische Universität Hamburg (Hamburg University of Technology) [TUHH]. (n.d.-a). ArtRoom Project. International Office TUHH, Hamburg University of Technology (TUHH). Retrieved on October 09, 2020 from https://www.tuhh.de/artroom/homepage.html

Technische Universität Hamburg (Hamburg University of Technology) [TUHH]. (n.d.-b). Guest Researchers from abroad. International Office TUHH, Hamburg University of Technology (TUHH). Retrieved on October 09, 2020 from https://www.tuhh.de/alt/tuhh/international/guest-researchers.html

Technische Universität Hamburg (Hamburg University of Technology) [TUHH]. (n.d.-c). Incoming Students: Orientation & Integration. International Office TUHH, Hamburg University of Technology (TUHH). Retrieved on October 09, 2020 from https://www.tuhh.de/alt/tuhh/international/incoming-international-students/counseling-contacts.html

Technische Universität Hamburg (Hamburg University of Technology) [TUHH]. (n.d.-d). International Office TUHH. International Office TUHH, Hamburg University of Technology (TUHH). Retrieved on October 09, 2020 from https://www.tuhh.de/alt/tuhh/international/international-office.html

Technische Universität Hamburg (Hamburg University of Technology) [TUHH]. (n.d.-e). Internships at TUHH. Subtitle: Erasmus Traineeship. Definition Guest Researcher. International Office TUHH, Hamburg University of Technology (TUHH). Retrieved on October 06, 2020 from https://www-dev.tuhh.de/alt/tuhh/international/incoming-international-students/visiting-international-research-students/internships-projects-at-tuhh.html

Technische Universität Hamburg (Hamburg University of Technology) [TUHH]. (n.d.-f). Orientation Program at TUHH: Online Orientation Weeks – Preliminary Program (in English unless otherwise announced). International Office TUHH, Hamburg University of Technology (TUHH). Retrieved on October 09, 2020 from https://www.tuhh.de/welcome/orientation-networking/welcome-weeks.html

Technische Universität Hamburg (Hamburg University of Technology) [TUHH]. (n.d.-g). Welcome @ TUHH: You are not alone!: Contact Us. International Office TUHH, Hamburg University of Technology (TUHH). Retrieved on October 04, 2020 from https://www.tuhh.de/welcome/about-us/contact-us.html

Technische Universität Hamburg (Hamburg University of Technology) [TUHH]. (n.d.-h). Contacts & International Team. International Office TUHH, Hamburg University of Technology (TUHH). Retrieved on December 08, 2020 from https://www.tuhh.de/alt/tuhh/international/contacts-international-team.html

THE World Universities Insights Limited [THE]. (n.d.). World University Rankings 2021: Ranking of General Engineering. THE World Universities Insights Limited. Retrieved on September 19, 2020 from https://www.timeshighereducation.com/world-university-rankings/2021/world-ranking#!/page/0/length/25/subjects/3066/sort_by/rank/sort_order/asc/cols/stats

Tran, L. T. (2020). Teaching and Engaging International Students. Journal of International Students, 10(3), Xii-xvii. https://www.ojed.org/index.php/jis/article/view/2005/1115

TUM Technische Universität München (TUM Technical University of Munich) [TUM]. (n.d.-a). TUM Global & Alumni Office. Homepage of TUM Global & Alumni Office, TUM Technical University of Munich. Retrieved on October 04, 2020 from https://www.international.tum.de/en/home/

TUM Technische Universität München (TUM Technical University of Munich) [TUM]. (n.d.-b). Welcome Services for International Researchers. TUM Gloabal & Alumni Office, TUM Technical University of Munich. Retrieved on October 04, 2020 from https://www.international.tum.de/en/welcomeservices/

TUM Technische Universität München (TUM Technical University of Munich) [TUM]. (n.d.-c). Help with your relocation and integration at TUM. TUM Global & Alumni Office, TUM Technical University of Munich. Retrieved on October 04, 2020 from https://www.international.tum.de/en/welcomeservices/help-with-relocation-and-integration/

Urban, G. (2001). Metaculture: How Culture Moves through the World. Public worlds: v.8. University of Minnesota Press.

van der Zee, K., & van Oudenhoven, J. P. (2013). Culture Shock or Challenge? The Role of Personality as a Determinant of Intercultural Competence. Journal of Cross-Cultural Psychology, 44(6), 928–940. https://doi.org/10.1177/0022022113493138

VERBI Software (2020). MAXQDA 2020 Analytics Pro (Version 2020) [electronic]. Verbi GmbH. Berlin, Germany: Available from maxqda.com.

Vereinigung der Bayerischen Wirtschaft (Bavarian Industry Association) [vbw]. (2012). Bavarian Industry Association (Ed.) Gutachten: Vol. 2012. Internationalisierung der Hochschulen: Eine institutionelle Gesamtstrategie (1. Auflage) [expert opinion: Vol. 2012. Internationalization of Higher Education Institutions: An Overall Institutional Strategy (1st edition)]. Waxmann. https://www.pedocs.de/volltexte/2017/13997/pdf/Internationalisierung_der_Hochschulen_Gutachten.pdf

Ward, C., & Kennedy, A. (1994). Acculturation strategies, psychological adjustment, and sociocultural competence during cross-cultural transitions. International Journal of Intercultural Relations, 18(3), 329–343. https://doi.org/10.1016/0147-1767(94)90036-1

Ward, C., & Rana-Deuba, A. (1999). Acculturation and Adaptation Revisited. Journal of Cross-Cultural Psychology, 30(4), 422–442. https://doi.org/10.1177/0022022199030004003

Ward, C. (2001). The A,B, Cs of Acculturation. In D. R. Matsumoto (Ed.), The handbook of culture & psychology (pp. 411–445). Oxford University Press.

Ward, C., Bochner, S., & Furnham, A. (2001). The psychology of culture shock (2nd ed.). Routledge.

Wegner, A. (2016). Internationale Nachwuchswissenschaftler in Deutschland. Motivation – Integration – Förderung: Ergebnisse einer bundesweiten Studie. (Schriftenreihe Hochschulmarketing, 12) [International young scientists in Germany. Motivation – Integration – Promotion: Results of a nationwide study. (Publication series University Marketing, 12)]. W. Bertelsmann Verlag. https://www.ssoar.info/ssoar/bitstream/handle/document/53019/ssoar-2016-wegner-Internationale_Nachwuchswissenschaftler_in_Deutschland_Motivation.pdf?sequence=1&isAllowed=y&lnkname=ssoar-2016-wegner-Internationale_Nachwuchswissenschaftler_in_Deutschland_Motivation.pdf.

Wit, H. de (Ed.). (2009). Measuring success in the internationalisation of higher education. EAIE Occasional Paper 22. European Association for International Education (EAIE).

Yan, Z. (2020). Acculturation and Well-Being Among International Students: Challenges and Opportunities. In U. Gaulee, S. Sharma, & K. Bista (Eds.), Rethinking Education Across Borders: Emerging Issues and Critical Insights on Globally Mobile Students (1st ed., pp 305-315).

List of Figures

Figure 1.1: Selection of Links for Guest Researchers 108

List of Tables

Table 1.3: Recognition of Master's Degrees of Interview Partners 98
Table 1.4: Services for International Researchers 106

Communication patterns in a digital context

Anna Carolin Uhlig

Abstract

The growing importance of digitalization, its influence on daily work-routines and communication processes needs to be examined. This is also true for negotiations, especially those affected by intercultural settings. To meet the demands of a fruitful process and outcome, the question arises: "How do low and high context communicators resolve their differences in video-based international negotiations?"

Results suggest that negotiation using digital technology reinforces already existing peculiarities of intercultural communication in a specific way. It is thought that virtual negotiations pose a greater challenge for high-context communicators than for low-context communicators. This is primarily due to the technically induced restriction of the perceptual capacity which ultimately leads to a specification and concentration on structures, processes and behavioral aspects.

Using qualitative ethnography, and a scenario-based case study, I conduct semi-structured interviews evaluated by using open and axial coding. Participants are corporate negotiators in an international context and have different cultural backgrounds. The findings of how virtual settings impact negotiation behavior are presented in this paper.

Introduction

International business negotiations always take place within a broad intercultural acting field. Encounters, face-to-face or virtual, pose numerous challenges to all participants – not only because of the complexity of its content, but also due to intercultural influences, the observance of which ensures a supporting atmosphere of negotiation.

Negotiators with different cultural backgrounds must address these differences to gain joint understanding. Virtualizing negotiations reduces the full range of communication and raises the risk of critical incidents between the participants. This risk increases in an intercultural context and requires specific consideration and respective preparation.

The reduction of the communication spectrum is caused by the limited transmitted verbal and non-verbal message content. This message content is of significant importance to all communication participants. This is especially true for high-context (h/c) speakers, who rely on context and nuances hidden within the message sent. Misunderstandings are likely to occur due to not being fully able to decode messages. Additionally, in an intercultural context, the same message can be either sent or decoded in different manners.

Furthermore, virtual technology sharpens the inability and insecurity in dealing with this type of communication. This leads to the particular situation of high and low-context (h/l-context) speakers and how they might struggle with a limited quality level of communication. This paper examines how negotiators deal with the changed communication context, taking into account their own h/l-context pattern of communication. The intention is to recognize, avoid, and solve critical incidents.

The study was carried out in an international German-based medium-sized, family-owned company. Interviewees have difference jobs within the company, having gained comprehensive experience in complex international negotiations. Participants have different cultural backgrounds. These will be compared with respective communication patterns based on E.T. Hall's concept of h/l-context communication. The aim is to help understand the extent to which the existing frictions of intercultural cooperation can be overcome.

Literature review

As it comprises different nuances and interpretations the range of communication is complex. Simplified by characteristics, communication is the process of transferring signals and messages. It is related to interactions between machines, humans and machines, and between different human individuals (Broszinsky-Schwabe, 2017). In the context of this work communication is used in the sense of an understanding between human individuals, (by using means of technology) purpose-oriented on a shared target within a negotiation setting.

According to some researchers, receivers not only decode subject information but listen to the information received. This means, the receiver must analyze facts, but also understand messages the transmitter sends about themselves. Furthermore, details about the message might be hidden in the relationship between transmitter and receiver and the feelings which those messages create in the receiver (Schulz von Thun, 2015).

The multiplicity of misunderstandings and misinterpretations might create uncomfortable and disturbing situations. Conflicts are defined as a process of confrontation. They based on different interests of individuals or groups and can be carried out in different ways (Bartscher, n.d.).

There is rarely a single cause for a conflict, in most cases it originates from various influential factors. Understanding the cause of a conflict can help to resolve it, as appropriate adjustments can be made. A distortion in perception can trigger and intensify conflict. Differences are perceived stronger than commonalities. Misinterpretation of body language and facial expressions can be interpreted as deception and draw uninvolved parties into conflict. The attitude of the involved parties can increase conflict by showing aggressive, uncooperative behavior, often accompanied by accusations, disparagement and exploitation. Tasks are not always processed effectively and others are blamed for mistakes (Preuß-Scheuerle, 2016).

Glasl (cited in Scheuerle) distinguishes between three main phases of conflict. The first phase starts with the *hardening-up of a situation*, followed by *polarization and debate,* leading to both parties *putting their words into action*, meaning both sides observe the actions of the other with suspicion and mistrust, losing empathy for each other. At this point of time there is still a chance for a win-win outcome (Preuß-Scheuerle, 2016).

At the next stage, both parties have *concern about image and coalitions,* black and white thinking spreads followed by *loss of face*. Deliberate malice and actions are assumed. Parties use *threatening strategies*. Here the conflict might not be solved internally, help of external advisors is needed to avoid a win-lose result.

The final phase is shaped by acts of destruction directed against the opponent, which increase to a point of fragmentation in order to destroy opponents' power and livelihood. This often ends with both parties losing. A hierarchical power such as a supervisor or a court should decide on the next steps. Such escalation levels show the consequences that unresolved conflicts can have. Misunderstandings in communication lead to misinterpretation and severe issues. Business set-ups are characterized by contrasting views and interests, which can lead to complications. One of these scenarios is negotiation.

While conflicts are seen as an uncomfortable and disturbing situation, a solution can only be found if all parties involved have a positive attitude towards solving the problem. Solutions to be developed should achieve a satisfactory result for both parties on factual and relationship levels (Preuß-Scheuerle, 2016).

Characteristics of negotiation

Negotiation is a type of communication which is characterized by opposing interests, motives, needs and points of view aiming for aligning and finding options for mutual gain. Negotiations take place in various aspects of life (Helmold, Dathe, & Hummel, 2019). In this paper, negotiations are business related such as commercial discussions, legal agreements or M&A transactions.

The social setting of negotiation situation entails specific necessities. It needs an involvement of two or more parties who share the aim of finding a mutual agreement. This requires striving for a balance of diverting interest with the readiness for conflict resolution on all sides.

Negotiations call for a broad range of skills to achieve the desired outcome. This is especially true for business negotiations. Together with technical and strategic knowledge and an orientation towards process, social competencies such as perseverance, persuasiveness, flexibility and cultural understanding are needed. The formative components for this kind of negotiation are described by Bierbrauer.

Figure 1.1: Components of business negotiations

(Author's conception of Bierbrauer, 2009)

Every negotiation has different stakeholders. They differ in nationality and ethnicity or their professional or organizational functions and roles. This requires the adaption of strategies and tactics. The external, unchangeable contextual conditions, i.e. venue, seating arrangements, participants, time frame or status, influence the structure of the negotiation itself. Negotiating parties should be clear on their strategy, they must decide how they want to reach their goal (i.e. competitive or accommodating, individualistic or collectivist-oriented etc.). During the process, the communication forms main part of the negotiation. It is about relationships, exchange of interests, concessions, agreements, persuasion and tactics. The results depend on stakeholders, strategy and process (cultural aspects influence results)[1]. Overall, the negotiation itself and the outcome should be perceived as 'fair' by parties involved (Bierbrauer, 2009).

Culture and its influence

Culture is a social phenomenon that serves as an orientation and reference system, exercised by a group or society. This can include, for example, nationalities, societies, organizations, regions and generations. Culture serves as an identification feature and comprises ideas, signs, symbols and meanings, shared among all members of a group. They are considered as natural behavior and learned through socialization. Although similar problems exist in all cultures, different approaches to solve them are preferred in each case. This leads to potentially contradictory solution patterns (Barmeyer, 2012).

Edward T. Hall (1981) shares this view and emphasizes that "various facettes of culture are interrelated" (p.16). He points out that sharing these defines the boundaries of different cultures.

---

1 Western cultures consider a contract as a result, for non-western cultures contracts don't mark the end but the beginning for further relationships (Bierbrauer, 2009).

When different cultures meet, something new emerges.

Figure 1.2: The Own, the Foreign, the Intercultural

```
┌─────────────────────┐          ┌─────────────────────┐
│     The "Own"       │ ───→     │    The "Foreign"    │
│                     │ ←───     │                     │
└─────────────────────┘          └─────────────────────┘
           │                                │
           ▼                                ▼
      ╭─────────╮   ╭──────────────╮   ╭─────────╮
      │   Own   │   │cultural overlap│ │ Foreign │
      │ Culture │   │   situation   │  │ Culture │
      ╰─────────╯   ╰──────────────╯   ╰─────────╯
                           │
                           ▼
              ┌─────────────────────────┐
              │   The "Intercultural"   │
              └─────────────────────────┘
```

(Adapted from Thomas, 2013b, S. 46)

Interculturalism describes the joint process of exchange, collaboration, understanding, interpretation, causing astonishment and irritation when cultures do not share values, meanings or knowledge. Individuals often assume similarity to themselves in culturally different oriented partners regarding the way of thinking, feeling, or behavior[2] (Barmeyer, 2012).

Ethnocentric thinking causes behaviors that are likely to be misunderstood, inducing the possibility of critical incidents. Critical incidents are remarkable situations in intercultural encounters. When different cultural systems clash, transmitted behaviors and information are often considered perplexing, peculiar or even upsetting (Barmeyer, 2012).

---

2 This attitude is called ethnocentric thinking.

The situation of interculturalism creates the room in which overcoming differences becomes possible. Cultural concepts help to recognize, interpret and classify these differences.

In general, cultural models provide a schematic and abstract depiction of culture. Therefore, they provide an instrument to make cultural phenomena explicable. Cultural models offer possibilities of understanding, decoding and classifying cultural features[3]. Cultural concepts and dimensions are used to describe, characterize and compare social systems as groups, organizations or societies. They allow for better understanding of cultural specifics such as different perceptions, thoughts, feelings and behaviors (Holtbrügge, 2022).

Cultural concepts[4] were developed due to the growing interest in cultural studies in the 1950s and 60s. While early models originated from disciplines such as anthropology, ethnography and psychology, which were adapted for business, subsequent cultural models[5], were developed and introduced by management scholars (Holtbrügge, 2022).

In this paper, two cultural models are highlighted. The dimensions according to E.T. Hall describe differences in the context-orientation of communication. The cultural standards according to A. Thomas, contrast different, formative cultural characteristics, without enforcing a binary structure.

Cultural constructs by E.T. Hall

Hall's culture model has been frequently used since the 1970s. At least three dimensions include h/l-context, time-orientation and space-orientation. Time orientation refers to monochronic behavior (linear, one thing at a time, punctuality) vs. polychronic (non-linear, multiple things at a time, flexible approach to time). Space-

---

3 To interpret cultural characteristics adequately, is necessary to understand and plan individual behavior and the course of negotiations.
4 In context of this work the expression of cultural concepts will be used synonymous with the expression of cultural dimensions
5 As by Geert Hofstede

orientation describes the feeling of private and public space / sphere an individual might have. This varies across cultures (Holtbrügge, 2022). In this paper the author focuses on context orientation. E.T. Hall classifies two categories; h/l-context cultures. They differ either in an explicit or implicit way of expression (Holtbrügge, 2022). Context means "Context is the information that surrounds an event; it is inextricably bound up with the meaning of that event" (Wiegmann, 2009).The different characteristics are shown in the table below.

Table 1.1: High vs. low-context cultures

Low-context cultures	High-context cultures
Focus is on *what* is said; everything is said explicitly.	Focus is on *who* says *what, when, were* and *how*.
Large part of information is included in the content of the message.	Information is largely embedded in the relations between the participants (age, location, time).
Good communication is precise, simple and clear.	Good communication is nuanced, sophisticated, and layered.
Are at loss when context when high context people do not provide enough background information.	Become impatient and irritated when low-context people provide information they do not need.
Agreements are written, final and binding.	Agreements are spoken, flexible and changeable

(Adapted from Holtbrügge, 2022, p. 77)

This tabular comparison illustrates the potential for misunderstandings between h/l-context speakers, even if they share the same language. It requires a deeper understanding of the counterparts' intentions to decrypt h/c messages and to avoid a pre-judgment of l/c speakers as rude.

Cultural standards by Thomas

Thomas states that if culture is an orientation system, it should have orientation marks which are typical for this specific culture.

These orientation marks can be called cultural standards. Members of a culture see these standards as normal, natural, typical and binding. Behaviors that differ (own and foreign) are evaluated and regulated based on these standards They are types of perception, thought patterns, judgments and interactions. Some of these cultural standards may be shared, some might have a different or less important meaning and others might be missing or replaced by more important ones. The effectiveness of cultural standards results from an analysis of critical incidents. Therefore, cultural standards might encourage a learning process to gain intercultural competence (Thomas, 2013a). Cultural standards only become visible in contact with foreign cultures and their effects on interaction with others (Thomas, 2013b).

For an effective collaboration, Thomas (2013b, 2013c) states that both partners need to show the ability and readiness to fit foreign cultural standards into their own patterns of perception, thinking, evaluation and action. The following overview shows the cultural standards relevant to this thesis for selected regions.

Table 1.2: Selected cultural standards by A. Thomas.

Central Europe	Northern Europe	Eastern Europe	Latin America	South Asia
Subject-orientation	Equality, inclusion	Emotionality	People-orientation (sympathy, family, emotionality, representational orientation)	Emotionality
Appreciation of structure and rules	Equality, flat hierarchy, pragmatism	Hierarchy	Hierarchy	Hierarchy as an organizational principle
Rule-oriented, internalized sense of duty	n/a	Group-orientation	Polychronic understanding of time	Hierarchy as an organizational

				(non-binding arrangements, flexibility)	principle Collectivism
and responsibility (obligation)					
Time planning	n/a	Group-orientation		Polychronic understanding of time (Present-orientation)	Polychronic understanding of time, time flows, cyclic understanding of time
Central Europe	**Northern Europe**	**Eastern Europe**		**Latin America**	**South Asia**
Weak contextual reference as a communication style	Conflict-avoidance	Emotionality, (indirect communication in conflicts)		Positive communication behavior (Communicative, conflict-avoidance)	Conflict-avoidance, indirectness
Separation of private and professional life	n/a	Emotionality		People-orientation	Collectivism
Individualism	n/a	Group-orientation		n/a	Collectivism

(Adapted from Schroll-Machl, 2016, pp. 260-261)

Cultural standards create an incentive to reflect the respective situation, one's own and the counterpart's behavior. They indicate how potential critical encounters can be interpreted and resolved in intercultural negotiation.

Influence of culture on negotiation

Different contexts in communication can lead to critical incidents in negotiations. It can be assumed that h/c speakers send and receive a lot of information on the relationship level, while l/c speakers mainly communicate on the subject level. As h/l-context speakers do not necessarily understand each other's communication pattern, the appeal hidden in a message cannot always be decrypted in an appropriate manner. This is likely to result in a situation, where people not really communicating with each other and loose track in the process.

The potential risk of not being able to decrypt each other's messages in addition to language barriers needs high attention. To stay on the same page requires the participants to go back and forth in the process. This approach can have its strategic benefits, but also can be interpreted as avoiding the topic (Harkiolakis et al., 2016). This again might cause irritation with l/c speakers as they need precise information. The critical incident might be that l/c speakers are focused on the results, while h/c speakers are focused on the negotiation itself.

Social settings embedded in the negotiation itself are subject to cultural differences and negotiators have different values and self-images. These preconditions result in different approaches in compromising, resolving conflicts and decision-making (Lewis, 2018). The context of an intercultural negotiation is particularly challenged when the social setting of a face-to-face encounter changes.

Virtual contexts and negotiation

The intercultural negotiation already poses challenges to negotiators involved. An additional challenge comes when participants do not meet face-to-face but online. Virtual and mobile work, in the context of increased application of home office, indicate the need to deal with the topic of virtual negotiation. Special conditions, advantages and challenges of virtual negotiation are briefly described in their main features.

While working virtually was something rarely done in early 2000s, several developments in the past years accelerated the spreading of virtual teams. Due to the covid crisis at the end of 2019, a general option for home office and remote work as well as declining prices for technology influenced the development of virtual teams (Lindner, 2020).

Smartphone use in business communication increased to almost 90% in 2021 (approx. 60%, 2018), videoconferencing to almost 70% (<50%, 2018) and collaboration tools to about 50% (approx. 30%, 2018) (Brandt, M., 2021). While before covid only 4% of employed people in Germany were working from home, this number peaked during the first lockdown in April 2020 by 27%. Although the number of home office workers fluctuated over the year, it still comprised under a quarter (24%) of all employed workers in January 2021 (Hans-Böckler-Stiftung, 2021). A study carried out in Germany among 602 companies' states that 68% of employees wish to maintain or even extent their level of videoconferencing in the future rather than meeting face-to-face.

The biggest risks of virtual communication are said to be the lack of face-to-face encounters (81%) and networking opportunities (46%) (Airplus, Statista, 2022a). The most annoying factors are poor internet connections (69%), technical glitches (50%) and the frequency of virtual meetings (46%). Additionally, unprofessional behavior and disruptions by 3rd parties are mentioned (kress.de, 2021). The most important reasons for personal meetings are the building of relationships and trust (84%), negotiations (76%), emotional communications (73%), as well as confidential and critical contents (71%) (Airplus, Statista, 2022b).

The advantages of working in virtual teams arise from the extended possibilities of team composition (no spatial boundaries), reduced costs (no travelling or similar). It offers opportunities for workplace and time flexibility. Digitalization facilitates access to, and distribution of information. Furthermore, virtuality can help to reduce hierarchical levels by horizontal integration and to skip bureaucratic hurdles (Kremer & Janneck, 2013).

There are some challenges that need to be addressed. Technical aspects such as data protection and the complex and expensive acquisition of equipment should be considered. Additionally, social aspects such as cultural and linguistic barriers influence the collaboration as well. There are increased demands on self-organization by employees, a more complex management situation and more difficult conditions for maintaining motivation due to a lack of personal contact (Kremer & Janneck, 2013). The psychological effect of physical non-formal social meetings should not be underestimated as it helps to build trust between participants. Independent of their cultural backgrounds, members of virtual teams struggle with a reduced identification with their colleagues, their company and its values due to increased distance. Lack of transparency about work processes causes inefficacy. Moreover, virtual context makes it more difficult to assess every team member performance and workload, so trust and communication within the team is indispensable (Kremer & Janneck, 2013).

In the social field of impact, the communication process, independent of technical media, plays a dominant role and uses established communication models. This interaction is shaped by individual characteristics. The technical field of impact is characterized technical faults and errors, such as malfunctions. The choice of the appropriate media tool is necessary to reach the desired goals. Finally, the communicative media process describes automated software feature as algorithms and filters.

The complexity of communication is shaped by different ways of interpreting the message and dealing with conflict. Negotiation, which by definition is characterized by divergent opinions, is additionally affected by the special challenges of interculturality. The increase in virtual negotiations introduces a further barrier to communication that needs to be overcome.

Harkiolakis et al. (2016) explicitly mention limited perception and the lack of sensory data as a challenge for e-negotiations, as humans depend on visual information. They describe the tendency to replace missing information with imagination, ideals, and experiences which do not necessarily fit the reality. Furthermore, they attach the feeling of "mutual invisibility" to showing less empathy when feeling protected by "anonymity and distance" resulting in the assumption of not being held accountable for actions, behaviors and words. They describe the measures for developing a relationship in virtual encounters – shift form proximity – in face-to-face encounters to shared interests. As proximity cannot be reached online, finding similarities between both parties moves to the foreground. Trust is highlighted as important in establishing a working relationship over distance. Missing information such as body language is restricted in virtual negotiation, making it more difficult to decode cultural expressions and to adapt the "own" behavior. Language barriers increase risks of misunderstandings, moreover, the preparation style of negotiation varies culturally, whatever the respective negotiator might seek as a desirable outcome (Harkiolakis et al. 2016).

Research question

The research question of "How do low- and high context-oriented negotiators resolve their differences in video-based international negotiations?" is considered relevant, as it is expected that video conferencing will continue to gain increased acceptance within the business world, in which international negotiation plays an important role.

The combination between the challenges of intercultural communication and the influences and impacts of a virtual setting is worth being analyzed and evaluated. An identification of potential critical incidents is necessary to adapt competencies to changed conditions. The assumption in this paper is that cultural differences influence negotiation in terms of communication and relevant behavior. Besides differences in communication behavior (h/l-context), there are variances in the perception of the counterpart's and one's own role in joint interaction. Further, the virtual setting has an additional impact on perception and behavior.

The first issue of relevance are differences in communication patterns and consequently in negotiation approaches of h/l-context speakers. Secondly, it is important to evaluate how these effect negotiation behaviors and to understand how differences and critical incidents could be overcome. Intercultural communication and interaction in a face-to-face setting comprise a risk of failure. The virtual setting and the screen size reduce the immediate and direct contact, operating just like a filter. A lot of non-verbal signals, especially important for h/c speakers, are restricted and deteriorate in transmission. Simultaneously this filter effect might weaken the communication behavior of l/c speakers, as their l/c manifestations are increased.

Negotiations are characterized by contrasting interests and by overcoming the resulting differences. Reaching an agreement requires openness in finding supporting attitudes and respective techniques or methods of getting to yes. Consequently, h/l-context speakers need to be sensitive towards their counterparts' communication behavior focused on opportunities, not threats.

Methodology

This study is based on qualitative ethnography and structured as a scenario-based case study. Due to the limited scope of this work, only four of six elements find consideration. Following Ellet (2018), these elements will be considered: identification of the subject, criteria selection, criteria-based analysis and overall evaluation.

The **identification of subject** describes what the case is about, which is vital to understand to be able to carry out an evaluation (Ellet, 2018). An appropriate **criteria selection** allows an evaluation of the case itself. These criteria are much dependent on the respective case (Ellet, 2018). Categories generated are used for **criteria-based analysis.** Results of coding categorizing are presented to learn about positive, negative or both aspects resulting from selected criteria (Ellet, 2018). This is followed by **overall evaluation**, dealing with insights gained from applying the criteria to the subject. Again, positive and negative findings are presented and reflected to allow deeper evaluation.

For this research, primary data were used by carrying out qualitative, semi-structured interviews. Each interviewee was presented with the same eight questions. A semi-structure approach allows the author to ask additional, supplementary questions. The intention was to obtain additional information, to clarify statements and to give interviewees the opportunity to contribute some of their own ideas.

Interviews were mainly carried out in English, with one exception. It should be noted that for some interviewees interview questions two and three needed further explanation. Three of seven interviews were carried out virtually, due to participants' schedule and availabilities, the others face-to-face. The duration of the interview varied between 23 to 64 minutes.

The study was carried out at a German, medium-sized, family-owned business. The company is internationally active in the chemical and energy sector.

Seven employees were asked to take part, among them former employees. Participants work(ed) in different functions and have experience in strategic negotiations. They had different levels of responsibility, ranging from skilled professionals to upper management. All participants are graduates and were selected for different characteristics (i.e. experience in international (video-based) negotiations, position company and cultural background).

Questions refer to the individual negotiator (h/l-context), the situation of the intercultural negotiation, possible differences that may occur, and approaches to solutions (resolving differences) as well as the specific social setting of virtuality. The cultural standards which could have an influence on the h/l-context orientation of a participant were given special consideration. Thus, when framing the questions, aspects such as individualistic and collectivistic orientation or hierarchy were indirectly asked for, without being explicitly addressed first.

There is no clear evidence that indicates setting interview length in relation to the h/l-context of interviewees, as there are other personality-related influences on duration.

As qualified data cannot be measured, in the sense of formal and content characteristics, criteria must be defined and selected in a different manner. Open and axial coding allow for a classification and clustering of criteria, with the aim of moving from general to specific scenarios. These scenarios could then be evaluated and compared to gain understanding of the obvious and hidden meanings in the statements.

The interviews were analyzed for clues and themes, with respect to the research question, by using open coding. Individual phenomena were combined into concepts and categories to break down the data. Core issues were then identified by asking questions such as: what, who, why, when, where, what for (Universität Augsburg, n.d.).

This analysis resulted in a few hundred codes, which were listed in a common code list, sorted alphabetically and revised several times by combining related codes that shared a meaning into preliminary categories. These preliminary categories / concepts were then redefined and differentiated in the next step of axial coding and cut into final categories. These were set in relation to one another. The aim was to understand causes, consequences, intervening conditions and strategies that link different statements about the study (Döring, Bortz, & Pöschl, 2016; Universität Augsburg, n.d.).

Results & discussion

The statements by participants could be easily divided into three core categories. There is no indication that there is a difference between h/l-context speakers as they have prioritized these three categories equally.

Most attention was drawn towards the formal framework of negotiation and the influence of the individual negotiator scored. The focus is less on the technical aspects than on the effects of virtual negotiation. The following figure gives an overview of the structure of core and the respective sub-categories.

Figure 1.3: Overview of core and sub-categories

The negotiation framework (46%)	The role of the individual negotiator (39%)	The virtual context (15%)
Organization & struture (16%)	Negotiation attitude (12%)	Technological impact (5%)
Negotiation Management (6%)	Behavior and perception (11%)	Assessment of virtual negotiation (10%)
Critical incidents (9%)	Steering communication (9%)	
Getting to yes (8%)	Role and competence (7%)	
Relation and collaboration (7%)		

The context-orientation of the interviewees move along the spectrum of Hall's h/l-context model. Although tendencies of the participant's context-orientation – according to Hall's findings – were confirmed, it is noticeable that there were swings in the opposite direction for both h/l-context speakers. Some of these are set out in an exemplary manner within the discussion section.

Participants were Taylor (Northern Europe), Jordan, Cameron and Alex (Central Europe), Sasha (Eastern Europe), Ellis (South Asia) and Austin (South America).
The following figure shows context-orientation tendencies of the respective interview partners according to Halls dimension and the author's assessment.

Figure 1.4: Assessment of participants on the scale

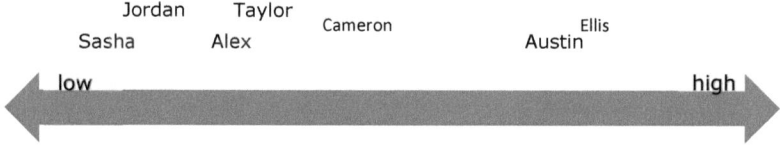

The negotiation framework

Due to the coding and categorizing, most important topics in question refer to the negotiation framework of organization and structure of the negotiation process. Five subcategories emerged from this.

Since negotiation itself is characterized by opposing positions, a view to structuring the process and the observation of leading principles is important. These organizing principles were summarized as **organization and structure** and is considered the most important element by h/l-context speakers. Jordan explained: 'proper preparation prevents poor performance.' To avoid getting lost Alex recommended to 'keep it simple and small.'

Bierbrauer (2009) refers to "structure", "process" and "result" as components of business negotiation. This is in line with the statements of the interviewees regarding the need for a structured approach considering stakeholders and the results pursued.

Attention was paid towards handling these organizing principles and could be supplemented by subcategory of **negotiation management**. Interviewees aimed to ensure a smooth adjusted process. This was done by focusing on designing and shaping the effected phases of the negotiation process. They recommended setting clear rules for managing the changed settings.

A good negotiation process depends on how negotiators deal with disruptions. Participants are aware of the necessity to handle **critical incidents** within the intercultural context. In particular, emotions, the ability to deal with or avoid conflicts and professionalism were mentioned. H/c participants showed more sensitive to this topic than l/c participants.

Helmold, Dathe, & Hummel (2019) define striving for "balanced interest" and "conflict readiness" as characteristics of negotiation. Consequently, **getting to yes** had an importance to participants. L/c speakers gave it a higher priority than h/c speakers. The contributions of h/l-context speakers indicate that under the influence of the virtual context the essential elements of the negotiation framework are of high importance. A dysfunctional communication would jeopardize a good result. To avoid these disruptions, collaboration is essential.

"Relationship", "fairness" and "equality of power" are necessities for negotiation. Further, "result-orientation", "value creation", and "target setting" are significant elements (Helmold, Dathe, & Hummel, 2019). Bierbrauer (2009) speaks of "results" and Helmold, Dathe, & Hummel (2019) "shared aims" as a joint understanding of the purpose of negotiation.

One of the fundamental difficulties of virtual negotiations mentioned by all participants was the potential lack of **relation and collaboration**. Without building connection and fostering personal interaction no negotiation is possible. The quality of the outcome is dependent on these issues. It is interesting to see that this is more important for l/c interviews than initially assumed.

The role of the individual

In addition to the importance of the framework conditions of the negotiation, the significance of the negotiator, and the **role of the individual**, now takes center point. So far, this research showed that the **negotiation attitude** is given similar attention by h/l-context speakers. It is the negotiator who shapes and imprints the negotiation. Consequently, soft factors and the ability to adapt to cultural peculiarities are vital. These were summarized as **behavior & perception.** This category also includes the ability to admit differences.

Interviewees of both contexts acknowledged the importance of being able to perceive needs and expressions. In an interview Cameron states 'aber dann muss man erstmal sehr viele Monate investieren, um eine Vertrauensbasis zu schaffen'[6]. Austin addressed potential misunderstandings due to the need to interpret words and emotions 'you cannot take everything for granted as they are not native speakers.'

Steering communication focused intentional communicative actions. Interview partners emphasized that it is important to become aware of the effectiveness of one's own communication. This includes the willingness to intervene in an appropriate manner and to reflect one's own viewpoint. A closer look revealed that h/c speakers focus their counterparts by adapting their communication, l/c speakers prefer clear and direct communication when addressing issues.

An additional relevant factor was recognized, **role and competence,** which support the navigation within negotiation and emphasized the importance of finding one's own role. Interviewees mentioned that experience is essential to ease this process.

---

6 Translation: But then you first have to invest a lot of months to create a basis of trust.

The virtual context

The ***virtual context*** was seen as something being added to the process, as a technical tool, making certain things easier. It was considered as increasing efficiency, but not something to be considered as first choice.

Results in terms of the ***technological impact*** show that in addition to general technical disruptions, interviewees described difficulties in picking up gestures and facial expressions. The technology reduced or completely filtered out their transmission.

Respondents commented on the number of negotiation participants. Technology offers the option of adding more people, as there are no travel costs or special availabilities to consider. Others noted that a negotiation situation could quickly become confusing if too many participants were to be seen in individual boxes on the screen.

The ***assessment of virtual negotiation*** focused on the social setting. It became apparent that participants saw advantages and disadvantages in the approaches of virtual and face-to-face negotiation. The choice of the approach depends mainly on the complexity of the issue to be negotiated. According to the participants' assessment, since a relationship in the team and with the other person is important, the establishment of such a relationship is vital. In general, interviewees preferred a hybrid model with a sensible combination of virtual and face-to-face meetings rather than committing to one option.

Discussion

After the results were collected and structured, it was necessary to shed light on whether and how they contribute to answer the research question. The aim was to clarify how h/l-context oriented negotiators solve their differences in international, video-based negotiations.

Current research shows little results on virtual intercultural negotiations. However, there are findings on facilitation in virtual meetings and workshops (Lange, 2020), as well as on virtual knowledge exchange in scientific intercultural teams (Balasubramanian, 2020). To a certain extent, some of their findings can be applied to this paper. This is especially true for general statements on the advantages and challenges of virtual cooperation as well as on aspects of perception.

The negotiation framework combines the subcategories of organization & structure, negotiation management, critical incidents, getting to yes and relation & collaboration. While the first two emphasize functional aspects, the others refer to behavioral ones. Negotiation characteristics, necessities and components – as sketched in the literature review – were transferred from a face-to-face to a virtual setting.

Organization & structure / negotiation management

All participants attach great importance to the framework conditions. It can be concluded that this need is intensified in the virtual context, as orientation markers get lost in terms of perception and information. Interviewees describe it as having 'strategy & structure', 'milestones' (Taylor), 'set rules', scripts & stencils (Cameron) and 'know your topics' (Austin).

Virtual negotiations need 'higher preparation which can also save time at the end and may result in a better outcome' (Taylor), but 'one must be more focused in a virtual setting' (Alex). All participants refer to body language and other non-verbal signals. A proper technical set-up allows for a better grasp of at least some of the signals from the negotiating partners (i.e. Jordan, Sasha, Alex). The measures for organization and structure help to bridge the gap of face-to-face encounters.

Lange (2020) describes that in virtual meetings and complex situations, special care should be taken towards preparation, giving room to the multiplicity of topics and the involvement of participants. Negotiators need orientation and clarity by careful adjusted organization and structure, proper preparation and excellent technical tools. This was also expressed in the idea to have one's BATNA[7] ready (Jordan, Alex). An exit option might be also important to h/c negotiators as it serves their need to adapt situations to own preferences.

Critical incidents

Particular problems arise in the perception of critical incidents, as recognition depends on the full communication context. Subject-oriented factors, such as not making progress (Sasha) indicate issues to l/c interviewees. Alex notices it when 'people are not talking to each other but are simply repeating positions.'

Observing the attitude, behavior and body language provide 'shortcuts to solution' (Austin) confirming his/her h/c attitude, emotion awareness and people and collectivistic-orientation. 'Excessive agitation over trivialities', 'accusations' (Ellis), 'Arroganz, frech werden, ablehnende Haltung'[8] (Cameron), show other types of conflict-promoting behavior.

Interviewees clarify questions, untangle problems (Alex), 'break the elephant into smaller pieces' (Taylor) or 'put the fish on the table' (Austin) to address issues. Participants try to find 'common understanding and wording' (Jordan) and 'stepping in the shoes of the other party' (Taylor). Austin puts company needs before personal ones and shows collectivistic behavior. According to Taylor the threshold to bring up misunderstandings is lower, although it takes longer to solve. Sasha states: 'I wouldn't say that there are

---

7 Best Alternative to a Negotiated Agreement
8 Arrogance, becoming cheeky, negative attitude.

anymore (issues), like aren't different to real-life negotiation'[9]. Taking a break is the method of choice for all participants when conflicts arise. Austin suggests to mute quarreling parties in virtual negotiations and initiating a break.

Although, h/c speakers have a tendency of conflict avoidance, the respective interviewees favor addressing issues and put high attention towards this matter. This might seem surprising. On the other hand it can avoid escalation and supports collectivistic behavior patterns, in terms of 'I understand your problem', 'let's find a good outcome'. This attitude of h/c interviewees might be an indicator for their experience in negotiation. It can be assumed that h/c negotiators address critical incidents in the sense of group-orientation and l/c negotiators with regard to the negotiation result.

The emergence of critical incidents cannot be prevented as they are caused by the intercultural situation itself. By recognizing and applying appropriate methods to resolve, negotiators can make them manageable. Splitting up issues and breaks are considered as helpful. A key element is to control one's own emotions. The nature of differences and arising conflicts does not seem to have changed, but only the way they are dealt with.

Getting to yes

The study shows different types of process monitoring. Some of them refer to quantitative measures (Austin), defined as 'results', 'desired outcomes' (Sasha) 'open-points lists', 'mark-ups' (Jordan) and 'goals' (Taylor). Ellis and Alex use soft indicators as perceiving and interpreting body language. Body language of supervisor's guide Ellis, showing emotion-orientation, hierarchy-awareness and collectivism. Alex orients on these marks as well, but also sets

---

9 The choice of words is interesting. It might indicate that Sasha has issues to perceive virtual negotiation as 'real'. Unfortunately, there are not enough indicators to support that this is true for him/her. Nevertheless, Balasubramanian also mentions the risk that virtual communication might not be considered as 'real' (2020).

measurable indicators for progress (goals). The overall atmosphere of the negotiation provides orientation h/l-context negotiators.

H/l-context speakers both use qualitative and quantitative measures to assess the progress. As all participants show the desire to achieve an adequate negotiation result, differences are smoothed out a bit. L/c interviewees pay higher attention on getting to yes, this can be explained with a higher goal focus, while h/c interviewees are more relationship-oriented. The virtual limitation causes a greater focus on aspects such as structuring the communication to gain a joint understanding.

To reach an agreement, those involved have to know what they want to achieve and know the status of the process. It is essential that negotiation parties have an elementary motivation to reach an agreement and therefore to overcome differences.

Relation and collaboration

Having personal interaction is important to all participants. It is 'super difficult' for Austin to build trust because of reduced human connections. 'Introductory rounds' (Taylor) help to build trust. The missing opportunities for coffee breaks and 'chit-chats' make it harder for Jordan to do so. There is a tendency to have as much personal contact as possible to 'build bridges' (Austin).

Surprisingly, trust is not necessarily top priority, as 'you don't have to be friends', if a contract settles everything (Sasha). S/he admits that trust is necessary in long-term relationships and handshake agreements. This is a typical attitude for l/c speakers. The motivation for building relationships can be derived from an atmospheric perspective or it can establish trust to come to terms. Meetings that require intensive exchange and participation are held in person for this very reason (Lange, 2020). The quality of relationship is a mean to overcome differences. A good relationship and trust make this step easier. Relation and collaboration work as a lubricant to the technical and structuring aspects of the negotiation process.

Regarding negotiation attitudes, no clear causality can be established here with regard to h/l-context communication behavior. The negotiator is at the center of negotiations, indicating why interviewees feel that the basic process of the negotiation has not changed that much. The results depend on his/her skills. In most cases, there is no adaptation of the negotiation approach because the need is not seen, or maintaining authenticity is considered more important. Also, in most cases, participants exhibit compromise-oriented negotiation tactics. There are individual tendencies (Austin & Sasha) that illustrate the typical behavior patterns of their communication context.

Sasha does not intend to change his/her negotiation approach. Austin would 'tailor-make' and 'design' his/hers in virtual relationships, proving h/c and people-orientation. A detection and evaluation of changes is not easy for Cameron and Alex, as they wish to retain authenticity.

Most participants follow a compromise-oriented approach. They state to 'propose instead of argue' (Ellis) and show a pragmatic attitude 'das ganze Leben ist ein Kompromiss'[10] (Cameron). Alex explains 'a good outcome is always, if both sides think they have given too much (...) then in reality both sides have given equally'. Sasha declares: 'If you got what you want, it's a good outcome, and didn't get what you want then it's a bad outcome.'

A differentiated viewpoint provides the basis for a good negotiating climate. It is good to express appreciation by working to understand the others' perspective. Compromise by give and take opens the field for clarifying differences, without giving up one's authenticity.

---

10 The whole life is a compromise.

Aspects which promote or disrupt negotiation have remained the same, as these are fundamentally socially acceptable behaviors. It is rather about the way negotiations are carried out. What has changed is the more difficult perception and classification of these behaviors. Therefore, the body language still perceivable and context is important for both h/l-context speakers.

In virtual meetings 'you see the screen but not what is around it' (Taylor), and according to Austin, making it more difficult to orientate, causing passive behavior. Jordan explained that it is easier if one knows and trusts the counterpart for quite a while, as one knows what kind of behavior to expect. Ellis pointed out conflict-avoiding attitude and face-saving behavior by claiming the necessity to communicate carefully and 'massage feelings'. On the other side s/he claimed: 'you can't just be defensive, but come back in the same tone', which contradicts conflict-avoidance by showing a l/c tendency.

Balasubramanian (2020) points out that communication gaps may arise in case there is no sense of social presence, "i.e. the degree to which people are perceived as being real" (p.15). He states that participants may try to minimize collaboration in order to avoid uncertainty and risk.

Participants name supportive behaviors that could also apply in face-to-face settings, such as an open, trustful, respectful atmosphere. They need their counterparts to show a win-win attitude, professionalism (Jordan / Cameron), flexibility, willingness to deplore, engage and listen (Sasha) and the ability change perspective (Austin / Alex). Likewise, disrupting behaviors such as 'blocking away', 'not listening', 'not taking time' (Jordan), excessive emotions, accusing or mocking (Ellis) do not specifically apply to virtual situations.

Lange (2020) also discusses the problem of a lack of resonance (mimics, gestures, tone, team dynamics) in virtual meetings. Associated with this is the problem of capturing and resolving difficult situations in particular. It is important to develop an increased mindfulness to absorb missing resonances as well as paying special attention. to listen carefully. The virtual setting requires the facilitator to pay special attention to team members, be it in terms of communication or any concerns (Lange, 2020).

This again documents the significance of the negotiators ability to cope with the different communication situations. This also includes the readiness to admit differences and the willingness to engage in these issues.

Steering communication

The different levels of a message are recognizable in the participants' answers. L/c participants are more likely to send and understand messages on the subject-level, while h/c speakers were more likely to send and understand messages on the relationship-level. Misunderstandings are very likely and l/c speakers need to catch the hints and nuances of non-verbal signals.

Misunderstandings arise due to language and cultural barriers. Alex describes it as a 'lost in translation' risk and according to Austin there are possible misunderstandings among non-native speakers. Ellis and Cameron watch gestures and mimics to see if the counterpart is still integrated in the negotiation.

H/l-context interviewees agree to clearly address issues as soon as they came up. It can be assumed that the approach and timing to do so, differs between h/l context speakers. This is exemplified by h/c reserved behavior when it comes to actively join the negotiation. For example, Ellis waits until she gets invited to say something in a negotiation. Sasha would just step in.

Participants do not intend to change their habits. Habits are shaped by the respective cultural background. This means that h/c speakers feel the need to adapt anyway, as it corresponds with the natural behavior (people/context-orientation). In turn, individualistic, l/c speakers do not perceive this adaptation as necessary.

Additional channels like messenger services allow further clarification and alignment among team members when necessary (Alex, Jordan, Taylor). Lange (2020) underlines the importance of visual impressions through use of rich communication channels. Harkiolakis et al. (2016) describe the limits non-native speakers have in expressing themselves, due to different sounds and idioms. They also state that in intercultural negotiations all participants have to go back and forth in the process to make sure everyone is still on the same page. Interviewees do this by asking questions, observe counterparts and the overall process.

The steering of communication consists above all in the fact that everyone makes contribution towards the desired result. The degree, timing, manner and extent of participation is determined by cultural aspects.

The virtual context analyzed

It could be stated that all participants emphasize quality of the technical equipment. Interviewees need the camera switched on and/or a good audio transmission, as otherwise a lot of non-verbal information is lost. Sasha, Austin and Cameron require limiting participants in virtual negotiation as it would get confusing. In general, it is easier for Sasha to read signs in virtual settings, but it is more difficult for him/her to 'create rapport'. Alex has difficulties 'to read the room' and grab the atmosphere. For Ellis, non-verbal signals are easier to read in virtual settings, if the setting (i.e. equipment, lighting) was good. Austin requires good technical equipment to understand the nuances of speech. S/he finds it harder to read body language in virtual settings, which compromises performance, a typical issue for h/c people.

According to Ellis, the attention span in virtual settings is lower. Austin adds that the learning curve in personal meetings is much better. The social component of sharing information and bonding influences focusing capabilities. Interviewees notice very similar disruptions as stated by Airplus and Faktenkontor such as, missing human connection, lack of networking opportunities (Airplus, Statista, 2022a), technical hick-ups and unprofessional behavior (kress.de, 2021).

All participants attached great importance to the quality and reliability of the technology to bridge limitations in perception. They were almost equally affected by virtual filters severely affecting perception and the decoding of non-verbal signals. Candidates were aware of the limitations and disruptive potential of virtuality. It can be assumed that this awareness has shaped their answers to the other questions.

Some scholars recommend having visual content sharing options in virtual workshops, especially with demanding objectives. Breakout rooms and virtual pin boards could also be used for this purpose. Information should also be made available at an early stage. She also emphasized the tiresome effect of virtual meetings and the lack of personal resonance (Lange, 2020).

Differences between virtual and face-to-face meetings are about the use of technology and the ability to "read people". The negative effects of a negotiation are amplified through the virtual context. In principle, there is a constructive attitude towards technology, and the advantages are perceived and appreciated. However, a connection is seen between the effective use of technology and the complexity of negotiations. The higher the complexity, the greater the desire for face-to-face negotiation.

This is confirmed by Lange (2020). She explains that face-to-face meetings (missing resonance) should not be permanently replaced by virtual collaboration, but rather supplemented.

The figure below shows the interrelation of virtuality and personal involvement connected with the complexity of the negotiation issues. Different levels of interaction can be chosen depending on the scope of negotiation and needs of the participants.

Conclusion

This paper has provided a deeper insight into the communication patterns and the performance of negotiators in international video-based negotiations. The purpose of the study was to examine how h/l-context negotiators solve differences that arise due to the virtual social setting. This paper has argued that there is an approach that will support the handling of critical incidents resulting from the combination of an intercultural and virtual setting.

Facing cultural differences within a virtual negotiation setting takes place in three fields: the negotiation framework, the role of the individual and the virtual context. The core element to all negotiators is to achieve an appropriate negotiation result.

Virtual limitation causes a greater focus on aspects as structuring the communication to gain a joint understanding. Negotiators try to compensate the limited perception and orientation through anticipatory preparation, conscious structuring and the use of high-quality technical aids. These formalistic parameters deliver orientation marks. Managing these topics make the handling of critical incidents easier.

The emergence of critical incidents generally cannot be prevented, as the intercultural setting is characterized by these. Building relationships and cooperation were vital for prevention. The driving force differ by cultural orientation. The quality of relationship is a mean to overcome differences. Relation and collaboration ease the handling of technical and structuring aspects. H/c negotiators prioritized the communication process itself, the l/c speaker the result of the negotiation. For experienced negotiators it was easier to act within this environment and to adapt communication patterns adequately.

In addition, the study showed the strong importance of the role of the individual, being the dominant factor. His/her abilities, skills and competencies determine the way of resolving critical incidents.

This also includes the readiness to admit differences and the willingness to engage in these issues. In that sense it is supportive to express appreciation by acknowledging the different perspectives. This leads to a give and take approach and provides options for clarifying differences. As everybody delivers contributions for the desired result, the intentional steering of communication, subject to resolving differences is essential.

In this context roles and competencies were seen as steering elements, but there was no clear statement of how to apply it. The cultural background influences the allocation of roles but is also shaped and exercised by experience and the situational context.

There is an awareness for the potential of disruption induced by the technology. Quality and reliability of the technology used are an indispensable criterion. The higher the quality of the technical transmission, the lower the risk of information loss.

Regarding the assessment of virtual negotiations participants agreed that it is not their first choice. It turned out that the higher the need for personal involvement, the higher the need for face-to-face negotiation.

A limitation of the study is that there are barely any literature and research studies available combining negotiation, interculturalism and the virtual setting. Recently, studies involving virtual collaboration were introduced, but they dealt rather more with collaboration in general and not with the specific setting of virtual intercultural negotiation.

Furthermore, the small sample size did not allow a universal statement about the behavior of h/l-context negotiators, but the results rather confirmed tendencies towards existing studies and models. Notwithstanding the limited sample size, this work offers valuable insights into how negotiation in a virtual setting were perceived by experienced negotiators. It is very interesting to see that, in general, negotiators cope quite well with the new necessities posed.

Additional research might explore as to whether a common (artificially constructed) negotiation culture might overrule national cultures to a certain extend. It might also explore how links between experience, ability, and willingness to agree on a shared negotiation culture might increase the chances of a good negotiation outcome.

References

Airplus. (2022a). Größte Risiken bei virtueller Geschäftskommunikation in Deutschland 2022. Retrieved from https://de.statista.com/statistik/daten/studie/1318246/umfrage/risiken-virtueller-geschaeftskommunikation/

Airplus. (2022b). Wichtigste Gründe für persönliche Geschäftstreffen in Deutschland 2022. Retrieved from https://de.statista.com/statistik/daten/studie/1318280/umfrage/wichtigste-gruende-fuer-persoenliche-geschaeftstreffen/

Anspruchsgruppen. (n.d.). Gabler Wirtschaftslexikon. Retrieved from https://wirtschaftslexikon.gabler.de/definition/anspruchsgruppen-27010/version-250673

Balasubramanian, V. (1st of Feb. 2020). Facilitating Information Exchange in Intercultural Virtual Teams. Intercultural Journal, 19(33), 13–25. Retrieved from https://www.interculture-journal.com/index.php/icj/issue/view/48

Barmeyer, C. (2012). Taschenlexikon Interkulturalität. Göttingen: Vandenhoeck & Ruprecht

Bierbrauer, G. (2009). Interkulturelles Verhandeln. In F. Haft, & K. von Schlieffen (Eds.), Handbuch Mediation. Verhandlungstechnik Strategien Einsatzgebiete (2 ed., pp. 433-453). München: Verlag C.H. Beck.

Bitkom Research. (24th of Nov. 2021). Wie werden Sie künftig mit den aufgrund der Corona-Pandemie eingeführten Digitalisierungsmaßnahmen verfahren? Retrieved from https://de.statista.com/statistik/daten/studie/1283537/umfrage/corona-bedingten-digitalisierungsmassnahmen-in-unternehmen/

Brandt, M. (11th of May 2021). Corona verändert die Unternehmenskommunikation. Retrieved from https://de.statista.com/infografik/24831/von-unternehmen-zur-kommunikation-genutzte-kanaele/

Broszinsky-Schwabe, E. (2017). Interkulturelle Kommunikation: Missverständnisse und Verständigung (2 ed.). [Springer-link version]. Retrieved from https://link.springer.com/book/10.1007/978-3-658-13983-4

Corporate Training. (n.d.). Virtuell verhandeln. Verhandlungstraining – Online Live. Retrieved from https://www.corptrain.de/produkt/verhandlungstraining-virtuell-verhandeln-online-live/

Döring, N., Bortz, J., & Pöschl, S. (2016). Forschungsmethoden & Evaluation in den Humanwissenschaften.[Springer-link version]. Retrieved from https://link.springer.com/book/10.1007/978-3-642-41089-5

Ellet, W. (2018). The Case Study Handbook. A Student's Guide (Revised ed.). Boston: Harvard Business Review Press.

Fisher, R., & Ury, W. (2011). Getting to yes. Negotiating an agreement without giving in (3 ed.). (B. Patton, Ed.) London: Random House.

Hall, E. (1981). Beyond Culture. New York: Anchor Books.

NLP Hamburg. (n.d.). Was ist Rapport. Retrieved from https://www.nlphamburg.de/rapport/

Hans-Böckler-Stiftung. (16th of Feb. 2021). Anteil der im Homeoffice arbeitenden Beschäftigten in Deutschland vor und während der Corona-Pandemie 2020 und 2021. Retrieved from https://de.statista.com/statistik/daten/studie/1204173/umfrage/befragung-zur-homeoffice-nutzung-in-der-corona-pandemie/

Harkiolakis, N., Halkias, D., & Abadir, S. (2016). e-Negotiations. Networking and Cross-Cultural Business Transactions (2 ed.). Retrieved from https://www.thalia.de/suche?sq=e-Negotiations.+Networking+and+Cross-Cultural+Business+Transactions+

Helmold, M., Dathe, T., & Hummel, F. (2019). Erfolgreiche Verhandlungen. Best-in-Class Empfehlungen für den Verhandlungsdurchbruch. [Springer-link version]. Retrieved from https://link.springer.com/book/10.1007/978-3-658-23969-5

Hofmann, T. (2020, 4 24). Verhandlung 4.0: Virtuelle-Verhandlungen in Zeiten von Social-Distancing. Retrieved from: https://verhandlung.blog/virtuelles-verhandeln/

Holtbrügge, D. (2022). Intercultural Management. (N. Waters, Ed.) Los Angeles. London. New Dheli. Singapore. Washington DC. Melbourne: Sage.

Konflikt. (n.d.). Gabler Wirtschaftslexikon. Retrieved from https://wirtschaftslexikon.gabler.de/definition/konflikt-41120/version-264491

Kremer, M., & Janneck, M. (2013). Gruppendynamik und Organisationsberatung. Kommunikation und Kooperation in Virtuellen Teams. Retrieved from: https://link.springer.com/article/10.1007/s11612-013-0227-x

kress.de. (21st of Feb. 2021). Was nervt an Online-Meetings am meisten? Retrieved from https://de.statista.com/statistik/daten/studie/1227262/umfrage/die-nervigsten-dinge-an-online-meetings-in-deutschland/

Lange, M. (2020). Virtuelle Moderation: Über die Gestaltung einer konstruktiven Gesprächsatmosphäre in virtuellen Meetings & Workshops. Intercultural Journal, 19(33), 117–123. Retrieved from https://www.interculture-journal.com/index.php/icj/issue/view/48

Lewis, R. D. (2018). When Cultures Collide. Leading accross cultures (4 ed.). London. Boston: Nicholas Brealey Publishing.

Lindner, D. (2020). Virtuelle Teams und Homeoffice. [Springer-link version]. Retrieved from https://link.springer.com/book/10.1007/978-3-658-30893-3

ManagementCircle. (2020, 11 09). Virtuelle Verhandlungen – auf was es wirklich ankommt. Retrieved from https://www.managementcircle.de/blog/virtuelle-verhandlungen.html

Moll, M. (n.d.). Intercultual Communication II. Hamburg: Europäische Fernhoschule Hamburg.

Preuß-Scheuerle, B. (2016). Praxishandbuch Kommunikation. Überzeugend auftreten, zielgerichtet argumentieren, souverän reagieren. [Springer-link version]. Retrieved from https://link.springer.com/book/10.1007/978-3-8349-4721-5

Schroll-Machl, S. (2016). Beruflich in Babylon. Göttingen: Vandenhoeck und Ruprecht.

Schulz von Thun, F. (2015). Miteinander reden: 1. Störungen und Klärungen. Allgemeine Psychologie der Kommunikation (52 ed.). Reinbek bei Hamburg: Rowohlt Taschenbuch Verlag.

Thomas, A. (2013a). Kultur als Orientierungssystem und Kulturstandards als Bauteile. In A. Thomas, Leben und Arbeiten in internationalen Kontexten (pp. 85-139). Berlin: LIT Verlag Dr. W. Hopf. (Original work published 1999)

Thomas, A. (2013b). Psychologie der interkulturellen Zusammenarbeit. In A. Thomas, Leben und Arbeiten in internationalen Kontexten. Schriftensammlung zur interkulturellen Kompetenz (pp. 45-83). Berlin: LIT Verlag Dr. W. Hopf. (original work published 2011)

Thomas, A. (2013c). Psychologie interkulturellen Lernens und Handelns. In A. Thomas, Leben und Arbeiten in internationalen Kontexten. Schriftensammlung zur interkulturellen Kompetenz (pp. 178 – 236). Berlin: LIT Verlag Dr. W. Hopf. (Original work published 1993)

Universität Augsburg. (n.d.). Empirische Forschung mit audiovisuellen Medien. Retrieved from: https://onlinekurslabor.phil.uni-augsburg.de/course/text/3865/3580

Wiegmann, D. (2009) Die Herausforderungen der Interkulturellen Kommunikation für den Europäischen Kulturkanal Arte. Das interkulturelle Seminar als unternehmensinterne Maßnahme. (Diplomarbeit). Universität Leipzig

List of Figures

Figure 1.1: Components of business negotiations 129
Figure 1.2: The Own, the Foreign, the Intercultural.. 131
Figure 1.3: Overview of core and sub-categories 143
Figure 1.4: Assessment of participants on the scale 144

List of Tables

Table 1.2: High vs. low-context cultures 133
Table 1.2: Selected cultural standards by A. Thomas 134

Impact of cultural dimensions on airline booking behavior: A quantitative analysis of structure-seeking behavior of a multinational airline group

Daniel Thal

Abstract

This research is primarily concerned with investigating the potential correlation between the degree of uncertainty avoidance exhibited by airline passengers and their corresponding flight booking behavior. To answer the posed research question, an ex post facto research design was created, analyzing sales and booking data of European Airlines within a defined research framework. Booking patterns are compared between origin countries characterized by either a pronounced tendency towards high or low uncertainty avoidance. Through the execution of a quantitative analysis, employing the methodology of the Mann Whitney U test, a statistically significant correlation between the observed degree of uncertainty avoidance and the discerned flight booking behavior has been ascertained.

These findings can be of commercial value for airlines as they offer valuable insights into the dynamic customer willingness to pay at distinct booking intervals. Furthermore, marketing strategies employed by airlines can be optimized if a preferred booking window of their customers is identified. As there currently is a scarcity of scholarly literature within this field, this study may be considered as starting point in the domain of cultural behavioral research in the context of the aviation industry. It is plausible that further investigations may be pursued, studying the correlations between diverse cultural dimensions and their impact on consumer behavior among airline passengers.

Introduction

The aviation industry and culture are two fields which are closely interlinked in our modern society. Bill Gates summarized the relationship of the two areas with the following words "The Wright brothers created the single greatest cultural force since the invention of writing. The airplane became the first World Wide Web, bringing people, languages, ideas, and values together" (Humphreys, 2023, p. 1). This description is directly reflected in the mission statement of Lufthansa Group, being one of the leading global airline groups. The goal is "Connecting people, cultures, and economies in a sustainable way" (Lufthansa Group, 2022, p. 18). This objective underscores the pivotal role that airlines assume in facilitating global cultural interconnectivity by enabling the seamless linkage of diverse cultural communities across the globe. However, cultures are not just connected by the aviation industry, they in reverse also have an impact on the airlines themselves and their business model. Since aviation is a truly global industry, flight tickets can be purchased from practically everywhere in the world, especially by using online booking platforms like airline websites or online travel agencies. This also means that a plethora of different cultures purchase flight tickets every day and by that directly influence airlines and their ticket sales, respectively their revenues.

The main objective of this research is to investigate if the cultural background of airline passengers effects their flight ticket purchasing behavior and if theoretical cultural tendencies can be confirmed within that practical context. Since cultural factors are often considered as rather intangible, this study aims to approve or decline qualitative assumptions by applying quantitative research methods. The GLOBE (Global Leadership and Organizational Behavior Effectiveness) study will serve as main theoretical cultural framework, specifying nine different cultural dimensions (Wolf, 2006). In this study, the focus will largely be on the dimension of uncertainty avoidance (UA) which emphasizes the behavioral elements "orderliness, consistency, structure, formalized procedures, and laws" of a specific culture, according to the GLOBE study (House et al., 2004, p. 603). To narrow down the behavioral aspect of UA to the context of flight bookings, the term of structure-seeking behavior (SSB) is introduced to describe this notion in an adequate manner.

As UA varies heavily across different cultural backgrounds, the assumption is that SSB in reverse has a significant impact on flight booking behavior in an international airline context. This statement leads to the following research question: Is there a correlation between SSB and flight booking behavior? To answer the question if a correlation between the different variables exists, real-life sales- and booking data of European Airlines (EA) will be compared and analyzed in an ex post facto research design. Depending on the results of this empirical investigation, it may be possible to derive concrete conclusions that can be directly attributed to the cultural dimension of uncertainty avoidance. In a practical context, this could support airlines in better understanding their customers by increasingly observing cultural tendencies when implementing marketing and pricing strategies.

Literature Review

Culture is a comprehensive term that has been defined in many ways in the literature. However, there are multiple recurring elements which are often considered components of culture. Generally, culture is behavior of a distinct group or society that differ from other ones which lead to a diverging perception of values or beliefs and increased variability (Crotts & Litvin, 2003). This means that within a culture, there usually is a greater homogeneity and thus more between-group differences than within-group differences (Reisinger & Crotts, 2010). Furthermore, culture is a phenomenon that is not stagnant but constantly evolving due to the influence of different factors like the media, social exchanges, or the usage of non-familiar products (Polat, 2019). Besides values and beliefs, the culture of an individual might also be observed in knowledge, morals, or norms. The expression of those elements often reflects what is usually desired within that culture or what is generally accepted as standard behavior (Ahn & McKercher, 2015).

To underline perceived cultural differences, different models have been created with the goal to generalize notions of a culture to enable comparability. Despite many approaches, it is widely agreed that differences across the multiple cultures are significant enough to assume diverging tendencies of behavior and beliefs (Reisinger & Crotts, 2010). The largest and most commonly used models regarding cultural dimensions are based on the studies of Hofstede and GLOBE. The theory on cultural dimension by Hofstede has been used in many studies across various fields. While it is a central hypothesis of Hofstede that cultural tendencies influence behavior and beliefs, the study has been criticized as it is claimed that culture has been oversimplified by using six dimensions only. It furthermore has been noted that the study of Hofstede is mainly based on monocultural views, largely dominated by western general cultural values (Ahn & McKercher, 2015).

In parallel, the GLOBE study attempted to correct the weaknesses of Hofstede's study by including a broader research scope comprising more than 170 scholars and a surveyed population of 17'000 managers across 62 countries within 951 organizations (Alipour, 2019). GLOBE, used as acronym for Global Leadership and Organizational Behavior Effectiveness, especially examined the cultural practices ("how certain things are done") and values ("how certain things should be done") based on Robert Redfield's perception of culture which manifests itself in acting (Wolf, 2006). Therefore, GLOBE included societal practices (as situation is) as well as societal values (as situation should be) in their survey, adding an extra informative layer (Alipour, 2019).

Furthermore, three additional dimensions in comparison to Hofstede have been identified leading to a total of nine cultural dimensions comprised in the research of GLOBE, indicated in Figure 1.1:

GLOBE's nine cultural dimensions

Figure 1.1: Own visualization displaying the different cultural dimensions identified by the GLOBE project.

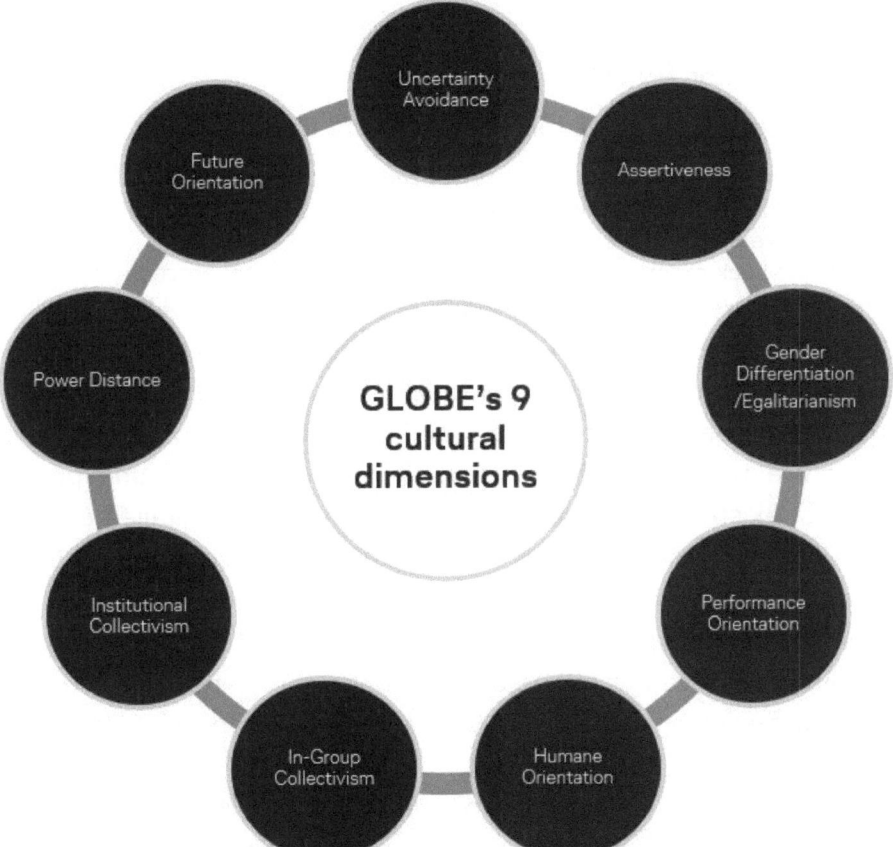

(From Culture, Leadership, and Organizations: The GLOBE Study of 62 Societies, by House et al., 2004, SAGE Publications.)

Ultimately, Voss et al. (2014) acknowledged the study conducted by the GLOBE project as "a significant advance, as it constituted an effort benefiting from complete foresight about what cultural features to measure, as opposed to relying on the equivalent of data mining, which was admittedly the case with the original Hofstede model" (Voss et al., 2014, p. 66).

Based on the outlined advantages compared to study of Hofstede, the theoretical framework and information presented in the GLOBE research will be applied in this thesis to distinguish between different cultural tendencies.

Uncertainty Avoidance

UA has been defined as follows within the GLOBE study:

> "The extent to which a society, organization, or group relies (and should rely) on social norms, rules, and procedures to alleviate unpredictability of future events. The greater the desire to avoid uncertainty, the more people seek orderliness, consistency, structure, formal procedures, and laws to cover situations in their daily lives." (House et al., 2004, p. 11)

While the exact definition of UA slightly varies across the studies of GLOBE and Hofstede, four core elements have been identified by the GLOBE project: Orderliness and consistency, a high degree of structure within people's lives and minimization of unexpected events, existence and focus on laws and rules and detailed expression of requirements of how to act in a social environment (House et al., 2004). When examining the definition of UA, particularly the element of seeking a significant degree of structure is assumed to be directly related to airline booking behavior. Hence the notion of structure-seeking behavior (SSB), acting as a subset of UA, is especially relevant in the context of this research. According to Alipour (2019), the primary aim of cultures with a high degree of UA is to reduce uncertainty while increasing predictability at the same time. Compared to other cultural dimensions, Ahn and McKercher (2015) state that UA is most relevant when attempting to predict and study cross-cultural behavior. Based on those insights, UA and SSB are the main dimensions to be investigated in this research.

UA in tourism and travel

Overall, Crotts & Litivn (2003) have detected that the cultural dimensions UA and masculinity/femininity are most suitable when researching travel behavior (Crotts & Litvin, 2003). This finding is represented in the fact that many studies, aiming to study travel and tourism behavior, are utilizing UA as most decisive cultural dimension. There are nevertheless exceptions, like the study of Broekhuizen et al. (2017) in which they found out that UA also has a direct impact in the field of business management when it comes to innovation or trademarking activities. It was detected that there is a correlation between a high degree of UA and rather cautious entrepreneurial behavior like increased trademark protection and overall, less product innovation (Broekhuizen et al., 2017). However, the focus of UA related research has been mainly on the field of travel, due to the complexity and greater number of assumed risks.

This can be further sub-divided in different travel stages: before-travel and during-travel (Manrai & Manrai, 2011). They summarized multiple elements within the before-travel stage, having the objective to reduce risk perceived by the traveler: usage of travel agents in the booking process, and detailed planning of travel activities in advance or pre-payment of travel components.

The hypothesis that travelers originating from high uncertainty avoidance cultures show a more cautious travel behavior in the before-travel stage has been confirmed in individual studies (Crotts & Litvin, 2003; Money & Crotts, 2003). They detected that risk- and UA-reducing measures like pre-booking multiple elements or pre-payment to a greater extent have been taken by travelers from high uncertainty avoidance cultures in comparison to tourists originating from low uncertainty avoidance cultures (Manrai & Manrai, 2011). In parallel, it was found that also in the during-travel stage, travelers from high UA cultures displayed a more cautious behavior compared to travelers originating from low UA cultures. This has been visible by a generally shorter duration of stay, less visited destinations, and preferably travel in a larger group by cultures with a high degree of UA. Those findings coincide with the study of Crotts & Litivin (2003), highlighting that uncertainty avoiders in general visited fewer destinations, had shorter stays, and travelled with larger parties.

One field of application of those results is marketing if it comes to the question on how to address travelers from certain cultures and what elements might be of high value to them (Reisinger & Crotts, 2010). This has also been confirmed by Manrai & Manrai (2011), pointing out that differences in cross-cultural consumer behavior represent a significant focus of research studies within the area of marketing. Closely related to the field of marketing is also the topic of pricing and the question of how much customers are willing to pay. The findings of this thesis potentially provide further insights of the impact of cross-cultural behavior on marketing and pricing approaches.

The airline industry

The passenger airline industry is a truly global field and is characterized by three central terms: complexity, dynamic and growth (Roucolle et al., 2020). The starting point of the industry was identified in the period between 1950 and 1970 – the dawn of the jet age (Oxley & Jain, 2015). As Figure 1.2 points out, the amount of global air passengers has remarkably increased over 70 years, despite many external shocks that have impacted the industry. This growth in passenger numbers can be attributed to several factors. Rapid technological enhancements led to decreased cost for air travel – resulting in a more affordable mode of transportation for the customers (Oxley & Jain, 2015; Cohen, 2009). Furthermore, the growing share of people joining the middle class (especially in developing countries) has led to an ever-growing amount in air travelers. This continuous economic development also plays a significant role in airline passenger forecasts for the upcoming decades (Oxley & Jain, 2015).

Development of global air passengers within the period of 1950-2014

Figure 1.2: Increasing trend of global air passengers, despite external shocks affecting the industry.

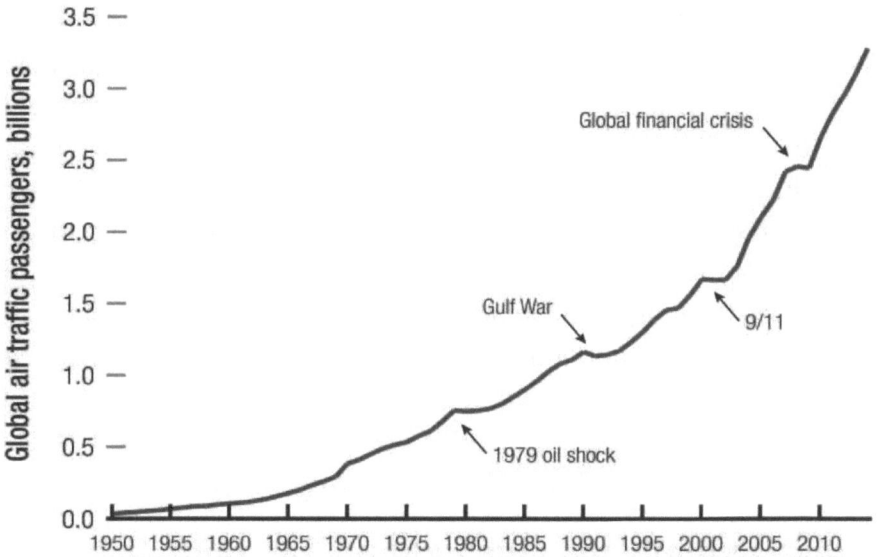

(From Global Air Passenger Markets: Riding Out Periods of Turbulence, by Oxley & Jain, 2015, The Travel & Tourism Competitiveness Report 2015.)

This increasing trend of passenger air transportation resulted in a peak in 2019, recording the busiest day in history as 225,000 flights operated on Wednesday, July 24, 2019 (Slotnick, 2019). With the trend of more seats per flight, leading to an average of 142 seats per flight in 2017, almost 32 million seats are offered in only a single day (Wyman, 2017). Assuming a high seat load factor, the number of transported passengers in a day is comparable to the population of Australia or three times the population of Portugal (Worldometer, 2023). The growth development is widely believed to be further accelerated in the next decades. According to Grous (2019), 4.3 billion passengers have been transported in 2018 while the number is expected to increase to 16 billion by 2050.

However, the industry growth has not always been linear. Figure 1.2 highlights external shocks like 9/11 or the Global financial crisis, leading to a temporary stagnation of air travelers. The resilience of the industry is underlined by an overall increasing trend, despite those individual crises. This has been put to the test again in 2020 when the airline industry faced an unprecedented external shock with the Covid-19 pandemic. Revenues and passenger numbers reduced to less than 50% of the volumes in 2019 – comparable to values around the year 2000 (Nicolau et al., 2022). While crises in the past often had the characteristic of only leading to a passenger stagnation without impacting the fundamental intention and behavior of air travelers, this changed with the latest event of the pandemic. Besides the significant drop in passenger numbers, the customer behavior and intention has been strongly affected and led to an even more competitive post-pandemic airline environment in which revenue management (RM) practices are a key tool for airlines to remain competitive (Nicolau et al., 2022).

Airline revenue management and marketing strategies

The importance of airline RM approaches has been underlined by Chiou & Liu (2016), stating that RM strategies became an integral part of commercial airlines' success as unit revenues have been under pressure throughout the last decades.

While business travelers have been characterized with a higher WTP and a preference for flexibility and corresponding product components, this differs to the other three customer segments which can be summarized as predominantly leisure-driven: individual tourists, visiting friends and relatives (VFR) and tour operator passengers. While the individual tourists and VFR passengers are considered as more price-sensitive than business travelers, they on average account for highest shares of passenger volumes. Tour operator passengers in comparison are the most price-sensitive customer segment (Cramer & Thams, 2021). Knowing the different WTPs of the customer groups is an essential component of the airline industry, not only in the context of RM and pricing strategies but also towards marketing management and regarding product developments (Breidert et al., 2006). This was confirmed by Lufthansa, highlighting the importance of a proper customer segmentation if it comes to offering the right services and products (Avram, 2019).

To effectively establish different segments, individual customers need to be clustered based on relevant aspects like buying habits, purchasing power, geographical location or buying attitudes. This helps to address customers in a targeted way if it comes to marketing campaigns and tailored communication about products and services, highlighting the distinctive benefits (Avram, 2019). With contemporary technological advancements, the segmentation approaches become more data-driven, leading to a greater marketing effectiveness by exploiting competitive advantages. This results in more sales and increased customer loyalty. As the focus in the passenger airline industry is on customer-centricity, tailor-made marketing plays a crucial role. This entails knowledge about flight purchasing behavior and the understanding about when, how and which product customers purchased to draw conclusions towards future actions (Avram, 2019). A close collaboration between pricing and marketing activities is essential to realize the commercial optimum. According to Raza et al. (2019), understanding culture and underlying consumption patterns can lead to additional competitive advantages if it comes to global advertising and the promotion of campaigns.

Aside from the indication of a specific customer segment, Zhang et al. (2021) discovered that the ToB can reflect the travel psychology of airline customers (Zhang et al., 2021). This has become apparent during the Covid-19 pandemic in which there was strong tendency visible of passengers booking their air tickets exceptionally close to departure. This has been predominantly triggered by a strong uncertainty regarding travel in direct correlation with imposed travel restrictions (Zhang et al., 2021). According to Wittmer & Hinnen (2016), the manifold cultural background of travelers is an aspect that impacts customer segmentation as well (Wittmer & Hinnen, 2016). The paper will further investigate if a correlation between cultural background and flight booking behavior can be discovered.

Hypotheses

Some studies concluded that travelers originating from high uncertainty avoidance cultures show a different travel behavior than travelers from low uncertainty avoidance cultures (Money & Crotts, 2003; Crotts & Litvin, 2003). It will be examined if the tendency of more cautious behavior by high UA travelers correlates with their respective flight booking behavior – resulting in an earlier ToB compared to passengers originating from low UA cultures. Within this research, the cultural dimension UA and its subset SSB represent the independent variable and it will be analyzed if a correlation with the dependent variable can be determined. The dependent variable in the context of this study is the flight booking behavior, reflected by the ToB, indicating the point of time a passenger booked an individual flight ticket.

Derived from findings in similar studies, the following hypotheses have been formulated with the objective to research if a correlation between the independent and dependent variable can be detected.

- **H0 (Null Hypothesis):** Cultures with a high score of uncertainty avoidance are not more likely to book their flight at a

different point of time than cultures with a significantly lower score of uncertainty avoidance.
- **H1 (Alternative Hypothesis):** Cultures with a high score of uncertainty avoidance are more likely to book their flight at an earlier point prior to departure than cultures with a significantly lower score of uncertainty avoidance.

Methodology

To address the research question regarding the potential correlation between SSB and flight booking behavior, it is imperative to employ an appropriate research design. This study adopts a quantitative approach to examine whether a relationship exists between the independent and dependent variable. Consequently, a correlational research design has been selected. This framework has the objective to examine the strength and direction of two or more variables while the data has not been manipulated by the researcher (Bhandari, 2023). The chosen research design is well-suited for drawing generalizations from intricate real-world scenarios, as it allows for the assessment of the strength of the correlation and the significance of the impact of the individual variable. This is especially relevant in a complex setting where an impact of other external variables cannot be excluded. Furthermore, this research is considered as an ex post facto study as the investigation commences after a fact has occurred without a manipulation from the researcher (Silva, 2023). This quasi-experimental study design explores the effects of cultural tendencies (SSB) on the flight booking behavior (ToB) in this research scenario.

Operationalization of variables

As outlined above, the independent variable represents cultural behavior in the context of this research. The concrete behavior is SSB, acting as a subset of UA in this study. To operationalize this variable, scores of the GLOBE study (House et al., 2004) were selected as foundation. Those scores represent UA societal practices on country-level which have been determined in the GLOBE research and act as main proxies (House et al., 2004). To create sub-groups with a significantly different behavior according to the findings of GLOBE, the mean (4.17) and the standard deviation (0.60) of all 62 country scores were calculated. An exhaustive overview of all 62 scores pertaining to UA societal practices can be found in Appendix A. Consequently, the formation of two distinct groups was undertaken to represent cultures exhibiting either a pronounced inclination or a minimal inclination towards UA.

Switzerland (5.37) and Germany (5.22) were at least one standard deviation above the mean while Columbia (3.57), South Korea (3.55), Greece (3.39) and Hungary (3.12) were one standard deviation below. Based on those significant differences, a different SSB between the countries with high and low UA scores was assumed. Furthermore, those countries were selected as direct flights between high uncertainty- and low uncertainty avoidant countries were carried out.

The dependent variable in this study is the flight booking behavior, operationalized as the time of booking (ToB). This variable captures the specific timing at which passengers made their individual flight reservation, offering insights into the number of days in advance the bookings were made prior to the scheduled departure of the flight. The data examined in this study pertains to actual sales transactions of a multinational airline group, referred to as European Airlines (EA). The data provides information on the ToB between selected country pairs, such as indicating how many passengers booked their ticket 90 days before departure (DbD) on their flight from Germany to Columbia. Based on the highlighted significant differences on SSB, two groups were formed containing booking information departing from a high UA country to a low UA country and vice versa. Table 1.1 illustrates these distinct groups, along with the corresponding departing and arriving countries:

Table 1.1: Different groups (based on the significantly different SSB) indicating the analyzed country scopes and absolute number of total recorded bookings (195'704) in the utilized data set

Group A		
Departure Country	Arrival Country	Recorded bookings
Germany	Columbia	2'209
Germany	South Korea	6'711
Switzerland	Hungary	29'181
Switzerland	Greece	120'490
Group B		
Departure Country	Arrival Country	Recorded bookings
Columbia	Germany	1'422
South Korea	Germany	7'299
Hungary	Switzerland	9'174
Greece	Switzerland	19'218

(Own visualization by author)

The dataset originating from an internal database utilized in this study comprises bookings recorded during the period from May 1, 2022, to March 31, 2023. This timeframe was selected due to the diminishing external impact of COVID-19 on airline customer booking patterns, which became less significant starting from May 2022. To ensure the exclusion of the Easter holiday period in 2023, the investigation of booking data concludes in March 2023. The departure country in the data is based on the point of commencement (PoC) of the entire journey, meaning that in the scenario of departure country Germany and arrival country South Korea, the travel commences in Germany and ends in South Korea. In the context of this study, exclusively round-trip bookings are used. The study will assume that bookings made in a particular country are done by those with a cultural background of that country, as opposed to expatriates. Crotts and Litvin (2003) have substantiated this finding, as they observed that the country of residence exhibits greater resilience in cultural dimension research when compared to the country of birth or nationality (Crotts & Litvin, 2003). To streamline the analysis, the dataset exclusively encompasses bookings made for economy class on direct flight connections.

To derive proxies from the recorded bookings between the chosen country pairs, the author created five clusters to categorize the time horizon into distinct booking clusters. These time intervals were determined based on the author's professional judgment. It is assumed that all five purchasing period alternatives are simultaneously accessible to passengers with perfect information. Figure 1.3 presents an overview of the clusters and the resulting proxies:

Figure 1.3: Five different clusters illustrating the different advanced booking horizons and derived proxies, based on different days before departure (DbD) intervals

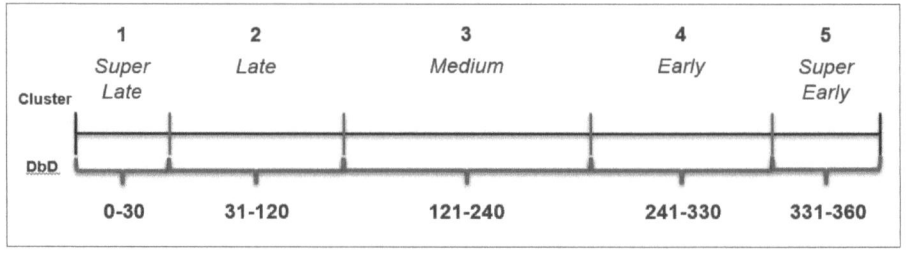

(Own visualization by author)

The formulated clusters are also used to compare the data that is based on behavior of Group A and Group B.

To assess the ideal test type, the data was examined by observing the descriptive statistics of the data set illustrated in Table 1.2 on the next page:

Table 1.2: Descriptive statistics of the data in the scope of both groups, indicating the central tendency of the data set, its variability and an indication if the data is normally distributed

	n	Mean	SD	Median	Trimmed	MAD	Min	Max	Range	Skew
Group A	158'591	75.7	68.7	52.0	65.7	53.4	0.0	362.0	362.0	1.2
Group B	37'113	44.7	47.5	30.0	35.6	28.2	0.0	362.0	362.0	2.4

(Own visualization by author)

Overall, it is visible that the total number of recorded bookings per group ("n") is not equal, but more bookings have been recorded in Group A. However, the minimum, maximum and the range of values is identical among both groups. Regarding the central tendency of the data set, it is observed that Group A exhibits higher values for the mean, median, trimmed value, and median absolute deviation (MAD). This finding can be confirmed by an examination of the standard deviation (SD), providing an indication about the variability, where the SD is higher for Group A.

In addition to the descriptive statistics, the data was tested if a normal distribution can be identified to select a suitable statistical test. The histogram presented in Figure 1.4 provides a visual indication about the distribution of the data:

Figure 1.4: Histogram that highlights the distribution of the data set in regard to how many days before departure a booked has been made (x-axis) and the overall frequency of bookings made in that point of time (y-axis)

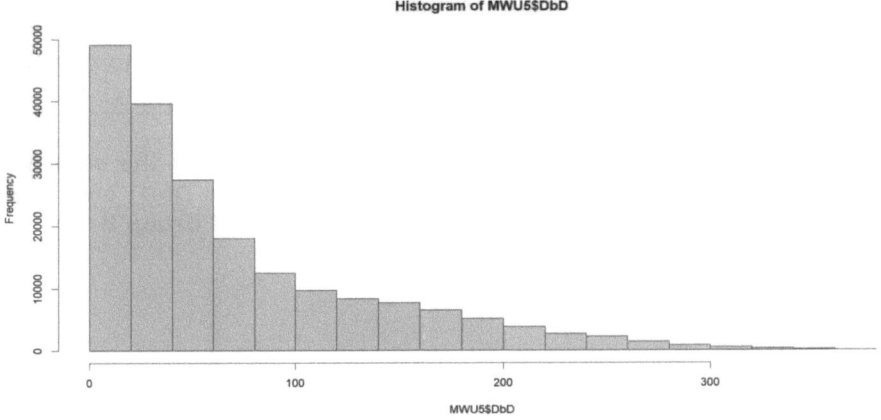

(Own visualization by author using RStudio)

The Kolmogorov-Smirnov normality test was selected to test if a normal distribution of the data can be identified, utilizing the mean and SD of the data set. The calculation was carried out in RStudio and the result of the Kolmogorov-Smirnov test indicates that the data is not normally distributed, D = 0.15301, p = < 2.2e-16.

Based on the findings, it can be inferred that a non-parametric testing method is appropriate for analyzing the data, as it the data distribution is not normal.

Consequently, the Mann Whitney U Test (also known as Wilcoxon Rank Sum Test) has been selected as suitable statistical test approach. The test compares two groups with the objective to assess if the groups are likely to derive from the same given population (McClenaghan, 2023). Transferred to this research, the Mann Whitney U (MWU) test studies if the two populations (Group A and Group B) are equal or not. This correlates with the formulated hypotheses: while the null hypothesis assumes the groups are equal, the alternative hypothesis imputes a difference between the populations represented in a varying flight booking behavior. With the objective to confirm or refute the hypotheses, the p-value was calculated and subsequently the effect size to give an additional indication on the significance of the outcome.

Results

The boxplot presented in Figure 1.5 shows the distribution of the data on the scale of DbD in Group A compared to Group B:

Figure 1.5: Boxplot that provides a visual indication on the distribution of the booking data (translated into DbD) on the y-axis for the individual Group A ("0") and Group B ("1")

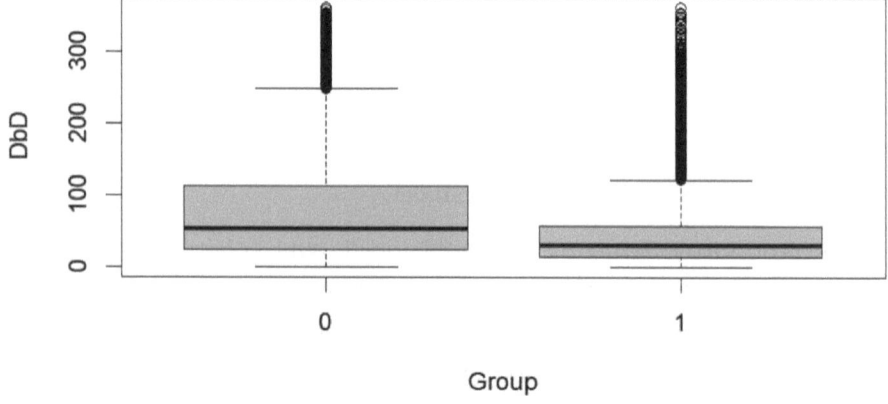

(Own visualization by author)

Considering this visual depiction of the recorded bookings across both groups, the interquartile range (IQR) of the samples differs noticeably. While the IQR for Group A ("0") appears comparably wide, it is rather narrow for Group B ("1"). This perception was further emphasized through an analysis of the documented allocation of bookings, grouped according to the predefined booking clusters. Figure 1.5 offers a comprehensive illustration of the distribution among the five designated clusters. While the cluster "Late" appears as booking interval with the highest share of recorded bookings for Group A, the cluster "Super Late" comprises the highest amount of bookings for Group B. Differences across both samples are visible in the "Medium" cluster as well. As the histogram indicated earlier, an overall skewness of the dataset towards a booking horizon closer to departure can be identified.

Resulting from the Wilcoxon Rank Sum Test carried out in RStudio, flight booking behavior originating from high uncertainty avoidant countries (Mdn = 52) significantly differed from the flight booking behavior shown by passengers originating from low uncertainty avoidant countries (Mdn = 30), $W = 3763115721$, $z = -83.721$, $p < .001$, $r = -.19$.

Consequently, the initially formulated null hypothesis (H0) is rejected while the alternative hypothesis (H1) is confirmed. This results in the finding that a correlation between SSB and flight booking behavior has been detected. Given the significant correlation between SSB and the booking data, an exploratory data analysis (EDA) was carried out.

While a statistically significant correlation between SSB and the ToB was concluded between Group A and Group B, further analysis has been executed as part of the EDA. Initially, a more comprehensive investigation was conducted into the correlation existing between the individual country pairs of departure and arrival. This examination focused on the allocation towards country origins displaying a significant disparity in SSB. As a result, subsequent analysis of the following country dyads (each belonging to Group A or Group B) were carried out (from – to and vice versa):

- Bookings from Germany to Columbia
- Bookings from Germany to South Korea
- Bookings from Switzerland to Hungary
- Bookings from Switzerland to Greece

The descriptive statistics overview of the defined country pairs indicates differences considering the central tendency and variability of individual samples. Furthermore, the amount of absolute recorded bookings varies across the dyads. While there are 3'631 bookings in the sample of flight bookings between Germany and Columbia, 139'708 recorded booking have been analyzed between the country pair Switzerland and Greece. Pertaining to the central tendency of the data, substantial disparities between the samples have been detected. Figure 1.6 presents a visual depiction of the central tendency of the data. Significant differences towards the mean and median were discovered. While the averages of the dataset values are rather similar on the left boxplot (Germany and South Korea), the values seem to differ substantially on the right boxplot (Switzerland and Greece):

Figure 1.6: Two boxplots that provide an indication on the central tendency of the data samples. While on the left side the bookings between Germany (Group "0") and South Korea (Group "1") have been plotted, the right boxplot presents a visual indication on bookings between Switzerland (Group "0") and Greece (Group "1").

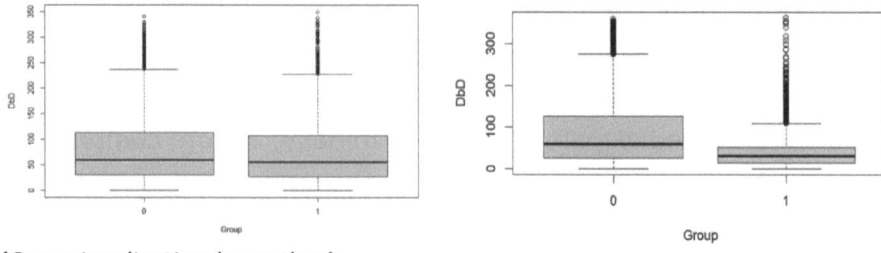

(Own visualization by author)

Additionally, the variability, represented by the SD, is noticeably divergent between those data samples. While the SD is almost the same regarding the data sample of flight bookings between Germany and South Korea, the difference is most significant concerning bookings between Switzerland and Greece. The same observation applied to the IQR.

Analogously to the initial data analysis, the MWU test (Wilcoxon Rank Sum Test) was chosen to examine if the detected correlation between SSB and flight booking behavior is also visible between the individual country pairs. Moreover, the effect size was analyzed. Starting with the smallest dataset of recorded flight bookings between Germany (Mdn=59) and Columbia (Mdn=43), the results indicated that the samples are significantly different from each other $W = 1856656$, $z = -9.28$, $p < .001$, $r = -.15$. A significant divergence was also observed for data samples of flight bookings from Germany (Mdn=59) to South Korea (Mdn=55), with however a very small effect size $W = 25404779$, $z = -3.82$, $p < .001$, $r = -.03$. Also, the samples of flight bookings from Switzerland (Mdn=34) to Hungary (Mdn=22) vv proved to be substantially different $W = 166447108$, $z = -35.24$, $p < .001$, $r = -.18$. Last in sequence, a significant difference between the dataset of flight bookings from Switzerland (Mdn=58) to Greece (Mdn=29) has been identified, with the largest effect size in comparison to the other country pairs $W = 1600557229$, $z = -85.28$, $p < .001$, $r = -.23$.

According to Cohen (1992), small effect sizes are considered to be within an interval of .10 and .30 while medium effect sizes are regarded to be between .30 and .50. Consequently, it has been detected that the populations of flight bookings between high uncertainty avoidant and low uncertainty avoidant countries in all four individual observations have been significantly different from each other, with however on average small effect sizes. Hence, also in this examination a correlation between SSB and flight booking behavior can be concluded.

The second part of the EDA further examines the five identified booking clusters based on the different DbD intervals. The data of the initially determined Group A (departure country with high tendency of UA) and Group B (departure country with low tendency of UA) in a distinctive cluster will be compared to investigate if the datasets of both groups differ within a defined cluster. As presented above, the distribution of recorded bookings is significantly different distributed among the clusters. While the Super Early booking period only comprises 277 bookings in total, the Late cluster records 86'324 bookings representing the largest of the five distinct periods.

Regarding the central tendency, the datasets within the time periods are naturally closer together between both groups as an interval was previously defined. However, clear differences are visible by examining the mean and median within cluster Late and Super Late. While for the Late cluster a difference across the values is recognizable, the data between Group A and B within the Super Late booking period is almost identical. This pattern is also confirmed when examining the variability between both groups within a defined cluster.

In sum, significant differences between the data samples comparing high uncertainty avoidant countries with low uncertainty avoidant countries were discovered in all tests. The corresponding effect sizes mostly were identified as small. In contrast, significant differences between Group A and Group B within a selected booking cluster were just partially identified. However, the effect size of the results has been constantly below or around the threshold of a small effect.

Discussion

The main objective of this research is to answer the posed research question if a correlation between SSB and flight booking behavior exists. Real-life sales- and booking data of EA has been analyzed by applying quantitative methods. Two groups were formed, consisting of departure countries that either have a high tendency of UA behavior (Group A) or respectively a low tendency of UA behavior (Group B).

The findings of the initial data analysis revealed a correlation between SSB and flight booking behavior, hence rejecting the null hypothesis while confirming the alternative hypothesis. Derived from the detected significant result, an EDA was additionally carried out. While the differences of the data samples between all country dyads have been found to be statistically significant, the differences between the groups within defined booking clusters were partially significant.

The findings support the answer to the research question, indicating that a correlation between SSB and observed flight booking behavior exists. Within the given research setting, this confirms the assumption that culture does have an impact on the consumer behavior if it comes to flight bookings. Especially in the realm of aviation, specifically regarding customer behavior in this domain, there has been a noticeable scarcity of research, resulting in a shortage of literature on the subject. Therefore, this thesis may serve as starting point to further study consumer behavior in commercial aviation. Regarding the contribution to the field of research, the discovered results within this thesis can be used in the context of several scenarios.

To begin with, the findings could provide an indication on a different WTP regarding a specific ToB. This can be attributed to the divergent countries that either have a high tendency of uncertainty avoidant behavior or a low tendency of uncertainty avoidant behavior. While per earlier examined literature, cultures that have a high degree of UA allocate value towards safety and certainty, this can be translated in assigning value towards earlier bookings windows. Consequently, a passenger culturally originating from a highly uncertainty avoidant country perhaps is willing to pay more at an earlier ToB to secure a flight booking. While only Germany and Switzerland have been researched in this study, this result may be transferred to other countries with similar scores of UA.

Airlines could take advantage of this behavior by adjusting pricing strategies and capitalizing on a higher WTP. In addition, airlines could include the findings of this research in their marketing and communication strategy. With the confirmation that passengers originating from a specific country of origin tend to make their flight booking at an earlier or later point of time, airlines could benefit by maximizing their return on investment when launching a marketing campaign. If passengers originating from a specific origin book at a particular point of time, marketing strategies that focus around that ToB could contribute to greater commercial success for an airline. In reverse, if higher flight booking activity is observed closer to departure, an early marketing communication might not generate the desired return of investment. Lastly, the discovered correlation between SSB and flight booking behavior can help airlines to predict booking forecasts to answer the question if bookings are still expected or if most potential passengers already booked their flight. This is a very valuable indication if it comes to the question of planning a certain aircraft type on a flight route, especially regarding the number of offered seats.

Besides the importance of the presented results for airlines, the findings also largely support the outcome of other studies. Research of Money & Crotts (2003) and Crotts & Litvin (2003) found that commonly travelers originating from high UA cultures show a more cautious travel behavior. This finding can be confirmed if a more cautious travel behavior is translated into booking a flight at an earlier point of time and respectively securing a seat. Similarly to this finding, also Manrai & Manrai (2011) revealed in their study that a higher degree of UA correlates with a rather risk-reducing behavior in the before-travel stage by increasingly planning travel components in advance. As an earlier ToB can be translated into planning a flight further in advance, the finding can be confirmed by the results of this research. When observing the shares of flight bookings within the defined clusters, it was detected in the EDA that for the country origins with a high degree of UA, the Super Late cluster was not the booking period with the highest number of bookings while it was for country origins with a low degree of UA. According to the study of Piga (2006), a high price volatility is observed in the last four weeks prior to departure (Piga, 2006). As an increased price volatility might be an aspect that is less appreciated by highly UA passengers due to the lack in predictiveness, since the assumption is that passengers mostly book their flight at an earlier point in time. This trend is confirmed in this thesis as the share of Group A bookings (high UA) during the last 30 days prior to departure is significantly smaller than the share of Group B bookings (low UA). To wrap it up, Zhang (2021) discovered that the Covid-19 pandemic resulted in a trend that air tickets have been booked very close to departure (Zhang, 2021). Although some bookings are recorded in the Medium, Early, and Super Early cluster, the overall booking data is still skewed towards a booking period closer to departure. Even though the chosen booking time frame (May 1st, 2022 – March 31st, 2023) is rather assumed to be "post-pandemic", the effect of a short-term booking behavior remains visible.

Limitations and future research opportunities

The findings of this thesis may be treated as starting point within the field of research as limited amount of similar literature exists. A reason for this could be the high complexity of the investigated topic. Not all external elements eventually impacting the discovered results were able to be regarded in this research.

One of the main challenges was to identify cultural proxies out of the existing sales- and booking data. As no passenger nationality is attached to the booking data, the point of commencement (PoC) was selected to be a suitable indication of the cultural tendency opposed to the point of booking (PoB). Nonetheless, it is imperative to acknowledge that while the PoC pertaining to a passenger may designate Germany as their point of origin, this may not align with the cultural predisposition of the customer in every instance. By only including round-trip bookings (and excluding one-way bookings) in the analysis, the confidence is increased that the passenger truly originated from the specific PoC. The PoB has the disadvantage that it can be manipulated by the customer when booking online by using a VPN connection to eventually seek a cheaper air fare or if a flight is booked by the passenger while being abroad. Furthermore, if a flight booking occurs via an online travel agency (OTA) the PoB of the OTAs headquarter is displayed in the data and not the true location of the actual passenger.

Additionally, further limitations of this study may exist based on the selected data set as only recorded bookings of EA were included comprising sales in the economy compartment and exclusively on direct flight connections within a defined time frame. Despite the considerable scale of the data sample, it is essential to note that it was exclusively derived from a single airline group, thereby exhibiting limitations in its capacity to offer a comprehensive portrayal of the entire market.

Ultimately, only one time period has been chosen in order to analyze the data sample. Even though this time frame may be considered less impacted by the Covid-19 pandemic, the ToB windows of flight bookings may keep on continuously changing. Consequently, the validity of the study could be increased if the data is not sourced from only one airline group and if multiple time periods were analyzed to eventually eliminate post Covid-19 booking behavior effects.

Finally, it is imperative to underscore one of the most prominent constraints inherent to this research, which pertains to the omission of price effects during the data analysis process. This is of particular significance, given that the price of a flight frequently exerts a notable influence on consumer purchasing decisions. Despite the large significance of this element, it is increasingly complex to include the information of a specific price at a certain point of time as prices have proven to be highly dynamic. According to Abdella et al. (2021), the price of a flight ticket might change up to seven times per day (Abdella et al., 2021). This fluctuating tendency resulted in the exclusion of this external factor, which however is also assumed to have an influence on the passenger flight booking behavior.

There are additional opportunities for future investigations in the field of cultural dimension research. To enhance the validity and robustness of the obtained findings during the investigation of the correlation between SSB and flight booking behavior, it is recommended to further control for extraneous variables. One of the most significant factors influencing the customer flight booking behavior is the addressed airfare pricing effect. The objective of a future research setting may be an analysis of the booking behavior while the price is identical over a certain period of time before the flight event to preclude an influence of this factor. Furthermore, the validity of the discovered results may be additionally increased by considering the varying purchasing power in different countries. Currency purchasing power, too, may exert an influence on flight booking behavior. An isolation of those effects will lead to a clearer result to which degree the cultural dimension of UA impacts passenger flight booking behavior.

Moreover, it is advisable to undertake additional research within the context of air travel, with a deliberate focus on different subject areas. In addition to the flight booking behavior, the online flight search activity is another topic that could be researched connected to SSB. A research question which might be answered within that setting could be the point of time when specific cultures start to plan their travel and search for flight options accordingly. Furthermore, this study holds the potential to provide valuable insights into the realm of marketing strategies, particularly regarding the optimal timing for communicating and promoting flight offers.

Possible future research could be connected to advanced seat reservations within flight events. As specific seat reservations often require an additional purchase, a research question could go into the direction on how much cultures with a high degree of in-group collectivism are willing to pay to ensure that the family or group sits close to another in a flight. This research possesses the potential to examine whether the WTP for seat reservations exhibits statistically significant variations among cultures characterized by differing levels of in-group collectivism. The outcomes of this investigation could be instrumental for airlines in reassessing pricing strategies, potentially leading to enhanced revenue generation. As outlined in the beginning of this chapter, there is currently a lack of scholarly literature within the domain of cultural dimension research pertaining to the aviation industry. Therefore, numerous opportunities regarding additional research in this field exist.

Conclusion

The core research question was formed in the introduction with the aim to investigate if a correlation between SSB and flight booking behavior exists. To answer the question if a relationship between the defined variables persists, sales- and booking data of EA was analyzed using an ex post facto research design. By responding to the posed research question and identify resulting findings, tangible outcomes concerning cultural dimension research in the context of the passenger aviation industry can be concluded with practical implications for airlines. The initial data analysis was carried out by applying statistical methods revealing a significant correlation between SSB and flight booking behavior, hence confirming the derived alternative hypothesis.

The discovered findings can be of considerable benefit for airlines by providing an indication on a different WTP concerning a specific time of booking. This result can be advantageous regarding optimizing pricing strategies and thereby increasing revenue by capitalizing on a higher WTP. In addition, the findings are of notable value regarding marketing strategies. Upon identifying that passengers departing from a particular country of origin exhibit distinct tendencies in the timing of their flight booking, airlines could enhance their return on investment through strategic optimization of their marketing campaigns. This research can be considered as a starting point in this field with a plethora of additional research opportunities still existing.

Just like the Wright brothers embarked on their journey of creating an aerial device, scientific studies in the field of cultural dimension research within the context of the aviation industry are just beginning. Given the growing trend towards an increased global interconnectivity, this domain of research deserves additional focus and dedication.

References

Abdella, J. A., Zaki, N., Shuaib, K., & Khan, F. S. (2021). Airline ticket price and demand prediction: A survey. Journal of King Saud University – Computer and Information Sciences, 33(4), 375–391. https://doi.org/10.1016/j.jksuci.2019.02.001

Ahn, M. J., & McKercher, B. (2015). The Effect of Cultural Distance on Tourism: A Study of International Visitors to Hong Kong. Asia Pacific Journal of Tourism Research, 20(1), 94–113. https://doi.org/10.1080/10941665.2013.866586

Alipour, A. (2019). The conceptual difference really matters: Hofstede vs GLOBE's uncertainty avoidance and the risk-taking behavior of firms. Cross Cultural & Strategic Management, Vol. 26 No. 4, pp. 467-489. https://doi.org/10.1108/CCSM-04-2019-0084

Avram, B. (2019). Airlines Customer Segmentation in the Hyper-Competition Era. Expert Journal of Marketing, 7(2), 137–143. https://EconPapers.repec.org/RePEc:exp:mkting:v:7:y:2019:i:2:p:137-143

Bhandari, P. (2023). Correlational Research | When & How to Use. Scribbr. Retrieved July 19, 2023, from https://www.scribbr.com/methodology/correlational-research/

Breidert, C., Hahsler, M. and Reutterer, T. (2006). A Review of Methods for Measuring Willingness to Pay. Innovative Marketing, 2, 8-32.

Broekhuizen, T., Giarratana, M. S., & Torres, A. (2017). Uncertainty avoidance and the exploration-exploitation trade-off. European Journal of Marketing, 51(11-12), 2080-2100. DOI: 10.1108/EJM-05-2016-0264, 10.1108/EJM-05-2016-0264

Buafai, T. & Khunon, S. (2016). Relationship between Hofstede's Cultural Dimensions and Tourism Product Satisfaction. International Journal of Economics and Management Engineering, Volume 10, Issue 8, 2984-2988.

Chiou, Y. & Liu, C. (2016). Advance purchase behaviors of air tickets. Journal of Air Transport Management 57. 62-69.

Cohen, J. (1992). A power primer. Psychological Bulletin, 112(1), 155–159. https://doi.org/10.1037/0033-2909.112.1.155

Cohen, J. (2009). Sustainable mobility transitions and the challenge of countervailing trends: the case of personal aeromobility. Technology Analysis & Strategic Management, 21(2), 249–265. https://doi.org/10.1080/09537320802625330

Cramer, C. & Thams, A. (2021). Airline revenue management current practices and Future Directions. Springer Gabler.

Crotts, J. & Litvin, S. W. (2003). Cross-cultural Research: Are Researchers Better Served by Knowing Respondents' Country of Birth, Residence, or Citizenship?. Journal of Travel Research, 42, 186-190.

Debus, M. E., Probst, T. M., König, C. J., & Kleinmann, M. (2012). Catch me if I fall! Enacted uncertainty avoidance and the social safety net as country-level moderators in the job insecurity–job attitudes link. Journal of Applied Psychology, 97(3), 690–698. https://doi.org/10.1037/a0027832

Federal Aviation Administration (2023). Economic Values for Investment and Regulatory Decisions. Retrieved September 10, 2023, from https://www.faa.gov/sites/faa.gov/files/regulations_policies/policy_guidance/benefit_cost/econ-value-section-4-op-costs.pdf

Glen, Stephanie (2023). Mann Whitney U Test: Definition, How to Run in SPSS. From StatisticsHowTo.com: Elementary Statistics for the rest of us! https://www.statisticshowto.com/mann-whitney-u-test/

Grous, A. (2019). Chapter 3: Capitalising on changing passenger behaviour in a connected world. London School of Economics and Political Science. https://www.lse.ac.uk/business/consulting/assets/documents/sky-high-economics-chapter-three.pdf

Groves, W., & Gini, M. (2013). An agent for optimizing airline ticket purchasing. In Adaptive Agents and Multi-Agents Systems (pp. 1341–1342). https://doi.org/10.5555/2484920.2485214

House, R. J., Hanges, P. J., Javidan, M., Dorfman, P. W., & Gupta, V. (2004). Culture, Leadership, and Organizations: The GLOBE Study of 62 Societies. SAGE Publications.

Humphreys, B. (2023). The Regulation of Air Transport: From Protection to Liberalisation, and Back Again. Taylor & Francis.

Jacobs, J., Klein, S., Holland, C. P., & Benning, M. (2017). Online Search Behavior in the Air Travel Market: Reconsidering the Consideration Set and Customer Journey Concepts. Annual Hawaii International Conference on System Sciences. https://doi.org/10.24251/hicss.2017.476

Kerkemezos, Y., & Karreman, B. (2020). On the Benefits of Being Alone: Scheduling Changes, Intensity of Competition and Dynamic Airline Pricing. RePEc: Research Papers in Economics. https://ideas.repec.org/p/tin/wpaper/20200042.html

Lufthansa Group (2022). Annual Report 2022. https://investor-relations.lufthansagroup.com/fileadmin/downloads/en/financial-reports/annual-reports/LH-AR-2022-e.pdf#page=19

Manrai, L. A., & Manrai, A. K. (2011). Hofstede's Cultural Dimensions and Tourist Behaviors: A Review and Conceptual Framework. Social Science Research Network. https://papers.ssrn.com/sol3/Delivery.cfm/SSRN_ID1962711_code1350781.pdf?abstractid=1962711&mirid=5&type=2

McClenaghan, E. (2023). Mann-Whitney U Test: Assumptions and example. Informatics From Technology Networks. https://www.technologynetworks.com/informatics/articles/mann-whitney-u-test-assumptions-and-example-363425

Money, R., & Crotts, J. (2003). The Effects of Uncertainty Avoidance on Information Search, Planning, and

Purchases of International Travel Vacations. Tourism Management, 24(2), 191-202.

Nicolau, J. L., Shin, H., Kim, B., & O'Connell, J. R. (2022). The Impact of Loss Aversion and Diminishing Sensitivity on Airline Revenue: Price Sensitivity in Cabin Classes. Journal of Travel Research, 62(3), 685–698. https://doi.org/10.1177/00472875221093014

Oxley, D., & Jain, C. (2015). Global Air Passenger Markets: Riding Out Periods of Turbulence. The Travel & Tourism Competitiveness Report 2015. https://www.iata.org/en/iata-repository/publications/economic-reports/global-air-passenger-markets-riding-out-periods-of-turbulence/

Piga, C. A., & Bachis, E. (2006). Pricing strategies by European traditional and low cost airlines. Or, when is it the best time to book on line? RePEc: Research Papers in Economics. https://econpapers.repec.org/paper/lbolbowps/2006_5f14.htm

Polat, H. (2019). Impact of Cultural Dimensions to Individualism, and Collectivism Dimension. Journal of Business and Economics, Volume 10, No. 12, pp. 1154-1164. DOI: 10.15341/jbe(2155-7950)/12.10.2019/003

Raza, S. A., Bakar, H. A., & Mohamad, B. (2019). The effects of advertising appeals on consumers' behavioural intention towards global brands. Journal of Islamic Marketing, 11(2), 440–460. https://doi.org/10.1108/jima-11-2017-0134

Reisinger, Y., & Crotts, J. C. (2010). Applying Hofstede's National Culture Measures in Tourism Research: Illuminating Issues of Divergence and Convergence. Journal of Travel Research, 49(2), 153–164. https://doi.org/10.1177/0047287509336473

Roucolle, C., Seregina, T., & Urdanoz, M. (2020). Measuring the development of airline networks: Comprehensive indicators. Transportation Research Part A-policy and Practice, 133, 303–324. https://doi.org/10.1016/j.tra.2019.12.010

Silva, C. (2023). Ex Post Facto Study. Sage Research Methods. https://methods.sagepub.com/reference/encyc-of-research-design/n145.xml#:~:text=Ex%20post%20facto%20study%20or,without%20interference%20from%20the%20researcher

Slotnick, D. (2019, July 25). Wednesday was one of the busiest recorded days in aviation history — and it's going to keep getting busier. Business Insider. https://www.businessinsider.com/most-flights-ever-225000-flightradar24-flight-tracking-2019-7?r=US&IR=T

Voss, R., Lucas, A. & Ward, S. (2014). Supranational Culture II: Comparison of Schwartz Value Survey Data against Hofstede, GLOBE, and Minkov as Predictors of Civilizational Affiliation. International Journal of the Academic Business World, Volume 8, Issue 2, 63-76.

Wittmer, A. & Hinnen, G. (2016). Air Transport Management: An International Perspective. Routledge.

Wolf, Thom (2006). Culture, Leadership, and Organizations: The GLOBE Study of 62 Societies [review] / House, R. J., Hanges, P.J., & Javidan, M., Eds., Journal of Applied Christian Leadership: Vol. 1: No. 1, 55-71.

Worldometer (2023) – Countries in the world by population (2023). https://www.worldometers.info/world-population/population-by-country/

Wyman, O. (2017). More seats, flying further. https://www.oliverwyman.com/our-expertise/insights/2017/jun/paris-air-show/more-seats-flying-further.html#:~:text=During%20June%202007%2C%20the%20average,20%25%20increase%20over%202007).

Zhang, L., Yang, H., Wang, K., Lei, B., & Zhang, X. (2021). The impact of COVID-19 on airline passenger travel behavior: An exploratory analysis on the Chinese aviation market. Journal of Air Transport Management, 95, 102084. https://doi.org/10.1016/j.jairtraman.2021.102084

List of Figures

Figure 1.1: Own visualization 169
Figure 1.2: Increasing trend of global air passengers 173
Figure 1.3: Five different clusters 180
Figure 1.4: Histogram 181
Figure 1.5: Boxplot 182
Figure 1.6: Two boxplots 184

List of Tables

Table 1.1: Different groups 179
Table 1.2: Descriptive statistics of the data 180

A disabler of cultural diversity: Unconscious bias in recruiting – How ethnicity affects the selection of applicants

Christiane Englert

Abstract

The current megatrends of digitalization, globalization and migration are shaping the worldwide labor market like never before and increase the need for skilled workers in international competition.

The German Federal Employer Agency presented entrepreneurs with a comprehensive analysis of the skilled workforce situation in Germany with the central question of how a foreseeable shortage of skilled workers could be averted in order to maintain growth and prosperity (2016). Although Germany passed 2006 the Allgemeines Gleichbehandlungsgesetz (AGG) (General Equal Treatment Act), a law providing protection against discrimination based on ethnicity, religion and worldview, age, gender, sexual identity and disabilities through employers, landlords and merchants, current studies reveal that applicants – in particular with a black phenotype as well as a Muslim religion – experience significant discrimination in recruiting.

In search of a possible disabler of cultural diversity, unconscious bias in recruiting is considered more closely. Thus, the following research question was raised:

How does ethnicity affect the selection of applicants due to unconscious bias?

The research question was examined through conducting seven semi-structured interviews with experts acting in the HR (Human Resources) sector for a minimum of three years. One of the most significant findings of the interviews was that although people are already working in an ethnically diverse working environment, this aspect of diversity is rarely included or promoted through specific diversity considerations and measures.

The results of this thesis may influence the future development of Diversity & Inclusion, and may help to develop and establish further recommendations that raise awareness and highlight the consequences of unconscious biases.

Introduction

The current COVID-19 pandemic has demonstrated that we all operate in a global environment. Globalization, digitalization and migration combine different cultures with economic growth and present societies with new challenges. Different cultures and ethnicities accompany us both privately and professionally.

Although many legal bases have been created in order to prevent discrimination in the most varied of forms and many companies operate with diversity management, current studies reveal that people of different ethnic origin still experience discrimination – in particular in recruiting. To investigate this matter, a disabler of cultural diversity is examined more closely: Unconscious bias. The following research question is the subject of this paper:

How does unconscious bias affect the selection of applicants of different ethnicities?

The paper seeks to move away from blame to appeal to the our responsibility. It closes with an outlook of possible future implications, which could affect the further critical discussion and developments regarding ethnic diversity.

The importance of ethnic diversity at the workplace in Germany

The term diversity comes from the Latin word "diversitas". The English term diversity is also often used in German and implies different social and ethnic backgrounds, gender, sexual orientation, different religious affiliations or worldviews, age, physical or psychological abilities or other characteristics. The main idea is that diversity deals not only with respecting and appreciating these differences but with generating integrative benefits for all (Lies,2018).

Demographic developments and structural change, change of job profiles and needed skills cause considerable difficulties in recruiting necessary skilled workers. The labor market is a very dynamic system in which employment is constantly started and terminated so that there are always vacancies and jobseekers. These vacancies become only problematic if their occupation takes too long or the search has to be cancelled because no suitable candidate is found.

In 2016, the BA composed a comprehensive analysis of the skilled workforce situation in Germany concerning a foreseeable shortage of skilled workers. One important factor was the integration of immigrants and refugees into the German labor market. 40 % of the refugees registered in Germany are in education and working age (between 25 – 45 years old).

With reference to the Fachkräfteengpassanalyse 2019 (Skilled labor shortage analysis 2019) of the BA (2020), most of the bottleneck occupations could be found in the health sector and field of care for children and elderly. The information technology (IT) sector and other technical professions, such as handicrafts and mechatronics as well as food production and sales, are also affected. Condensed, 185 professions are currently affected by a skilled labor shortage, which indicates that Germany will have to rely on attracting skilled staff from abroad to be able to adequately close gaps here.

Compared to other European countries, Germany is a main destination for migrants worldwide. Migration could be defined as a permanent change in the center of life i.e. place of residence. The reasons for migration are very versatile and could be realized within a country or across national borders (Bundesamt für Migration und

Flüchtlinge (BAMF), 2020, p. 42). In the period between 2000 and 2019, approximately 16.3 million emigrations were registered whereas 21.8 million immigrations were counted (BAMF, 2020, p. 45).

However, migration to Germany is changing: While humanitarian immigration has been steadily decreasing in the last four years, more and more immigrants are consciously choosing Germany with the aim to study or to work here (BAMF, 2020, p. 7). The number of foreign students who have enrolled at German universities has increased by 0.9 %. With a share of 10.4 %, China is the most represented country of origin here, followed by India (8.8 %), Italy (4.4 %) and Syria (4.3 %) (BAMF, 2020, p. 9).

In summary, 26 % of Germany's population had a migration background, i.e. 21.2 million people in German private households who either themselves or at least one of their parents had not German citizenship since birth. On average, migrants have lived for approximately 21 years in Germany, 35.5 % less than ten years (BAMF, 2020, p. 11).

All the above data indicate that the professional integration of people with other ethnic backgrounds is a central socio-political task to actively counteract a shortage of skilled workers.

Different terms for discrimination

The term discrimination (from Latin "discriminare", i.e. separate, distinguish) indicates the distinction between different people and/or groups mostly due to outer appearance and behavior. Therefore, it is an issue that affects all social classes and society as a whole. Every form of discrimination is associated with one or several characteristics and describes a process of building social categories (Beigang, Fetz, Kalkum & Otto, 2017, p. 12 ff.).

A distinction can be made between the following forms:

- Direct discrimination

- indirect discrimination
- intersectional discrimination
- structural discrimination and
- statistic discrimination

Direct discriminations are all explicit distinctions between individuals or groups, which enable equal opportunities and rights. Indirect discrimination includes superficial neutrality in regulations, criteria or procedures, which implies imbalances and inequalities between individuals or groups in practice. Thus, these measures are abused to disadvantage individuals or groups. (Beigang et al., 2017).

The intersectional approach includes several, multidimensional forms of discrimination to combine and create different modes of discrimination, e.g. gender & race, sexuality & religion or disability & physical appearance (Beigang et al., 2017). Structural discrimination refers to systematical generalizations and socio-economic disadvantages, e.g. in form of non-access to necessary resources, what could be found in e.g. educational or health care facilities (ibid, p. 14-15). Finally, statistical discrimination relates to an economic understanding and perspective, based on incomplete information. Representative and socio-statistical characteristics of a group (e.g. ethnic origin) are used for the theoretical assessment of the productivity of group members without adding information and facts.

Summarized, discrimination could be defined as a disadvantage or degradation of individuals and groups according to certain values, also due to unconscious attitudes or emotional associations. To justify social, cultural, economic, political and legal disadvantages, discrimination consists in the use of categorical distinctions, with which social groups are identified. Imbalance of power and inequalities are historically grown -but changeable with the help of new social learning processes (Scherr, 2016).

Nonetheless, it should be seen critically that research and data collection on discrimination are often based on reports of subjective perceptions of discrimination. Whether it is a question of discrimination in the scientific, socio-psychological or legal sense, can often not be determined with certainty. Thus, it is important to consider the common intersection as displayed in Figure 1.1:

Figure 1.1: Schematic representation of the connection between perceived discrimination and discrimination in the social science or legal sense

Abbildung 2: Schematische Darstellung des Zusammenhangs zwischen wahrgenommener Diskriminierung und Diskriminierung im sozialwissenschaftlichen oder juristischen Sinne

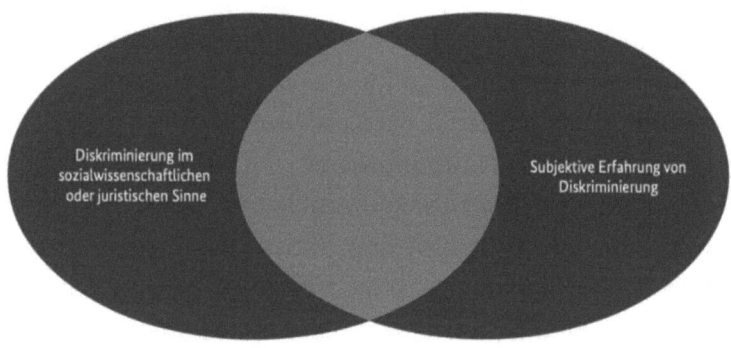

(Beigang et al., 2017, p. 20)

Furthermore, Zick, Küpper & Hövermann (2011) identify a certain normalization effect to discrimination. This habituation effect can be determined when people are confronted with discrimination on a regular basis so that they do not perceive it anymore as discrimination.

Stereotype, prejudice, privilege and bias

Incomplete knowledge and rather unemotional assumptions about a social group or an individual belonging to this group could be defined as a stereotype. A stereotype is expressed through neutral expectations e.g. how members of this group behave and act (Domsch, Ladwig & Weber, 2019).

Franken (2015) defines stereotypes as joint thinking patterns in form of a simplified representation of people and events. These neutral categorizations between people and/or groups cannot be scientifically confirmed, are based on individual subjective perceptions and mostly already shaped in early childhood. If stereotypes are charged emotionally, they become a prejudice. Prejudices could be described as the personal negative – less often positive – valuation about a particular social group. Prejudices are mostly generalizing and judgmental without sufficient background information (Domsch et al., 2019). Thus, the difference between stereotypes and prejudices is an emotionally manned or valued judgement. Prejudices serve to express mostly negative feelings and actions towards others. (Franken, 2015).

Racism

A scientifically value-neutral definition of racism is difficult. In research on racism, two important characteristics have emerged that are explicit in terms of content: first, the division of people into categories and hierarchies and second, an underlying ideology. Racial discrimination refers to discrimination based on the color of skin and ethnic origin (Weiß, 2013).

DiAngelo coined the term 'white fragility' and describes racism as a complex socially interconnected system in which discrimination takes place as actions based on prejudices – largely unconscious – including ignorance, exclusions and violence. She argues that not the differences are problematic, but misinformation and assumptions. People of color (POC) could also act racist, but without any institutional power in society (2018).

According to Arndt (2015), racism is based on forced misinformation and passive ignorance. She explains racism as a special form of xenophobia, which is also represented in racist language to legitimize oppression. The problem lurks in seemingly harmless terms in our everyday language, combined with an active process of denial. Often, this leads to an unconscious entering of racism as a dominance culture in our everyday life.

In sum, racism is a specific form of ideological discrimination in which individuals and groups are hierarchized based on their color of skin or ethnic origin.

Legal requirements in Germany

In order to prevent discrimination, Germany has created various legal instruments on various levels that are interpreted and applied together with human rights requirements of the United Nations (UN) and the Council of Europe. The basis for all protection against discrimination builds art. 1 of the Universal Declaration of Human Rights (UN, 1948), that all people are equal in dignity and rights. This equal treatment is further specified in Art. 3 of the Grundgesetz (GG) (German Basic Law), originally from 1949, that no one may be disadvantaged because of their gender, origin, race, language, ethnicity, as well as their beliefs or disability.

With the creation of the AGG, the Antidiskriminierungsstelle des Bundes (ADS) (Federal Anti-Discrimination Agency) was established to carry out advisory and public relation work as well as research in protection against discrimination.

Currently, the ADS reports more than a quarter of all requests for advice concern issues of racism and ethnic origin. Affected people report targeted ID checks by the police because of their color of skin or their appearance. In addition, problems when applying for an apartment with foreign-sounding names are often reported. The legal basis forms an important part of the anti-discrimination policy in Germany. However, legal proceedings on this are still rare due to the lack of a sort of anti-discrimination culture, where discriminations are often trivialized and ignored (Althoff, 2016).

Diversity Management

The origin of diversity management can be found in the protests of the civil rights, gay and women's movements in the USA. Various groups fought against discrimination in society and achieved many signal-pointing and especially legal changes, e.g. the Civil Rights Act in 1964. In the 90s, the idea of diversity came to Europe. The first German article appeared with the topic: "Managing Diversity: Postmodern Cultural Work in Companies" (Kiechl, 1993). In addition to the previously rather politically motivated considerations and actions, there were also economic ones. The increasing participation of women in employment, demographic changes and increasing migration confront society with new challenges. Diversity management must be seen as an opportunity and part of modern leadership.

Summarized, diversity management could be described as a combination of recognition as well as utilization of diversity in organizations with the aim to identify the success-relevant aspects and use diverse competencies, characteristics, attitudes and cultural backgrounds as a strategy to gain benefits for the entire organization (Lies, 2018).

Gardenswartz & Rowe (1995) created the Four Layers of Diversity model to illustrate the multidimensionality of diversity. The model is a holistic and inclusive approach. Despite the different arrangement of each factor, no priorities exist. Each layer leads both privately and professionally to different characteristics, skills and attitudes, which means that they are interconnected and influence each other. The two inner layers are immutable dimensions, while the outer dimensions are changeable, as portrayed in Figure 1.2 on the next page:

Figure 1.2: The Four Layers Of Diversity

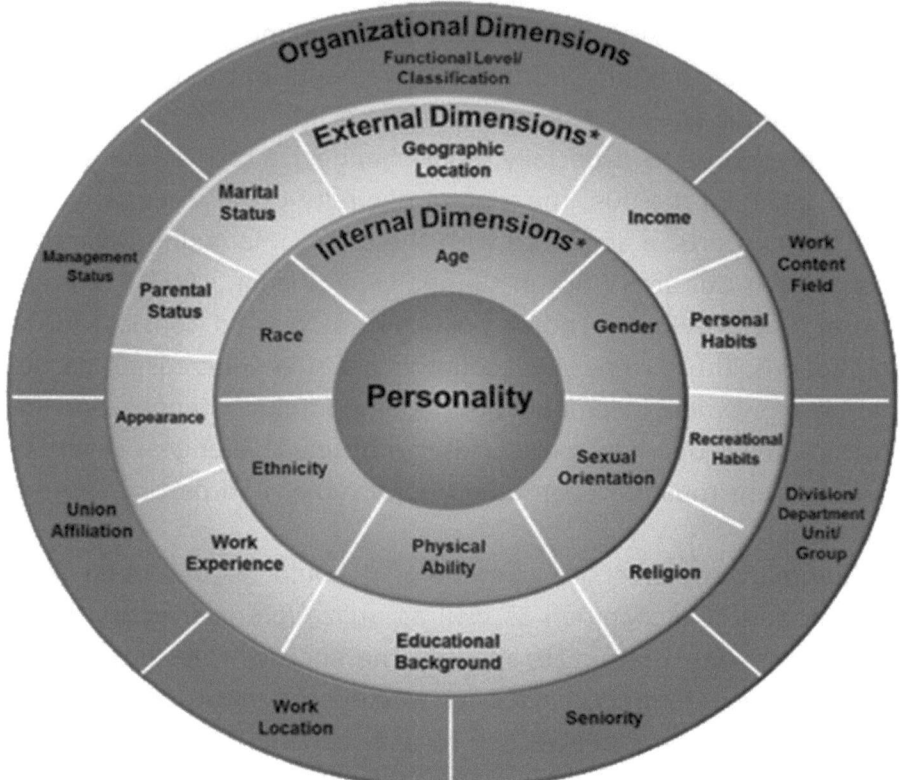

(©Gardenswartz & Rowe, located at https://www.gardenswartzrowe.com/why-g-r)

The outermost dimensions act as differentiations within a company or organization. Therefore, these dimensions are the most quickly influenced dimensions.

Schein (1988) has dedicated himself to the concept of organizational culture to demonstrate that all shared values, traditions and beliefs within an organization affect the behavior and actions of the people working within.

Diversity as a competitive advantage

Cox & Blake (1991) examined important competitive factors regarding diversity in the workplace. They identified the following six arguments:

1. cost argument
2. resource-acquisition argument
3. marketing argument
4. creativity argument
5. problem-solving argument
6. system flexibility argument

Krell, Ortlieb & Sieben (2018, p. 41 ff.) explain and discuss these points further. The cost argument is very versatile and often not tied to an exact number in currency. Employees who feel integrated and valued are more motivated, more willing to perform and have a lower absence rate due to health problems. Various teams can achieve better results through different perspectives, which also cause positive effects on potential customers. Correspondingly, the costs incurred to establish and implement a diverse workforce are well invested compared to the costs caused by e.g. legal actions against discrimination or poor reputation on the market.

The resource-acquisition argument relates to the current changes in the global labor market in terms of demographic changes and migration. Companies face the challenge of training young talents of diverse ethnic origins in order to secure skilled workers in the long-term (Krell et al., 2018).

The marketing argument refers to the signaling effect if diversity in the workforce is a core value of the company. Today, the best talents can choose the employer who corresponds to their values. Moreover, values are constantly changing. People tend to realize themselves individually and want to work more versatile and flexible to better combine work with private life. Employees want to be respected and integrated as who they are, without negating their origin.

The creativity argument is closely linked to the problem-solving argument. Not the used technology is in the foreground when promoting creativity, but the exchange of perspectives and experience in diverse teams. With different perspectives, a more versatile approach to problems is possible as well as a faster solution process. Critically seen should be that the pure fact diversity is not the decisive factor, but rather the cooperation and management of diverse teams (Krell et al., 2018).

The last argument referring to system flexibility assumes that the potential of a company is determined by the ability to change. Just as social conditions change, a company needs to be able to reflect these changes within the workforce. Therefore, diversity concepts can make a significant contribution to the overall organizational flexibility and resilience.

Already in 2015, Hunt, Layton & Prince studied 366 companies displaying a positive correlation between a diverse workforce and financial results. Diversity serves as a positive competitive factor so that companies with a diverse workforce are able to achieve better economic outcomes in comparison to their respective national industry medians.

Diversity Charter – Charta der Vielfalt

Already over 3,500 German companies and organizations with approximately 13.4 million employees are currently joining the Diversity Charter. Established in 2006 under the patronage of the Federal Chancellor, Angela Merkel, this voluntary commitment is used as a declaration to promote recognition, perception and representation of diversity in all its facets in German business. The Diversity Charter is not a regulatory authority, but a non-profit organization and initiative for awareness of the topic of diversity. In the center of this initiative is the signing of a certificate that literally encompasses the self-commitment to create a diverse working atmosphere filled with "acceptance, mutual trust and free of prejudices."

All companies, organizations, and foundations based in Germany can sign it as well as institutions from the public sector. All participants receive support in implementing the Diversity Charter values, can take part in diversity activities and are allowed to use the Diversity Charter Logo (Charta der Vielfalt, 2017).

Unconscious Bias

Unconscious biases are neuroscientific processes to filter essential features from perception while comparing them with what we have already have experienced and learned. In his international bestseller *Thinking, Fast and Slow*, he distinguishes in two modes of human thinking: System 1 and System 2. System 1 is the unconscious part. It is described as a sort of autopilot with fast, automatic and intuitive thinking, which requires no effort. System 2 on the other hand is the conscious part and stands out through slow, conscious, reasoning, and mindful thinking, which takes intentional effort to engage (Kahneman, 2011). Consequently, unconscious bias affects all levels, professionally as privately, institutionally as socially.

Tsipursky (2020) describes cognitive bias as so-called blind spots, which represent a predictable pattern of mental errors in implicit snap decision making by reacting instantly. According to Fuller, Murphy & Chow (2020), having unconscious bias is a natural part of the human condition. Implicit biases are time- and energy-saving shortcuts in the human brain, which often even contradict our stated values. Vedantam (2010) coined the term 'the Hidden Brain' and describes unconscious biases as hidden forces, which influence multiple factors in our daily life without our awareness or consent.

Fields of research on unconscious biases are very versatile. Therefore, classifying and organizing biases have been attempted in various ways. Benson (2016) orders 175 biases according to causes and strategies. He structures the biases into four central challenges that our brain is confronted with.

1. Biases that arise from:
2. too much information

3. not enough meaning
4. the need to act instantly
5. the limits of memory

Benson approaches the topic by focusing on the problem each bias tries to solve in order to understand why they occur.

Problem 1: Information overload

According to Agarwal (2020), several studies reveal that every second our brain is capable of processing about 11 million bits of information, of which our conscious mind can only handle approximately 50 of those. That fact illustrates that most of our processing takes place in the subconscious mind. Incoming information is unconsciously filtered and only a fraction is saved.

Problem 2: Lack of meaning

The second problem occurs when reduced information is received. When this reduced information is updated, the gaps will be filled with information we already think we know without verifying objective facts and logic.

Problem 3: Need to act fast

Tsipursky (2020) argues that to save time we are encouraged to trust our first intuition and to follow our instincts. With this sensed self-authenticity, we estimate to be confident in our ability to make an important impact. Solutions that appear simple and complete are preferred. The status quo should be retained to avoid mistakes.

Problem 4: Limited memory capacity

In order to be capable of storing all our memories, we reduce our experiences to some key elements. In order to form generalities, we discard many details. We save memories depending on the type of experience and ignore the context.

The "James-Lange theory of emotion" suggests that very emotional experiences are longer remembered. Emotions are often assumed to be judgements about a situation that cause feelings and physiological changes. Summarized, negative emotions increase more memory performance than positive emotions do (Wirtz, 2019).

Types of unconscious bias in recruiting

Recruiting is always about the evaluation of one person from another person (or a group of few) and is therefore prominent for unconscious judgement distortions. Many procedural errors are based on unconscious bias. Incorrect evaluation can hardly be uncovered in retrospect because it cannot be determined how many rejected people would have proven to be excellent candidates (Kanning, 2015). Many of the effects mentioned below also occur in combined forms, in varied expression and strength as well as at different stages in the recruiting process.

The overconfidence effect

Early at the beginning and central of the personnel selection process is the requirement analysis to define the specific skills and characteristics required from the candidate. However, the requirement analysis is often composed of only one representative (or a group of few) to determine the requirements intuitively, using very abstract competence terms such as "communication skills" or "customer orientation" without further job-specific definition. Real workplace content is often abstracted to the necessary or more likely desired competencies of the candidate (Kanning, 2015, p. 82 ff.). In addition, employees who actually perform the job are often not – or only barely – included in these considerations.

This is also confirmed through a study by Stephan & Westhoff (2002), wherein total 70 % of the 100 surveyed medium-sized (1,000 – 5,000 employees) companies reported having no differentiated definition of the expectation of the candidate. 12 % stated that they have no requirement analysis at all. 57 % reported that they work with a list of skills and characteristics, which they assume to be relevant for the advertised position.

Another study of Kanning, Pöttger & Gelléri (2007) with a survey of 97 larger companies (> 5,000 employees) verifies that even the design of an assessment center for the selection of executives is often only realized through questioning by one superior (54 %) or through other team members (58 %). Only 23 % combined these two perspectives. Thus, it can be concluded that the decision-makers trust preferably their intuition and subjective experience, which contributes to a restricted view. Therefore, candidates are often at the mercy of the decision-makers' gut instinct.

Tsipursky (2020) defines this mental pattern as a sort of illusory superiority. Decisions are made with the unconscious belief and false self-perception that individual instinct is unfailing. This is called the overconfidence effect.

Confirmation bias

To make a proper preselection of the candidates, the examination of the application documents is an important part of the recruiting process. Kreuscher (2000) examined that more than 70 % of the decision-makers have no binding criteria for how the various components of the application are to be assessed. Only 1.2 % had set formal selection criteria in advance. On average, less than 10 minutes are taken per portfolio – the negative selection is often made in less than 30 seconds.

According to a study by Machwirth, Schuler & Moser (1996), 90 % of the focus of the screening is based on formal criteria such as cleanliness of the documents, typing, grammatical errors or a professional sounding email address – even if these formal facts ultimately have nothing to do with the execution of the job.

By selecting and interpreting specific information that confirms the recruiter's expectation, false coherences are made and the own hypothesis is considered as confirmed. This cognitive bias is described as confirmation bias. The decision-makers unconsciously look for evidence to support their thinking and opinion. The overall picture of the candidate is disregarded and information that corresponds to workplace-related criteria is no longer perceived (Nalty, 2016).

Beauty bias & halo effect

How beauty and an outwardly well-groomed appearance are perceived, varies greatly from person to person and from one (corporate) culture to another. Concerning the external appearance of the candidate, the application photo still plays a prominent role. The English idiom "don't judge a book by its cover" – a metaphorical phrase which means one should not prejudge the worth or value of something only by its outward appearance – describes what happens unconsciously here.

The beauty bias argues that candidates, who are outwardly perceived as attractive, are unconsciously associated with positive character traits and competencies like intelligence, self-confidence or good leadership skills (Domsch et al. 2019, p. 7). Watkins and Johnston (2000) found that this is in particular practiced if other qualifications are not immediately noticed.

Hamermesh (2011) investigated the economic effects of beauty since 1990. He examined that beauty not only has a positive effect on the job employment but also on salary negotiations, promotions and loans with better terms. In several studies, he found out that beauty is attributed to youth and power. The effects of external improvements like clothing, cosmetics and even plastic surgery play a minor role because there is a global substantial agreement about facial symmetry, which is considered as good-looking. Although there are no differences in averages, there are differences about gender and ethnic origin: Women and white people are clearly preferred. Younger people are even rated on average more attractive than older people. Therefore, according to Hamermesh, the preference for beauty is purely discriminatory and affects society as a whole.

This cognitive mechanism also applies to what is known as the 'halo' effect. This implicit bias is demonstrated if one specific aspect outshines other characteristics so that the overall perception is reduced. The decision-maker only concentrates on one particular characteristic and does not consider other important aspects. This effect could be related to external characteristics as well as to individual behavioral characteristics or performance. (Domsch et al. 2019, p. 7).

These unconscious biases become even more evident when candidates visibly differ from other candidates e.g. due to their ethnic origin. In an experiment by Weichselbaumer (2016), with professionally identical 1,474 applications, clear discrimination against female Turkish migrants – especially when they own Turkish names and even more when they are wearing a headscarf – was detected in the application system. With positive feedback of 18.8 % of the overall callback rate, the applicant with the German name, Sandra Bauer, was the most successful. The applicant with the Turkish name, Meryem Öztürk, without a headscarf was contacted by 13.5 % of the companies whereas the applicant named Meryem Öztürk, wearing a headscarf, received only 4.2 % of the callback feedback. This is represented in Figure 1.3 on the following page:

Figure 1.3: Names and photographs, indicators for identity

Sandra Bauer   Meryem Öztürk   Meryem Öztürk

(Weichselbaumer, 2016, p. 22, Fig.1, located at http://ftp.iza.org/dp10217.pdf)

Methodology

Expert interviews have emerged as a special variant of the social science research routine. There are various methods in scientific work with regard to the implementation and, in particular, the evaluation of expert interviews (Bogner, Littig & Menz, 2009). To guarantee complete voluntariness, sampling in form of secondary selection through self-activation was used (Reinders, 2005).

Inquiries were made via the virtual social business network LinkedIn. Since the debate of unconscious bias should be handled sensitively, the researcher consciously decided for this method, as this ensures a high level of motivation and openness for the subject matter.

Expert status was granted through the researcher on the following basis:

- currently working in Germany
- currently working in the HR sector
- working with a minimum of three years' experience in the field of HR

In clear contrast to a layperson, experts own a form of substantive content representativeness i.e. that they perform as a representative of a group, which contains all important characteristics and aspects to be examined (Meuser & Nagel, 2009, p. 37-38).

The implementation and evaluation of expert interviews in this paper is a qualitative content analysis with the medium of expert interviews according to Meuser & Nagel (2009). The focus is on the overall content of the interviews with the aim to show the typical, similarities as well as differences of the current handling of unconscious ethnicity bias in recruiting from different perspectives.

With the help of semi-structured interviews of the experts, the researcher examined if and how the topic of unconscious bias is addressed in recruiting and if there is a strategy to prepare the recruiters regarding applications from different ethnic origins.

In total, seven people were interviewed to deliver a manageable number of cases. All interviews were realized through the researcher in person via video/telephone call and all interviews were used for the evaluation. Each interview lasted 20 minutes. All interview partners were assured of anonymity without naming personal data or companies. Therefore, no recording on a data carrier was made. The survey was written in English. However, all interviews took place in German.

An interpretative evaluation strategy by Meuser & Nagel (2009, p. 56-57) was used.

Stage 1: Conducting the interviews an paraphrasing the answers.

Stage 2: Categorization of the paraphrased answers and thematically compression.

Stage 3: Comparing and bundling of the content of the different categories.

Stage 4: Conceptualization and theoretical generalization.

Research questions

In designing the questions, the researcher's intent was to work out questions which are open, neutral, simple as well as clear. All interviews consisted of the following seven question blocks:

1. What is your current position in your company and since when have you been in this position?
2. Did you have another position before? How long have you have been at this company? How long have you been working in the Recruiting/HR?
3. Every organization has a different terminology regarding diversity, fairness, equality, etc. What is your company policy regarding equal opportunity in the hiring process? And what do you call this process?
4. Is the topic unconscious bias explicitly addressed in your company?

5. Are there any special seminars offered in your company for recruiters – to prepare for different ethnicities?
6. How many ethnicities are currently represented in your company?
7. Does the company have future plans to ensure a diverse workforce? If so, could you pls. tell me what they are?

The questions were put into these categories:

Category 1: Status Quo

The first and second questions aimed to ensure that the expert status is given as well as for the assessment of the researcher, which position and empirical value the answers may have.

Category 2: Unconscious Bias

Question 4 refers specifically to the issue unconscious bias to figure out, whether the topic already has been presented by name and content.

Category 3: Effects of ethnicity

Question 5 and 6 deal with the topic of different ethnic origins and/or groups to evaluate if there are already different ethnic groups represented in the company, as well as if (and in particular how) recruiters are being prepared.

Category 4: Future measures

The last question aims to determine which measures in the field of diversity are planned.

Research results & discussion

The results of the expert interviews clearly reveal major differences associated with the interpretation as well as design of diversity implementations at the workplace in Germany.

Status Quo

All experts the researcher talked to have extensive years of experience in the field of HR and recruitment in Germany. Two of the interview partners already studied with a focus on personnel management. All of them are in a leadership position and responsible for recruiting decisions – be it as a direct decision-maker or as an advisor with significant influence on personnel selection. Six experts are employed, whereas one expert acts self-employed as a trainer and consultant for recruiting in the tech branch. Six of the seven interview partners work in the private sector, whereas one person works in the public sector.

Six of the seven interview partners were female. This distribution also reflects the results of a study with 30 German companies that about 70 % of the employees in HR are female. Even future young academics in this field are predominantly female with a quota of approximately 80 % (Gorges, 2015).

Surprisingly, the topic of cultural diversity was a very familiar topic for all respondents even if the term, meaning, development and inclusion at the workplace had a completely different expression. This fact demonstrates that there are hardly any standardized designations and specifications in practical implementation in this field. Three experts stated that diversity forms a part and task of the HR department, whereas three experts have implemented this as a separate unit: Diversity Management, Diversity & Inclusion and Diversity & Equal Opportunities.

All experts mentioned the focus on gender-equal job advertisements. However, since January 1, 2019, this has also been a legal obligation in Germany according to the AGG. With the abbreviation "m/w/d" (male/female/diverse) also intersex candidates should be considered. According to a study of the ADS (2018), 97,8 % of German job advertisements do not contain any discriminatory language or formulations. However, 20% of job advertisements still don't address certain groups (e.g. women or people with a migration background) consistently.

This is also reflected in the interviewees' different policies regarding equal opportunities in the recruiting process. Three stated that they do not have any concrete fixed measures or standards.

Equality and fairness are only guaranteed through their corporate values and own judgements. On the other hand, three reported concrete measures from internal consultations and discussions, the use of AI tools to standardized documents and guidelines for the job interviews.

The experience of the trainer and consultant confirmed this picture. In particular, the tech branch in Germany needs to focus on people from abroad because of the shortage of skilled workers in this sector. In addition, there is often only one female application for every 10 applications, which explains a clear preference in this category for female candidates.

Consideration of unconscious bias in recruiting

When asked explicitly if the topic of unconscious bias is addressed in the company, it was engaging that all experts knew the term but three of all reported no reference in their work. Two stated that they see importance of that issue in their work, but that their working environment – regarding the executive board – is not yet open to it. Only one expert stated that personally and professionally no specific importance of unconscious bias is perceived.

One expert reported that unconscious bias is only addressed in an educational way as a reaction to conflicts due to e.g. cultural differences but not as a preventive measure for clarifications right from the beginning. Only once they offered intercultural training with the focus on one specific country's cultural background (here: India).

The consultant reported offering own training courses on this topic, particularly when using bias-free interview techniques. From the expert's point of view, this is seen as a priority. He experiences that many superiors or managers still select candidates due to purely personal preferences, which have nothing or only very little to do with the qualitative competencies of the candidate.

In contrast to all considerations of gender equality, there are no separate considerations regarding ethnic equality. Although the overall topic diversity is present and often represented through trainings, all experts reported the lack of seminars about different ethnicities – in particular in recruiting. Therefore, it remains unclear to what extent the thematic treatment of unconscious bias deals with ethnic diversity.

One expert mentioned that regarding ethnicity it is rather challenging to evaluate appropriate data in comparison to gender or age. Surveys with regard to this background could easily turn out as a form of exclusion instead of inclusion.

Prospect planning

Regarding further plans to ensure a diverse workforce, the answers were very versatile. Four experts reported continuing their work in diversity and equality but without any concrete and/or new measures or specific targets. Only two experts reported concrete aims like e.g. to offer unconscious bias trainings for all employees, create a survey to evaluate more about the needs of the workforce from different ethnical origin, or to achieve a certain quota of women in leadership positions until a particular date.

In this context, one expert reported planning to advertise all jobs in the future as part-time jobs – with the option to work as well full-time – to address more women in general. Two of the experts reported that the issue of work-life-balance, in particular for parents, is also a part of their strategic diversity work. So here, too, it is evident that in addition to the gender-sensitive language in job advertisements, the flexibility in working hours and the representation of a good work-life-balance also have an influence on who feels addressed by a job advertisement. Similar considerations were not mentioned with regard to other ethnicities.

Summarized, it could be concluded that in Germany the issue of gender is currently the most visible part of the diversity work.

Moreover, this mainly about increasing the pure number of women in the workplace – in particular in leading positions.

Although most companies already employ an ethnically diverse workforce, this factor of diversity seems not sufficiently considered. The impression given is that an increase in employees with different ethnic origins is perceived as a sort of automatic development due to increasing international or globalized working. Actions and measures are mainly initiated when problems or conflicts occur instead of proactively.

Therefore, it would be interesting in a possible next research step to focus on the ethnic diverse workforce itself in order to gain insights from the employees to figure out which measures have which impact and what needs to be in focus here.

Implications for Future Research

As can be examined from the expert interviews, future implications could be implemented and prioritized very differently. As Kahneman (2011) argues, having unconscious biases is a human disposition. All human judgements are biased in a way, but to be able to detect and visualize them makes it possible to recognize, understand and finally anticipate.

Worldwide, blind auditions are already used in the field of music to focus only on playing or singing rather than gender, age or ethnicity. The majority of German orchestras have been building this anonymized procedure for decades around their first round of applications. The curtain, wall or screen is considered a guarantee for equal opportunities, which in Germany has proven itself concerning the increasing number of women in orchestras: 41 % in 2019 compared to only 6 % in 1971 (Schmidt, 2020). Anonymized application processes could be suitable in all industries for reducing various forms of discrimination in the application process.

One of the challenges is to use suitable and practicable methods of anonymizing application documents. In the case of paper-based applications, previously defined characteristics could be defaced or deleted. In addition, a separate application form could be made available in which only neutral features are mentioned. Standardized online application forms must be adapted accordingly (Krause et al., 2010).

Besides the question of the appropriate method, the question of the scope of anonymization remains, i.e. which characteristics are affected? With reference to international experience, the following characteristics could be identified as anonymizable characteristics in application forms as well as in the curriculum vitae (CV) (Krause et al., 2010, p. 26):

- surname
- gender
- nationality and place of birth
- disability
- date of birth/age
- marital status and
- photo

In particular, the reference to language skills could allow indirect conclusions about the applicants' nationality or possible migration background. Therefore, an indication of the language skills according to objective scale (e.g. according to the Common European Framework of Reference for Languages) could be recommended (Krause et al., 2010).

Furthermore, certificates from abroad could also be a sign of a possible migration background. Besides, a critical question is how certificates from abroad are compared to German standards and ultimately evaluated. Since certificates are particularly important in applications in Germany, they must be made comparable and anonymized accordingly (Krause et al., 2010).

Nevertheless, anonymous application cannot be used for internal applications and regardless of the chosen method of anonymization, the question arises when is the appropriate time in the application process to remove anonymization.

Unconscious bias comes into play at the latest in the job interview when persons face each other. Therefore, the question remains whether such measures only postpone possible discrimination in the application process instead of preventing it entirely.

The use of algorithms & artificial intelligence in recruiting

According to Torsten Biemann, Professor at the University in Mannheim for Human Resource Management and Leadership (Siemann, 2017), it is important to differentiate between the different terms and to focus on the content and data used.

Algorithms can sort and analyze data and patterns and give further recommendations and instructions. Therefore, algorithms are already used for personnel selection to limit the applicant pool in a first step, e.g. matching algorithms generate a data comparison for job profiles out of the CVs. Depending on the job profile, the algorithm takes key terms such as certain competencies, skills and qualifications into account. This can be cost- and time-efficient.

In addition to subjective experience, algorithms can be used to support intuitive decision-making from a mechanical angle. However, it should be viewed critically, that every IT-based selection is only made according to the advanced programmed parameter by human hands, i.e. that the selection is only made on the basis of the variables previously recognized as important.

Furthermore, algorithms are already used to identify suitable channels (e.g. social media) for addressing potential candidates of a special target group. More and more recruiters are also using the candidates' personal profiles on social media to draw conclusions about their personality, interests and qualifications. Kosinski, Bachrach, Kohli, Stillwell & Graepel (2014) examined possible correlations in abstract metadata, like the profile used in social media. The researchers found only very low correlations with personality traits because social media is often used as a form of self-optimization or impression management.

The situation is different with the allocation of likes, browsing histories, search queries or purchase histories, which could reveal potential attitudes of the user. It should be discussed critically which abstract metadata are suitable for validly predicting personality traits (Kosinski et al. (2013). Therefore, it is important to discuss the bilateralism of the use of algorithms and AI in recruiting because the data used can be clearly subject to unconscious bias.

This problem is also attributed by West, Whittaker & Crawford (2019) to the lack of diversity on the part of AI developers: Female researchers at leading AI conferences worldwide comprise only 18 % – e.g. only 15 % of the employees in Facebook's AI department are women, 10 % at Google. Employees with a black phenotype are also in the minority. Only 2.5 % of the employees at Google are black, Facebook and Microsoft are each at 4 %. More data e.g. on other gender minorities was not published. Furthermore, they discuss the lack of transparency of the used AI systems. Since these systems are often protected by patents, their disclosure contradicts the business model of most manufacturers. Thus, many systems exist without publicizing for what purpose they are used.

In summary, algorithms and AI find their further way into our overall social life and diagnostic decision-making procedures. The human factor is always the decisive factor due to the programming beforehand and in the interpretation of the data afterwards. Furthermore, a system only works well if people accept it and are able to develop it and notice if errors creep in. Thus, long-term standardized solutions must be acquired in this field with regard to transparency, control and evaluation, data protection and business ethics.

Unconscious bias trainings

When we think of unconscious bias training measures, the question arises of how unconscious bias can be measured. In the scientific field of unconscious bias research, the Implicit Association Test (IAT) is often used as a psychometric tool. First introduced by Greenwald, McGhee & Schwartz (1998), this computer-based diagnostic is currently one of the best-known test procedures. In the different phases, various stimuli (words as well as images) are subsequently displayed to the test candidates, who must assign these to different categories. Within the assignment, response time and any incorrect assignment are noted, which are finally used to calculate the IAT effect to measure the strength of implicit association. IATs are mostly designed online for individual participants to raise the awareness of implicit biases.

However, Mierke & Klauer (2003) argue that the IAT effect could also occur without the presence of certain associations, e.g. due to insufficient or necessary context information. With regard to the different dimensions of diversity, different test results can be possible for one and the same person, which limits the retest reliability (Lane, Banaji, Nosek & Greenwald, 2007).

The offers for unconscious bias trainings range from workshops and webinars to keynote speeches and concrete consultations. They differ in duration, agenda and aim (e.g. pure sensitization or behavioral changes) and whether the trainings are instructed as voluntary or mandatory. Nevertheless, there is growing skepticism about the effectiveness of diversity trainings – in particular with regard to the lack of a standard curriculum as well as a standard certificate for the training provider. In addition, the design of the trainings is often not based on scientific data or theories (Forscher, 2020).

Most diversity trainings focus on the behavior and action of the individual or of a group like a team or a department. In contrast, Bohnet (2016), a behavioral economist, argues for a behavioral design of organizations, based on collected data and analysis. Her approach is to concentrate on the organizational processes instead of focusing on the people. She argues that many anti-bias trainings do not change behavior, in particular in the long-term, and have therefore rather no impact. But with changing the environmental conditions and personal experiences in practice, companies could be able to change also the individual's perception.

Conclusion

The researcher's aim in this paper was to discuss different facts of cultural diversity and to examine the impacts of unconscious bias in recruiting regarding ethnic origin. Based on the examined studies combined with own research, it could be determined that still too little importance is attached to this part of diversity. Therefore, it can be assumed, that unconscious biases still influence the selection of applicants from different ethnic origins – often in an unfair way.

As a country of immigration, Germany needs to deal more intensively with the issue of ethnic diversity in order to be able to secure a skilled workforce in the long term as a global competitive advantage. And besides all legal or organizational requirements, this starts with each of us.

Unconscious biases are more than a trendy buzzword and although they are natural, they are no justification for discriminatory behavior. Thus, people in HR who are responsible for the selection and evaluation of others should raise the recognition and awareness of this topic, because they define the possibilities for others.

Diversity is not just about gender. It should be in every company's own interest to fill vacancies with the most capable people – regardless of any preferences or (unconscious) biases to increase overall economic efficiency and social welfare. Diversity becomes increasingly important and is most fundamentally, about power balance. Equality at the workplace as well as in society will continue to gain strength in the following years. Global togetherness creates solidarity, understanding and mutual support and shapes companies to be more resilient in crises.

As Fosslien & West Duffy (2019) put it: *"Diversity is having a seat at the table, inclusion is having a voice, and belonging is having that voice to be heard."*

References

Allgemeines Gleichbehandlungsgesetz (AGG) (2006). Retrieved December 18, 2020, from: https://www.gesetze-im-internet.de/agg/AGG.pdf.

Althoff, N. (2016). Das Diskriminierungsverbot im nationalen deutschen Recht. In: A. Scherr et al. (Eds.). Handbuch Diskriminierung, Springer Reference Sozialwissenschaften. Wiesbaden: Springer Fachmedien.

Amstutz N., Müller C. (2013). Diversity Management. In: T. Steiger, E. Lippmann (Eds.). Handbuch Angewandte Psychologie für Führungskräfte. Berlin, Heidelberg: Springer. https://doi.org/10.1007/978-3-642-34357-5_17.

Antidiskriminierungsstelle des Bundes (ADS) (2018). Diskriminierung in Stellenanzeigen. Studie zur Auswertung von Stellenanzeigen im Hinblick auf Diskriminierung, Ausschlussmechanismen und positive Maßnahmen. Retrieved January 12, 2021, from: https://www.antidiskriminierungsstelle.de/SharedDocs/Downloads/DE/publikationen/Expertisen/diskriminierung_in_stellenanzeigen.pdf?__blob=publicationFile&v=5.

Antidiskriminierungsstelle des Bundes (ADS) (n.d.). Themen und Forschung. Ethnische Herkunft / Rassismus. Retrieved January 23, 2021, from: https://www.antidiskriminierungsstelle.de/DE/ThemenUndForschung/Ethnische_Herkunft/Ethnische_Herkunft_Rassismus_node.html.

Argarwal, P. (2020). SWAY. Unravelling Unconscious Bias. London: Bloomsbury Sigma.

Arndt, S. (2015). Rassismus. Die 101 wichtigsten Fragen. München: C.H. Beck.

Beigang, S., Fetz, K., Kalkum, D., Otto, M. (2017). Diskriminierungserfahrungen in Deutschland. Ergebnisse einer Repräsentativ- und einer Betroffenenbefragung. In: Antidiskriminierungsstelle des Bundes (ADS) (Eds.). Retrieved January 13, 2021, from: https://www.antidiskriminierungsstelle.de/SharedDocs/Downloads/DE/publikationen/Expertisen/expertise_diskriminierungserfahrungen_in_deutschland.pdf?__blob=publicationFile&v=7.

Benson, B. (2016). Cognitive Bias Cheat Sheet. Because thinking is hard. Retrieved January 28, 2021, from: https://betterhumans.coach.me/cognitive-bias-cheat-sheet-55a472476b18#.c14jwweaw.

Bohnet, I. (2016). What Works: Gender Equality by Design. Harvard University Press.

Bogner, A., Littig, B., Menz, W. (Eds.) (2009). Experteninterviews: Theorien, Methoden, Anwendungsfelder (3rd revised ed.). Wiesbaden: VS Verlag für Sozialwissenschaften.

Bryman, A., Bell, E. (2011). Business Research Methods (3rd ed.). Oxford University Press.

Bundesagentur für Arbeit (BA) (2016). Schwerpunktheft. Fachkräfte für Deutschland.

Zwischenbilanz und Fortschreibung. Retrieved December 18, 2020, from: https://www.arbeitsagentur.de/datei/dok_ba013186.pdf.

Bundesagentur für Arbeit (BA) (2020). Statistik/Arbeitsmarktberichterstattung. Berichte: Blickpunkt Arbeitsmarkt. Fachkräfteengpassanalyse 2019. Retrieved December 18, 2020, from: https://statistik.arbeitsagentur.de/DE/Navigation/Statistiken/Themen-im-Fokus/Fachkraeftebedarf/Fachkraeftebedarf-Nav.html.

Bundesamt für Migration und Flüchtlinge (BAMF) (2020). Migrationsbericht der Bundesregierung. Migrationsbericht 2019. In: Bundesministerium des Inneren, für Bau und Heimat (Eds.). Retrieved January 11, 2021, from: https://www.bamf.de/SharedDocs/Anlagen/DE/Forschung/Migrationsberichte/migrationsbericht-2019.pdf?__blob=publicationFile&v=10.

Bundesministerium für Familie, Senioren, Frauen & Jugend (BMFSFJ) (2021). Aktuelle Meldung. Zweites Führungspositionen-Gesetz. Meilenstein für mehr Frauen in Führungspositionen. Retrieved January 16, 2021, from: https://www.bmfsfj.de/bmfsfj/aktuelles/alle-meldungen/meilenstein-fuer-mehr-frauen-in-fuehrungspositionen/164124.

Charta der Vielfalt (2017). FAQ. Vor der Unterzeichnung. Retrieved January 15, 2021, from: https://www.charta-der-vielfalt.de/fileadmin/user_upload/Unterzeichner/FAQ_Unterzeichnungsprozess_092017_01.pdf.

Charta der Vielfalt (n.d.). Für Diversity in der Arbeitswelt. Retrieved January 15, 2021, from: https://www.charta-der-vielfalt.de/.

Cox, T. H., & Blake, S. (1991). Managing cultural diversity: Implications for organizational competitiveness. Academy of Management Perspectives, 5(3), p. 45-56.

DiAngelo, R. (2018). White Fragility: Why It's So Hard For White People To Talk About Racism. Boston: Beacon Press.

Dixon-Fyle, S., Dolan, K., Hunt, V., Prince, S. (2020). McKinsey & Company. Diversity wins. How inclusion matters. Retrieved February 1, 2021, from: https://www.mckinsey.com/~/media/McKinsey/Featured%20Insights/Diversity%20and%20Inclusion/Diversity%20wins%20How%20inclusion%20matters/Diversity-wins-How-inclusion-matters-vF.pdf.

Domsch M.E., Ladwig D.H., Weber F.C. (Eds.) (2019). Vorurteile im Arbeitsleben. Unconscious Bias erkennen, vermeiden und abbauen. Berlin: Springer Gabler.

Dreas S.A. (2019). Diversity Management: Grundbegriffe, historischer Ursprung und Ansätze. In: Diversity Management in Organisationen der Sozialwirtschaft. Basiswissen Sozialwirtschaft und Sozialmanagement. Wiesbaden: Springer VS. https://doi.org/10.1007/978-3-658-20546-1_2.

Dychtwald, K., Erickson, T.J., Morison, R. (2006). Workforce Crises. How to Beat the coming Shortage of Skills and Talent. Boston: Harvard Business School Press.

European Commission (n.d.). The EU Platform of Diversity Charters turns 10!. Here is why Diversity Charters matter today. Retrieved January 26, 2021, from: https://ec.europa.eu/info/policies/justice-and-fundamental-rights/combatting-discrimination/tackling-discrimination/diversity-management/eu-platform-diversity-charters-turns-10_en.

Fachkräfteeinwanderungsgesetz (FEG) (2020). Retrieved January 25, 2021, from: https://fachkraefteeinwanderungsgesetz.de.

Forscher, P. (2020): Unconscious bias training is no way to solve ethnic disparities. Retrieved February 5, 2021, from: https://capx.co/unconscious-bias-training-is-no-way-to-solve-ethnic-disparities/.

Fosslien, L., West Duffy, M. (2019). Retrieved December 28, 2020, from: https://twitter.com/lizandmollie/status/1150109074098253824.

Franken, S. (2015). Personal: Diversity Management. Studienwissen kompakt. Wiesbaden: Springer Fachmedien.

Frauen in die Aufsichtsräte (FidAR) (2020). WOMEN-ON-BOARD-INDEX 185 I. Retrieved February 3, 2021 from: https://www.fidar.de/webmedia/documents/wob-index-185/2020-11/201031_WoB-Index_185_I.pdf.

Fuller, P., Murphy, M., Chow, A. (2020). The leader's guide to unconscious bias. How to reframe bias, cultivate connection and create high-performance teams. London: Simon & Schuster UK Ltd.

Gardenswartz, L., Rowe, A. (1995). Diversity teams at work. Chicago: Irwin.

Gorges, H. (2015). HR braucht mehr Männer. In: Human Resources Manager. Retrieved February 1, 2021, from: https://www.humanresourcesmanager.de/news/hr-braucht-mehr-maenner.html.

Greenwald, A.G., McGhee, D. E., Schwartz, J. L. K. (1998). Measuring individual differences in implicit cognition: The implicit association test. Journal of Personality and Social Psychology, Vol. 74, No.6., p. 1464–1480.

Grundgesetz für die Bundesrepublik Deutschland (1949). Art.3. Retrieved December 19, 2020, from: https://www.gesetze-im-internet.de/gg/BJNR000010949.html.

Hamermesh, D. S. (2011). Beauty Pays: Why Attractive People Are More Successful. Princeton University Press.

Hunt, V., Layton, D., Prince, S. (2015). McKinsey & Company. Why diversity matters. Retrieved December 19, 2020, from: https://www.mckinsey.com/~/media/McKinsey/Business%20Functions/Organization/Our%20Insights/Why%20diversity%20matters/Why%20diversity%20matters.pdf.

Jablonski, H.W. (2019). Privilegien (an)erkennen und Potenziale richtig einschätzen. In: M.E. Domsch, D.H. Ladwig, F.C. Weber (Eds.). Vorurteile im Arbeitsleben. Unconscious Bias erkennen, vermeiden und abbauen. Berlin: Springer Gabler.

Kahneman, D. (2011). Thinking, Fast and Slow. Penguin Books.

Kanning, U. P., Pöttker, J., Golléri, P. (2007). Assessment Center Praxis in deutschen Großunternehmen – Ein Vergleich zwischen wissenschaftlichem Anspruch und Realität. Zeitschrift für Arbeits- und Organisationspsychologie, Vol. 51, p. 155–167.

Kanning, U.P. (2015). Personalauswahl zwischen Anspruch und Wirklichkeit. Eine wirtschaftspsychologische Analyse. Berlin, Heidelberg: Springer.

Katholische Nachrichten-Agentur (2020). In: zdf.de. Pläne der Bundesregierung – Grundgesetz: Begriff "Rasse" wird gestrichen. Retrieved January 3, 2021, from: https://www.zdf.de/nachrichten/politik/grundgesetz-rasse-lambrecht-100.html.

Kiechl, R. (1993). Managing Diversity: Postmoderne Kulturarbeit in der Unternehmung. In: Die Unternehmung: Swiss journal of business research and practice, Vol. 47, p. 67-72.

Koopmans, R., Veit, S., Yemane, R. (2018). Ethnische Hierarchien in der Bewerberauswahl: Ein Feldexperiment zu den Ursachen von Arbeitsmarktdiskriminierung. Discussion Paper. SP VI 2018-104. Retrieved December 18, 2020, from: https://bibliothek.wzb.eu/pdf/2018/vi18-104.pdf.

Kosinski, M., Stillwell, D., Graepel, T. (2013). Private traits and attributes are predictable from digital records of human behavior. Proceedings of the national academy of sciences, 110(15), p. 5802-5805. https://doi.org/10.1073/pnas.1218772110.

Kosinski, M., Bachrach, Y., Kohli, P., Stillwell, D.J., Graepel, T. (2014). Manifestations of user personality in website choice and behaviour on online social networks. Mach Learn. Vol. 95, p. 357–380. https://doi.org/10.1007/s10994-013-5415-y.

Krause, A., Rinne, U., Zimmermann, K.F. (2010). Anonymisierte Bewerbungsverfahren. IZA Research Report No. 27. Retrieved January 22, 2021, from: http://legacy.iza.org/en/webcontent/publications/reports/report_pdfs/report_pdfs/iza_report_27.pdf.

Krause, A., Rinne, U., Zimmermann, K.F. (2012). Anonymous job applications in Europe. IZA J Labor Stud 1, 5. https://doi.org/10.1186/2193-9012-1-5.

Krell G., Ortlieb R., Sieben B. (2018). Vielfältige Wettbewerbsvorteile. In: Gender und Diversity in Organisationen. Wiesbaden: Springer Gabler. https://doi.org/10.1007/978-3-658-20554-6_4.

Krell, G., Wächter, H. (2006). Diversity Management. Impulse aus der Personalforschung. Band 7. Trierer Beiträge zum Diversity Management. München, Mehring: Rainer Hampp Verlag.

Kreuscher, R. (2000). Lebenslaufanalyse – kürzer als das Rauchen einer Zigarette. Personalwirtschaft, Vol. 10, p. 64–68.

Kruger, J. M., Dunning, D. (1999). Unskilled and unaware of it: How difficulties in recognizing one's own incompetence lead to inflated self-assessments. Journal of Personality and Social Psychology, Vol. 77, p. 1121–1134.

Lane, K. A., Banaji, M. R., Nosek, B. A., Greenwald, A. G. (2007). Understanding and using the Implicit Association Test: IV. What we know (so far). In: B. Wittenbrink, N.S. Schwarz (Eds.). Implicit measures of attitudes: Procedures and controversies (p. 59–102). New York: Guilford Press.

Lies, J. (2018). Diversity Management. In: Gabler Wirtschaftslexikon. Retrieved January 2, 2021, from: https://wirtschaftslexikon.gabler.de/definition/diversity-management-53993/version-277052.

Machwirth, U., Schuler, H., Moser, K. (1996). Entscheidungsprozesse bei der Analyse von Bewerbungsunterlagen. Diagnostica, 42, p. 220-241.

Meuser, M, Nagel, U. (2009). Experteninterview und der Wandel der Wissensproduktion. In: A. Bogner, B. Littig, W. & Menz (Eds.). Experteninterviews: Theorien, Methoden, Anwendungsfelder (3rd. revised ed.). Wiesbaden: VS Verlag für Sozialwissenschaften.

Mierke, J., Klauer, K. C. (2003). Method-specific variance in the Implicit Association Test. Journal of Personality and Social Psychology, 85, p. 1180–1192.

Moscovici, S., Lage, E., Naffrechoux, M. (1969). Influence of a consistent minority on the responses of a majority in a color perception task. In: Sociometry, p. 365-380.

Nalty, K. (2016). Strategies for Confronting Unconscious Bias. Colorado Lawyer., Vol. 45 No 5, p. 45-52. Retrieved February 1, 2021, from: https://kathleennaltyconsulting.com/wp-content/uploads/2016/05/Strategies-for-Confronting-Unconscious-Bias-The-Colorado-Lawyer-May-2016.pdf.

Ogette, T. (2020). Exit Racism. Rassismuskritisch denken lernen (9th ed.). Münster: UNRAST-Verlag.

Reinders, H. (2005). Qualitative Interviews mit Jugendlichen führen. Ein Leitfaden. München, Wien: R. Oldenbourg.

Schein, E. H. (1988). Organizational culture. Retrieved January 29, 2021, from: https://dspace.mit.edu/bitstream/handle/1721.1/2224/SWP-2088-24854366.pdf.

Scherr A. (2016). Was heißt Diskriminierung?. In: Diskriminierung. essentials. Wiesbaden: Springer VS. https://doi.org/10.1007/978-3-658-10067-4_3.

Schmidt, H. (2020). Blind Auditions: Wer alle hören will, muss wohl doch sehen. In: Zeit Online. Retrieved January 17, 2021, from: https://www.zeit.de/kultur/musik/2020-08/blind-auditions-klassische-orchester-probespielen-vorhang-diversitaet-frauenanteil.

Siemann, C. (2017). E-Recruiting. Der Algorithmus ist nur so gut wie die Annahmen, auf denen er basiert. In: Personalwirtschaft. Retrieved January 29, 2021, from: https://www.personalwirtschaft.de/recruiting/artikel/der-algorithmus-ist-nur-so-gut-wie-die-annahmen-auf-denen-er-basiert.html.

Sozialgesetzbuch (SGB) III, § 448 (2019). Gesetz zur Förderung der Ausbildung und Beschäftigung von Ausländerinnen und Ausländern. Retrieved January 24, 2021, from: https://www.bundesregierung.de/breg-de/aktuelles/gefluechte-fruezeitig-foerdern-1635252.

Statististisches Bundesamt (Destatis) (2020). Bevölkerung mit Migrationshintergrund 2019 um 2,1 % gewachsen: schwächster Anstieg seit 2011. 52 % der Menschen mit Migrationshintergrund sind deutsche Staatsangehörige. Pressemitteilung Nr. 279 vom 28. Juli 2020. Retrieved January 10, 2021, from: https://www.destatis.de/DE/Presse/Pressemitteilungen/2020/07/PD20_279_12511.html.

Stephan, U., Westhoff, K. (2002). Personalauswahlgespräche im Führungskräftebereich des deutschen Mittelstandes: Bestandsaufnahmen und Einsparungspotential durch Strukturierte Gespräche. Wirtschaftspsychologie, Vol. 3, p. 3–17.

Strafgesetzbuch (1871). Retrieved December 22, 2020, from: https://www.gesetze-im-internet.de/stgb/StGB.pdf.

Tsipursky, G. (2020). The blind spots between us: How to overcome unconscious cognitive bias and build better relationships. New Harbinger Publications.

Tversky, A., Kahneman, D. (1974). Judgment under Uncertainty: Heuristics and Biases. Science. Vol. 185, Issue 4157, p. 1124-1131.

Ullrich, P. (2006). Das explorative ExpertInneninterview: Modifikationen und konkrete Umsetzung der Auswertung von ExpertInneninterviews nach Meuser/Nagel. In: T. Engartner, D. Kuring, T. Teubl (Eds.). Die Transformation des Politischen: Analysen, Deutungen und Perspektiven; siebentes und achtes DoktorandInnenseminar der Rosa-Luxemburg-Stiftung. Berlin: Dietz.

United Nations (UN) (1948). Universal Declaration of Human Rights. Art.1. Retrieved December 19, 2020, from: https://www.un.org/en/udhrbook/pdf/udhr_booklet_en_web.pdf.

Vedantam, S. (2010). The Hidden Brain. How our unconscious minds elect presidents, control markets, wage wars, and save our Lives. New York: Spiegel & Grau Trade Paperback Edition.

Verhaag, B. (1996). Blue Eyed. Indigo.

Watkins, L. M., Johnston, L. (2000). Screening job applicants: The Impact of physical attractivity and applicants quality. International Journal of Selection and Assessment, Vol. 8, p. 76–84.

Weichselbaumer, D. (2016). Discrimination against Female Migrants Wearing Headscarves. Discussion Paper No. 10217. Retrieved December 18, 2020, from: http://ftp.iza.org/dp10217.pdf.

Weiß A. (2013) Was ist Rassismus?. In: Rassismus wider Willen. Wiesbaden: Springer VS. https://doi.org/10.1007/978-3-531-93342-9_2.

West, S.M., Whittaker, M. and Crawford, K. (2019). Discriminating Systems: Gender, Race, and Power in AI. AI Now Institute. Retrieved from February 3, 2021, from: https://ainowinstitute.org/discriminatingsystems.pdf.

Wirtz, M.A. (Eds.) (2019). Dorsch. Lexikon der Psychologie (19th revised ed.). Bern: Hogrefe.

Zick, A., Küpper, B., Hövermann, A. (2011). Die Abwertung der Anderen. Eine europäische Zustandsbeschreibung zu Intoleranz, Vorurteilen und Diskriminierung. In: Friedrich-Ebert-Stiftung (Eds.). Retrieved January 14, 2021, from: http://library.fes.de/pdf-files/do/07905-20110311.pdf

List of Figures

Figure 1.1: Schematic representation 204
Figure 1.2: The Four Layers Of Diversity 208
Figure 1.3: Names and photographs, indicators for identity 216

The impact of culture on identity as evidenced through communication:
A case study on expat women

Maria Hehle-Fritsch

Abstract

Globalization has undoubtedly made our world more interconnected. Central to the discussion of how people from different cultural backgrounds can work and live together effectively is the reciprocal relationship between culture, identity and communication (Hortobágyi, 2009; Leary & Tangney, 2011; Martin & Nakayama, 2010).

This study aims to add to the body of literature on this discussion, while also contributing to the under-researched field of female expatriation (Mohan & Tabassum, 2017). The research project set out to investigate the impact of culture on identity in female expats and how this is evidenced in communication. Moreover, the study's aim was to test the hypothesis that identity is a communicative process. The research was exploratory and followed a case study design. Combining ethnography and discourse analysis, data for this study was obtained by means of semi-structured interviews and observations, and later analyzed through an inductive approach.

Overall the study's findings supported the hypothesis that identity is a communicative process. In this context, findings showed that some women employed code-switching as a communicative strategy to express group membership with either their original or host culture. In this process, cultural patterns such as collectivism and polychronism could be identified as having an impact on the women's identities. Additionally, a central theme that emerged from the study was that of identity gaps. In this respect, there was some evidence that high-context cultures emphasize the communal identity more strongly than low-context cultures. However, it was also found that regardless of cultural background, most women in the study population seemed to experience some degree of stress as a result of an identity gap occurring between the personal identity layer (self-image) and the enacted one (communicating this self-image). The small sample size, as well as the global pandemic happening at the time of the research presented some limitations to this study. Therefore, more research is needed to get a deeper understanding for the cultural factors that impact not only identity itself, but also the development of identity gaps. Further research could usefully explore how identity gaps are impacted by communicative competence.

Introduction

Since the restoration of the new global economy in the 1950s, our world has become increasingly interconnected (Jones, 2005). The UN's World Migration Report (McAuliffe, Khadria, & Bauloz, 2019) estimated a staggering increase of 120 million in international migrants between 2010 and 2020[1]. With such a sharp increase of people from different cultural backgrounds trying to work and live together effectively, understanding more about identity construction, how it is impacted by culture and expressed in interaction seems imperative.

In fact, while scholars disagree on how identity is formed, the swiftly growing body of literature on this subject seems to undergird the notion that it is a highly relevant topic (Leary & Tangney, 2011).Since identity, culture, and communication are intricately intertwined (Hortobágyi, 2009; Leary & Tangney, 2011; Martin & Nakayama, 2010), it is no surprise that many expatriates face internal

---

1 from 150 million to 272 million, of which 47.9% are women

struggles when learning a new language and cultural norms (Bochner, 2003).

While there is a vast body of literature on the male expatriate experience, not many studies have focused exclusively on women (Mohan & Tabassum, 2017). However, considering that female expatriates often hold important roles in their workplaces, families, and the wider societal context, investigating identity from their perspective could generate valuable insights about how culture, communication and identity interact.

Against this backdrop, this study aimed to explore the impact of culture on identity in female expats and how this is evidenced through communication. The research's primary focus lay in answering the following research questions:

RQ1: How does culture influence the way people experience and consequently express and manage their identities in interaction?

RQ2: How do people use communicative strategies to express and manage their identities?

The secondary focus was testing the hypothesis that identity is a communicative process, with culture playing a significant role in how people predominately experience and express their identities.

The study was exploratory and interpretative in nature and followed a case-study design. Applying ethnographic field-work methodology and observations, data was obtained by interviewing several female expatriates. An inductive approach was chosen to analyze the data by means of discourse analysis. Data was analyzed on how the participants employed code-switching as a communicative strategy to construct and manage their identities.

Furthermore, the content of the interaction was analyzed to identify possible identity gaps, which would show how the study participant's original culture may have impacted the way they predominately experienced their identities. The main objective with both approaches was to uncover possible cultural patterns that informed the participant's identity expression and management.

An additional focus in the study was the documentation and analysis of observations about how the study participants expressed and managed their identities in other settings. While it will be imperative to discuss the concept of identity, it goes beyond the scope of this study to provide an elaborate analysis of this subject.

Instead, the interconnection of culture, identity, and communication will be the main focus. While five semi-structured interviews that were analyzed in-depth provided the main data set for this study, for this the author also gleaned from observations of a minimum of 4 years that she spent with the study population. This allowed her to draw comparisons and notice differences in how study participants acted in various contexts.

Theorizing identity

While the question of who we are is not easily answered (Tatum, 2002), it is still a critical one to investigate since any interaction we have will automatically involve our identities (Ting-Toomey, 2012). Hortobágyi postulates that

> in intercultural communication in particular, for a proper decoding of the messages it is of paramount importance to recognize to what an extent people's identity contributes to formulate and convey the information (2009, p. 257).

Culture can further impact how we experience, construct and express our identities (Hecht, Jackson, & Ribeau, 2003; Markus & Kitayama, 2010). Therefore, identity is strongly intertwined with culture and communication, working together in an ongoing process of mutual influence (Hortobágyi, 2009; Leary & Tangney, 2011; Martin & Nakayama, 2010).

The purpose of this study is to explore the impact of culture on identity in female expats and how this is evidenced through communication. In this context, we are trying to answer the question how culture influences the way people express and manage their identities in interaction. Communication perspectives on identity

Two main concepts for identity have emerged in academia in recent years, namely the Social Science and the Interpretive Perspective. Each of these perspectives can provide critical insights into learning more about how identity is constructed and managed. Adopting a dialectic approach to identity as proposed by Martin and Nakayama (2010),we will take both research perspectives into consideration. However, since one of the aims of this study is to test the hypothesis that identity is a communicative process, we will prioritize the IP.

Table 1.1: **Perspectives on identity and communication**

Social Science Perspective	Interpretive Perspective
Identity created by self (by relating to groups)	Identity formed through communication with others
Emphasizes individualized, familial, and spiritual self	Emphasizes avowal and ascribed dimensions

(Adapted from Martin and Nakayama, 2010, p. 163)

The Interpretive perspective provides critical insights as to how identity is constructed and managed through interaction. The emphasis here is on identity as a communicative process. This is of further importance to our research question, because we try to answer how culture influences the way people express and manage their identities. While the SSP pays special attention to the reciprocal relationship between the individual and their social environment, The IP focuses on communication as a dynamic process through which identity is constructed (Hecht et al., 2003). Jung and Hecht (2004, p. 266) state that "people's identities are asserted, defined, and/or changed in mutual communication activities."

Theories such the *Face Negotiation Theory* (Ting-Toomey, 2012) suggest that identity is therefore constantly negotiated and managed when interacting with others. In this respect, the concepts of "avowed" and "ascribed" identity are important (Martin & Nakayama, 2010, p. 163).

Avowed identity refers to a person's self-image – the "labels" we use to describe ourselves based on personal perceptions. For instance, I may see myself as a diligent and loyal person, a coffee-lover and sports enthusiast.

Ascribed identity on the other hand, is the labels others put on us (Hortobágyi, 2009). For example, I may view myself as sensitive, while others might see me as empathetic or anxious. This shows that identity is not formed in isolation, but requires interaction with others.

The Communication Theory of Identity

A prominent identity theory called The Communication Theory of Identity is based on the notion that identity construction is a dynamic and communicative process. Having done extensive research on intercultural communication, Hecht et al. (2003) postulate that identity is experienced at multiple levels, and is continuously constructed and expressed when interacting with others. It "focuses on the mutual influences between identity and communication" (Jung & Hecht, 2004, p. 266) and comprises the following layers: "personal (self-perception), communication (enactment), relational (other's perception of us), and communal" (Hecht & Choi, 2012, pp. 140-142). Hecht et al. (2005) propose that a more comprehensive view on identity can be achieved when merging Western and non-Western approaches. Therefore, they argue that:

> the theory attempts to integrate the holism from Asian and African conceptions, polarity from the Greeks, harmony from African views, collectivism from Asian ideas and the individual orientation in the Greek perspective[2] (p. 259).

This attempt is reflected in the different identity layers as presented in the figure on the next page. While Hecht and his colleagues argue that individuals experience identity through all these

---

[2] Here we can understand „Greek perspective" as a Western way of thinking.

layers, they also stress their reciprocal relationship[3] (Hecht & Choi, 2012).

Figure 1.1: Identity layers of the CTI

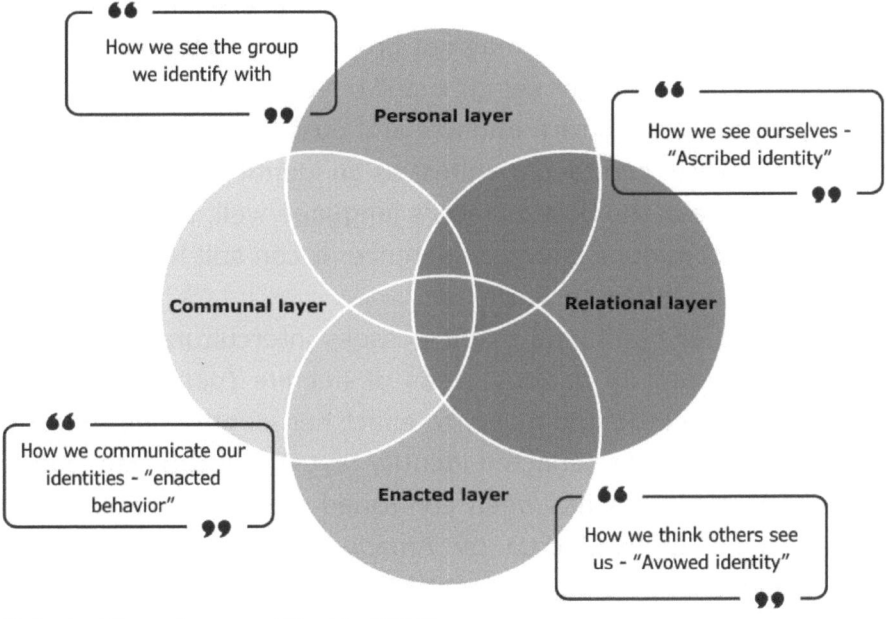

(Adapted from Jung and Hecht, 2004)

Since CTI regards communication itself as identity, "identity gaps can occur in the process of or as a result of communication" (Jung & Hecht, 2004, p. 315). Interacting cross-culturally may increase the risks for communication breakdowns and therefore identity gaps to occur. Both language as well as the cultural patterns, which inform how people interact with each other can act as barriers to congruency between these layers. For example, a person from a

---

3 This means that they influence each other. For example, I may see myself as a positive person (personal layer), which can influence how I present myself at a job interview (communication layer)

low-context[4] cultural background living in a high-context[5] culture may perceive herself as a "good communicator" (personal identity layer).

However, as she finds herself in a new cultural environment, her direct communication style may not prove very fruitful with locals, giving her a reputation of being "rude" or "overbearing" (relational identity layer). This in turn impacts and possibly changes her self-perception, which can then manifest as an identity gap. The person might even speak the host country's language well, but if she lacks intercultural communicative competence, it can still lead to people responding negatively towards her.

On the other hand, she might possess intercultural awareness and be competent in various areas of her life (personal identity layer) but if she lacks the ability to enact her identity due to insufficient language skills (enacted identity layer) this can also lead to an identity gap. This has been confirmed in current research on identity gaps as conducted by Amado, Snyder, and Gutchess (2020) and others (Jung & Hecht, 2008). They have found that particularly identity gaps between the personal and enacted layer are connected to acculturation stress. Discourse analysis

According to De Fina (2007) identity construction and management have language and discourse at their core. Gee (2005) refers to discourse as "language in use". Along similar lines, Moll (2012, p. 35-36) suggests that discourse is "how people use their language in order to achieve certain purposes". Martin and Nakayama (2010) contend for the centrality of language in intercultural communication and its close connection to identity construction. Since this

---

4 „A style of communication in which much of the information is conveyed in words rather than in nonverbal cues and contexts" (Martin & Nakayama, 2010, p. 228).
5 „A style of communication in which much of the information is contained in the contexts and nonverbal cues rather than expressed explicitly in words" (Martin & Nakayama, 2010, p. 228).

study has a special focus on communication in action, discourse analysis was chosen to analyze the research data.

Discourse analysis has been used in a plethora of ways and across various disciples (Brown & Yule, 1983; Johnstone, 2018; Jørgensen & Phillips, 2002; Phillips & Hardy, 2002). A simple, yet helpful definition of discourse analysis is that of Tannen (n.d.) who defines it as "the analysis of language 'beyond the sentence'".

Others such as Gee (2014) propose that rather than looking to one specific discourse theory as the correct or most applicable, discourse analysis should be viewed as a "tool box". This means that based on the research data, one discourse analysis theory may be favored over another. Within the context of communication studies, Tracy advocates that

> discourse analysis provides communication researchers with compelling a way to study how people present themselves, manage their relationships, assign responsibilities and blame, create organizations, enact culture, persuade others, make sense of social members' ongoing interactional practices, and so on (2001, p. 734).

Cultural patterns of communication: High context vs. Low context

This last statement by Tracy shows that culture can be enacted in discourse. Therefore, when discussing discourse, one inevitably must discuss culture.

When trying to define culture, we are once again faced with the reality that scholars have yet to find a common definition (Bochner, 2003). However, despite disagreements (Kinast, Schroll-Machl, & Thomas, 2010), one aspect all approaches seem to have in common is that culture involves human interaction[6] (Martin & Nakayama, 2010). This is further confirmation that culture and discourse cannot be separated.

---

6 Throughout this paper the words interaction and communication will be used interchangeably.

While Hofstede defines culture as "the collective programming of the mind" (Hofstede & Hofstede, 2001, p. 1), Ting-Toomey and Oetzel (2001) view it as a social learning process in which members of a group pass on patterns of thinking and acting.

E.T Hall was the first to coin the terms high context and low context communication, referring to them as cultural patterns. Moll, n.d. (p. 22) defines a cultural pattern as „ a behavior or a group of behaviors that is recognized and defined by the people who perform it".

Globalization has made our world increasingly interconnected and diverse. Hence, it is imperative to speak of cultural patterns or trends instead of making strict classifications (Moll, 2012). Here, Moll (2012) further stresses the contextual nature of cultural patterns. This means that how a cultural pattern (e.g. directness) is interpreted will largely be a matter of comparativeness.

That is why a discursive approach is helpful when discussing cultural characteristics. The figure on the following page shows the main pattern differences between high and low context cultures on a sliding scale. While these patterns are grounded in scientific research, there will always be variations and exceptions (Meyer, 2014; Moll, 2012). Hence, people will find themselves on different points on the sliding scale based on context.

Figure 1.2: Patterns of High context and Low context cultures

MORE HIGH CONTEXT COMMUNICATION PATTERNS	MORE LOW CONTEXT COMMUNICATION PATTERNS
• More indirect speech styles: communication nuanced and layered, messages spoken and read between the lines • More focused on collaboration and group interests: group needs above that of the individual • Focus on history and tradition • Polychronic time approach: relationship over tasks; time viewed as more fluid and/or cyclical • "Politeness" and face saving more important • Boundaries of social categories such as work, family, leisure, etc. less clear	• More direct speech styles: communication explicit, little "encoding" needed, focus on spoken word and content • More focused on individual needs and achievements: group important, but individual still emphasized • Focus on the present • Monochronic time approach: task over relationship; time viewed as sequential and something to be "managed" and "used" • Concept of face saving present, but less important • Clearer separation of social categories such as work, family, leisure, etc.

(Adapted from Meyer, 2014, p. 39, and Moll, 2012, pp. 50-54)

Code-switching

Having examined discourse and culture as it relates to communication patterns, we will now wrap up our discussion by looking into a communicative strategy called code-switching.

Code-switching (CS hereafter) refers to the use of two (or multiple) languages[7] within a discourse unit (Auer & Wei, 2008).

Since our research question deals with identity construction as a communicative process, this study is situated in socio-linguistic, or more precisely in an interactional sociolinguistics context.

---

7 Or dialects and accents (Martin & Nakayama, 2010)

Interactional sociolinguistics is a subdivision of sociolinguistic and was developed by John Gumperz. Building on Gumperz' understanding of communication as a social act, which asks for the participant's "coordinated efforts", (Gumperz, 1982, p. 1 as cited in Gafaranga, 2008, p. 283), Gafaranga argues that at the heart of this process lies the negotiation of meanings among speakers.

Hence, some of Gumperz' work focus on pragmatic aspects of code-switching. Anchimbe also emphasises pragmatics in code-switching, which is concerned with the intentions and meanings of the speaker. He argues that code-switching is

> as, quite often, a conscious activity by multilingual speakers who switch to other languages in order to perform a certain action, e.g. insult, warn, reproach, exclude, include, or denigrate, through the choice of words or expressions they use, and the social ramifications attached to them within the society. (2015, p. 140)

Similarly, Martin and Nakayama (2010, p. 249) propose that people code-switch in order to: „accommodate the other speakers, avoid accommodating others, or to express another aspect of their cultural identity."

While Baker (2011, p. 113) adds that people code-switch to facilitate communicating a message, but also to express "roles, norms and values", others stress the importance of code-switching as an act of identity expression and cultural closeness (Velásquez, ibid 2010, as cited in Abubakr, Hassan, & Muhedeen, 2019, p. 60).

While Martin and Nakayama list code-switching to express identity as separate action, it could be argued that the first two can function as a means to express and manage identity. For example, let us assume that a woman in her late 50ies moved 500 miles away from her hometown when she was 16 years old. She has very bad memories of her childhood and does not like going back to visit with family. She feels closely connected with her new community and has even picked up the local dialect. Each time she does visit family, she makes no attempt to code-switch dialects in order to accommodate her family members. In fact, she insists on having "unlearned" her family's dialect and talks to them in her new home community's dialect even more pronouncedly. This illustrates how she created as sense of "exclusivity" by choosing a specific dialect in order to expresses her "new"[8] cultural identity and group membership with the host community.

Expanding on the idea of communicating group membership, an important theory is Gumperz' "we/they codes". According to Gumperz (1982) code-switching practices are governed by semantic processes. To understand those, one must identify whether speakers in bilingual communities speak from a "we" or "they" perspective.

While "we-codes" are associated with the minority language representing "in-group" and "informal activities", "they-codes" are connected to the majority language and "associated with more formal, stiffer, and less personal out-group relations" (Gumperz, 1982, p. 66). Wodak, Johnstone, & Kerswill (2010) further propose that a speaker who uses "we-codes" does so to communicate their belonging with the local group.

Another important concept put forth by Gumperz is that of contextualization cues (Gumperz, 1982). Contextualization cues are "signaling mechanism" that speakers employ to communicate how their words should be interpreted (Gordon, 2014, p. 67). However, Gordon (2014) proposes that how a person utters the statement "I am not hungry", and is then encoded by the listener, will depend on their culturally informed understanding of the semantic meaning of these words. In most low-context cultures, "I am not hungry"

---

8 Since identity can be viewed as a communicative process, which is dynamic in nature, "new" may not be the most accurate word. The woman has been living in the host community for over 40 years. So, the cultural identity she has adopted is not new anymore. It may also continue to change. The same issue arises with the term host community. She sees herself as a local and has been accepted as a local. Hence, it's not necessarily her host community any longer, but her home community. Both of these terms were adopted for a lack of space to discuss their various definitions.

means just that. However, in some high-context cultures this statement may mean the opposite, and is used to demonstrate politeness.

The concept of contextualization cues is a vital consideration for our study when considering Gordon's argument that

> "Miscommunication and breakdown in intercultural encounters may result from unshared contextualization conventions, and may contribute to larger social problems such as ethnic stereotyping and differential access to opportunities" (2014).

Research Question & Methodology

Identity in the context of discourse is a multi-faceted issue (Scollon, 1996). Therefore, to gain a more in-depth understanding of the study participant's experience, a case study approach was adopted. Not only does a case study approach lend itself to obtaining detailed information on a subject, but it is also a recognized and widely used method (Crowe et al., 2011).

The author adopted a combination of ethnography and discourse analysis for her data analysis. While ethnography has been an established qualitative research approach in the social sciences for many years (Emerson, Fretz, & Shaw, 2011) its primary purpose is to "study culture" Wolcott (Wolcontt, 1999, p. 67).

Two ethnographic methods are semi-structured interviews and observations. These were used in the study to get a deeper understanding of the study participant's cultural backgrounds and how these impacted the way they expressed their identities.

While most data was collected through the semi-structured interviews, the author also drew on another convenience samples from her international environment (family network, church community, and work). Observations took place in a non-structured fashion by spending time with the participants in their daily lives, during non-profit work meetings, social gatherings, and other events.

The author applied a discursive approach drawing from both a social science and interpretive perspective to define identity. Since the core focus of the study was to consider how participants communicated their identities through verbal and non-verbal language, the author chose discourse analysis as the main method to analyze the research data.

Study population and sampling design

The study population consisted of expat women from different cultural and educational backgrounds and were of different ages and marital status. While the study participants were chosen based on convenience sampling, the author aimed at diversifying the study sample with regards to their cultural backgrounds. This was done to identify possible differences in how cultural patterns may impact the way study participants constructed and managed their identities in interaction. Moreover, the participants were selected based on the following parameters:
- Non-Swiss or Non-Austrian citizen
- Minimum of 0.5 years living (and working) in the Swiss or Austrian Bodensee region
- Proficient language level to conduct the interviews in English

Data analysis process

A study conducted by Van Hout and his colleagues (Van Hout, Pander Maat, & De Preter, 2011) has inspired the data analysis process for this research project. The research process was hence split into two phases: traditional ethnographic-fieldwork and discourse analysis.

Phase 1: Fieldwork
While the official time frame for this phase was between the end of September and the beginning of November 2020, the author has spent extended time with the study population for the last 5 years.

While fieldwork during that period lacked a systematic approach and no structured notes were obtained, the author allotted a considerable amount of time during the official research process on reflecting and documenting relevant research observations made during those 5 years.

Data collection through ethnographic interviews and observations: Semi-structured interviews

The interviews were conducted with a convenience sample of 5 female expatriates. The author received permission to record the interviews, which were then verbatim transcribed and analyzed. While the interviews were approximately 1 hour long in total, roughly 20-30 minutes were allotted for the actual interviewing process.

The reaming time was used for opening and closing the interview session (including rapport building, instructions, and follow-up questions). Due to time constraints for this study, only about 10-20 minutes of interview material was transcribed for in-depth analysis.

The questions below were asked during the interviews to identify how study participants use language to express and manage their identities, elicit information on how they experience their identities, and evaluate whether an identity shift has occurred in the acculturation process and if so, what has caused the shift.[9]

- How would you describe yourself?
- Please complete the following statement: "I am..."
- What is important to you in life?
- What is no longer important to you since moving to Switzerland/Austria?
- What is one piece of advice you would give to people moving to Switzerland/Austria?

---

9 Not all questions were asked, but rather chosen based on how the conversation flowed

- If you are willing, please share a challenging/embarrassing moment you had since moving to Austria/Switzerland and how it impacted you.

Observations: Ethnographic fieldnotes

After each interview, the author documented her observations within 48 hours through ethnographic fieldnotes. This was done to capture details of the context in which the interview took place, but also to identify some preliminary themes and rich points. However, the author also took regular notes "on the field", recording information that seemed relevant for the study.

Throughout the data collection process, the author continuously reflected on her notes to identify core themes (within as well as across each case study). More focused coding was applied in Phase 2 (Discourse analysis), when analyzing the interviews with the assistance of MAXQDA – a data analysis software.

Phase 2: Discourse analysis: Code-switching as a communicative strategy

The discourse analysis employed for this study focused on code-switching as a communicative strategy for the participants to express and manage their identities. Code-switching practices were analyzed in the context of the interview setting, while also drawing on observations of the participants in other settings. The aim was to identity how cultural patterns may have impacted the participant's identity and how this consequently became evident in their communication.

Figure 1.3: Impact of culture on identity as evidenced through communication

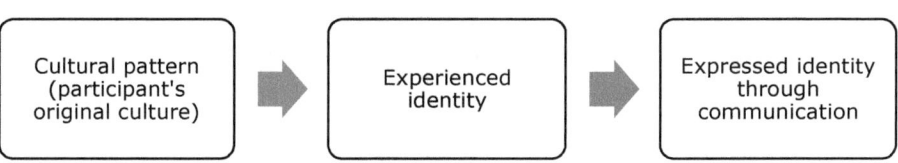

Referring back to Martin and Nakayama (2010) and others (Auer & Wei, 2008), code-switching has been associated with cultural identity expression and communicating a sense of separation or belonging. Moreover, code-switching can act as contextualization cues, which are "signaling mechanism" that speakers employ to communicate how their words should be interpreted. The speaker's intended meaning and the encoding that follows by the listener are culturally informed (Gordon, 2014, p. 67).

Discourse analysis: Identity gaps

A second emphasis in the discourse analysis was the s of identity gaps. Rather than looking at specific communication strategies, the author focused on how participants presented their "stories" of being a foreigner. The research questions were designed to elicit responses that would point to an identity gap rather than asking participants directly. The goal was to identify which identity layers were expressed, as well as between which ones there was discrepancy. This was done to glean insights into how cultural patterns may have impacted the way participants experience their identities.

Transcription

Phase 2 started with the transcription of the semi-structured interviews with a voice recording tool called Otter. While the recording tool made initial transcriptions of the interviews, a rigorous reviewing process was still necessary so that the interviews were transcribed verbatim. Due to time and word count constraints for this study, only about 15-20 minutes of the interviews were transcribed verbatim. Verbatim transcriptions allowed the author to study the discourse how it naturally flowed. In this respect, the author not only focused on recording the natural flow of the conversation (including grammar mistakes, pauses, etc.), but also documented aspects such as word intonation.

Inductive coding with the assistance of MAXQDA

The first round of coding involved the identification of broad topics such as "relationships" or "difficulties", "which served the purposes of obtaining a general overview of the content that was discussed in each interview.

Moreover, the author created code clouds for each participant, which included all words that were used at least twice in the verbatim interviews. This gave her a good overview of the main themes in each conversation. The code clouds were helpful in identifying connections when analyzing the data for code-switching strategies and identity gaps.

While the second round of coding focused on the overall structure of the conversation, identifying all situations in which the study participants employed code-switching during the interview process, the final step involved the analysis and interpretation of the main topics that emerged from the data set in the context of the research question and relevant literature.

Discussion

We will now discuss the main findings, answering:

- How culture influences the way people experience and consequently express and manage their identities in interaction
- How people use communicative strategies to express and manage their identities

Moreover, this section will provide evidence to support the hypothesis that identity is a communicative process, with culture playing a significant role in how people predominately experience their identities.

This discussion will take place in the context of identity gaps to show that culture can impact identity and consequently communication, but also to support the hypothesis that identity is a communicative process.

Code-switching as a means to express and manage identity

The following pages will present the first set of findings, which deals with language as a means to construct and manage identity. In that respect, we will attempt to show how cultural patterns are reflected in some CS practices the participants employed during the interaction.

Only two out of five study participant employed CS during the interview. While Case 3 engaged in CS three times during the interview, Case 5 did so seven times. While the other participants did not employ CS during the interview at all, all of them have been observed employing this strategy in other settings. While these observations were taken into consideration, the focus of this study was on the in-depth analysis of the interviews. The two study participants who engaged in CS had English as their second or third language and both were from a more high-context cultural background as compared to their host culture, or that of the English native speaking participants. While it is likely that in some cases CS was used to manage language competence, deeper analysis showed that this strategy was primarily employed to express and manage identity related aspects.

Of all cases in which CS was identified, two revealed that the participant's cultural backgrounds played a role in how they experienced, managed and expressed their identities. These two cases will be presented and discussed on the following pages.

Example 1
The following transcript is from an interview with a woman from a high-context cultural background, who has been living in Eastern Switzerland for 20 years. Throughout the interview she changed from English to the local language – Swiss German – several times. The excerpt below is an example of such an occasion. It demonstrates how cultural patterns can influence people's identities, and how this is then reflected in language use.

Figure 1.4: Code-switching: Case study example 1

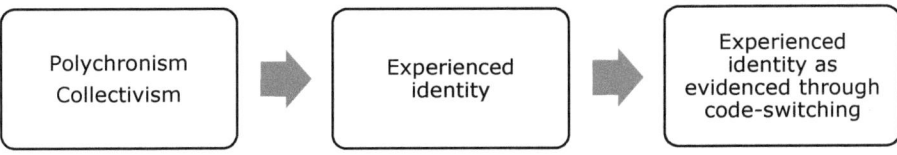

In the excerpt below the participant discusses differences in how people deal with time/appointments in her home and host country respectively. However, we can also see how she positions herself in this discussion, verbalizing her personal approach:

> I know I'm not <u>that</u> ah...stricted, you know, restricted, **and I'm more flexible,** you know. Because for me, you have time, but **you make time.** I'm more person like that. I can bounce off everything, cause I want to see you. **I make time, I'll make space on my calendar** if it is possible and everything [bumbling]... cause everyone is like, ah personally **they** say like, **"Oh, is it oh we cannot go <u>"Wanderung"</u> or something like that, because it might be windy, it's too cold."** For <u>me</u>, if it is in [her original culture]...if **we** already make an appointment on that day, that day...it doesn't matter rainy, <u>rainy, heavy</u> rainy, hot. **We**'ll find it out.

First, she stresses the fact that she sees herself as a flexible person and that people are more important than keeping a strict schedule. She supports these claims by saying: **"Because for me, you have time, you make time."** and **"I'll make space in my calendar"**.

In a later part of the interview, she also confirms her prioritization of relationships over "ideal circumstances" as follows:

Interviewer:
> "So, if I understand this correctly uhm, you don't look so much at the circumstances, but the relationship is in the focus?"

Interview participant:
> "Yes indeed...you **just put that first, regardless of the circumstances.**"

Interview participant:

"You know, because I think...if...**waiting on to the perfect time, then it means I put pressure for myself. Isn't it?**"

She also explains that circumstances like the weather are not a reason for canceling on people: **"For me, if it is in [her original culture]..if we already make an appointment on that day, that day...it doesn't matter rainy, rainy heavy rainy, hot. We'll find it out."**

From these short passages we can see how the woman constructed her identity as a "flexible person", who prioritizes relationships over tasks and is not concerned with "perfect" circumstances so that an event can take place. Referring back to Martin and Nakayama (2010), as well as Hecht et al. (2003) this could be an example of avowed identity or the personal identity layer as discussed in the CTI.

Furthermore, we could argue that the content of this discourse unit strongly indicates a polychronic approach to time. This is further supported when drawing on on-site observations from the interview. The author was invited for lunch at the participant house. While the official time for lunch was set for 12 pm, it was not served until at least an hour later. While the participant finished cooking the meal, she also showed the author around the house and introduced her to her family members who happily entertained the author while discussing various topics ranging from food to work.

Preparing an authentic dish from her home country and welcoming the author into her home, even though they have not known each other for very long, was a way of expressing her identity. In this context, it could be argued that her identity was influenced by the cultural pattern of collectivism, which typically place great emphasis on family (groups) (Meyer, 2014; Moll, 2012).

Interestingly, the participant chose to code-switch while discussing the topic of appointments by inserting the German word "Wanderung" into her English sentence: "*...cause everyone is like *ah personally **they say like, "Oh, is it oh we cannot go "Wanderung"** or something like that**, because it might be windy, it's too cold.***

In this case, it was clear that she did not employ code-switching to manage insufficient language competence, but rather to communicate part of her identity. Including the word "Wanderung"[10], and switching from a first person to a third person perspective ("they say...") provide strong evidence that she views herself as "different" from the locals, implicitly expressing her ethnic identity. This is in line with current research on code-switching, which posits that it can be used as a means to express identity (Abubakr et al., 2019; Gumperz, 1982; Martin & Nakayama, 2010; Myers-Scotton, 1995).

Moreover, this act of code-switching in combination with changing from a first person to a third person perspective could be an example of Gumperz' (1982) "we/they code" theory as discussed previously. This theory argues that "they-codes" are "associated with more formal, stiffer, and less personal out-group relations" (Gumperz, 1982, p. 66).

Example 2
This code-switching example is from a participant, who is from a typically more high-context culture now living in Eastern Switzerland. The example shows how the participant managed her identity during interaction, and used code-switching as a means to communicate group membership. Also, we will see how cultural patterns may have informed the participants identity, which led to an identity change when exposed to the new cultural environment.

---

10 „Wanderung" is the German word for „hiking", which is a very popular past time activity in Switzerland. Swiss typically enjoy the outdoors and value nature. These claims are based on the author's observations, having spent all her life living just few minutes away from the Swiss border, regularly visiting with family and friends. Moreover, she has observed that most expats she has met over the past 5 years have expressed an appreciation for Switzerland's rich nature.

Figure 1.5: Code-switching: Case study example 2

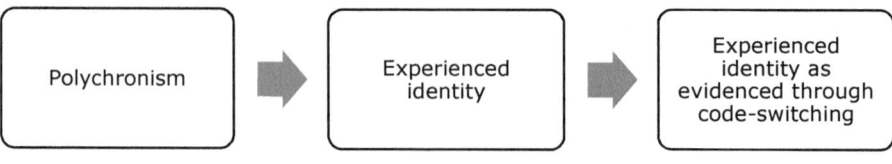

When asked what the participant appreciated about her host country, she reported the following:

> "And then I also feel like, people are very, they're very nice, you know, they're in general, very gentle. Very rarely will you find someone that's disrespectful to you, uhm… I would say there, the whole country, I mean, it's very clean. It's very **"In Ordnung".** Everything has **rules, and it's good**. You can go walking anywhere. **There's signs everywhere to know where to walk [brief giggle]. Yeah, it's all very organized**. I also like that. Yeah. It gives me, like security for my future. And it also gives me…kind of hope for my children, if I would have children, like, they would grow up in a country that I, like, everything is kind of [motions her hands parallel in front of her to show "order"] in a good system."

In the passage above we can see how the study participant employs code-switching by inserting the German word **"In Ordnung"**[11] while describing what she appreciates about the local culture.

In the last section she points out that **"everything is kind of in a good system"**, voicing her positive feelings about raising children in such an environment.

We could argue that in this context, the act of code-switching combined with the positive description of the local culture served as a means to communicate "group membership" or "in-group" language, which corresponds to Gumperz' "we code".

Interestingly, in the context of the code-switching act, the participant also pointed out that her host country was very organized. While saying this she giggled and also reported in a later section:

---

11 Which in English can have several meanings. It can be translated as "alright", but also "decent" or "orderly". In this context, the German word is used to describe something as well organized and put together. This does not only refer to a physical environment, but also to a person's behavior.

„that I really like, to be on time. Something I had to learn [laughs]."

The fact that she mentioned "having to learn to be on time" indicates that the participant initially had a polychronic approach to time, and that a shift has occurred in her personal identity as a result of being exposed to the new cultural environment[12], which has a more monochronic time approach.

Identity as a communicative process: Identity gaps

One of the findings that emerged in the context of identity gaps was that study participants experienced different degrees of acculturation stress as a result of an identity gap between the personal (self-perception) and enacted layer (how we communicate our identities). These results are based on the author's long-term observations working in the study field, as well as the data collected through the interviews. During the interviews, 3 out of 5 study participants voiced some degree of challenge in the adaption phase because of language deficiency. There was no clear evidence that age or marital status played a role in whether, or to which degree, participants experienced acculturation stress because of an identity gap. Moreover, there was no clear evidence that women from a low-context culture struggled more or less from acculturation stress as a result of an identity gap.

However, of the two concrete identity gaps that could be identified in the interviews, one was between the personal and enacted identity layer, and one was between the enacted and communal layer. While the first identity gap was found in a woman from a low-

---

12 While not explicitly stated, it is possible that her self-image has changed as a result of feedback that she got from her surrounding about her time management. She said she "had to" learn to be on time. This word choice strongly suggests that she was ascribed a certain identity (e.g. unpunctual) and that it was necessary for her to change in order to belong and survive in the local community.

context cultural background the latter was found in a woman from high-context culture.

While there is not sufficient data to support this as a general claim, the following excerpts demonstrates how women from different cultural backgrounds experience their identities differently, and how identity gaps can occur as a result of communication breakdown.

Identity gap between personal and enacted identity

One study participant from a high-cultural context background reported that language served as a tool to "enact" her identity as a successful businesswoman in her original culture. Moving to a new culture she described as a humbling process, since she lacked both language skills and a relational network:

> „I think uhm **coming to Switzerland humbled me**, because I was very confident in [her original culture]. I was very, very confident. I had a, a **good reputation**. Both amongst my family, my friends and my business...I, **I was known in the areas that I operated**. And coming to Switzerland humbled me, it, **it brought me right down to my knees.**"

The above excerpt indicates that her self-concept (personal identity layer), the identity she was ascribed[13] (relational identity level), and her ability to enact this identity were congruent in her original culture. Once in a new cultural environment, she must have experienced those layers in a different way, because she said that it "brough her right down to her knees." This statement strongly suggests that the participant experienced some degree of discrepancy between these layers. Language seemed to have played a critical factor in narrowing the identity gaps:

> „Ehm...six years down the line now I can communicate. I don't have great [emphasizes word great] language skills in German, but I can

---

13 Others must have ascribed a positive identity to her since she said she had a good reputation among family, friends and business partners.

[emphasizes word can] communicate. So that has **helped a lot**. That has given me **some** [emphasizes word some] **confidence**..."

In other parts of the interview, the study participant reported how obtaining a job that allowed her to express herself in her mother tongue led to positive results on various levels: "Because I was...teaching **English**, and I was teaching **a subject I knew**, and I was **able** [emphasizes word able] to **help people**."

Not only did it reshape her self-concept (personal identity layer), but she also experienced a new sense of belonging with local society (identity through group membership): "...I **had something** that I could **help people** with. They needed me. And I had **something to give**. And that made me feel valuable **again. I contributed** to society. I was **part of society**. I was **acceptable**."

Again, we can see how language can contribute to either opening or closing an identity gap, because identity is constructed through interaction. The next discourse unit shows how increased intercultural communicative competence helped the study participant to establish friendships:

"...I've, **I've come to know how to approach them [the locals]**. I've come to know how to **keep that distance**, how to **speak about safe subjects**, how **to get to know them**. And then once you do...they, they give you the go ahead, they actually open the door, **and then they are very, very faithful friends**".

This is in line with current findings in the field of intercultural communication, proposing that communicative competence can help a person to form bonds with others (López-Rocha, 2016).

Identity gap between personal and communal identity

We will now focus on identity as it is experienced through group membership (communal layer; SSP), looking at how an identity gap can form between the enacted and communal layer if a person's image of the group they belong to is not confirmed in another context. The following excerpt is taken from an interview with a participant from a high-context cultural background now living in a low-context culture.

Interestingly, when asked about how the participant would describe herself and what she values in life, she lists various relational aspects:

Interview participant:

"I am a **wife**. Already said that. I am **married**."

Interviewer:

"That seems very important to you".

Interview participant:

"Yeah. I am a **daughte**r. I am **a Christian**."
...Mm hmm. I would say the most important for me would be God. So like my spiritual life. And then yeah, my **family**."

These statements indicate that she experiences her identity very strongly through the relational and communal layer, which can be linked to her high-context cultural background.[14]

In a later section she reported the significance of people in exercising her faith on a communal level: "the relationships that I had with **my friends, which were at the church, they were like, everything to me**, you know. I could give my life for these people, no problem.

After moving to her new cultural environment, a mismatch appeared to have occurred between the concept she had of her group (Christian community) in her original culture and the way it was expressed in the host country. This assumption is based on the following statement:

„I found that **people here didn't live their Christian life in a way that I kne**w....and then you meet them outside, they're smoking, they're sleeping with their girlfriends. They're like fighting with each other. **And then there was like, a disconnect for me**..."

---

14 High-context cultures are typically more collective in nature – see Figure 1.2: Patterns of High context and Low context cultures

The fact that the study participant also reported that her spiritual life[15] became less important after moving to her new cultural environment strongly points to an identity gap. This identity gap may have resulted from the participant's inability to enact/communicate part of her identity (communal and/or personal level), which would be an example of how culture can impact the communicative process of identity construction.

Talking about spirituality, another noteworthy observation was that both women mentioned above emphasized the importance of faith/God and a faith community in their lives. This was also a rich point of discussion during the interview with at least one more woman from a high-context cultural background. Interestingly, while the woman from a high-context cultural background continuously emphasized her spiritual self, she did so within the context of community. Additionally, she continuously stressed the value of family and friends. This combination was also evident in another woman from a high-context cultural background in the sample group.

In contrast to the woman from a high-context culture, who highlighted the spiritual self and community, the woman with a low-context cultural background addressed the spiritual self too, but with less emphasis on a communal context. Cross-cultural psychologist Alan Roland (1991) has found that there are three universal identity layers: the individualized self, the spiritual self, and the familial self.

These are manifested and emphasized differently within cultural groups (Martin & Nakayama, 2010). We could argue that the individualized and familial self would equate to the CTI's personal and communal identity layer, respectively.

Interestingly, Martin and Nakayama posit that

---

[15] Not her relationship with God/faith itself (her spiritual identity), but exercising it on a communal level the way she was used to in her original culture.

identity development does not occur in the same way in every society. The notion of identity in India, Japan, and some Latino/a and Asian American groups emphasizes the integration of the familial and the spiritual self but very little of the more individualized self (2010, p. 165).

However, Roland (1991) stresses that while the individual self is predominant in Western societies, the familial self is also emphasized in women from Western societies[16]. This seems to support the above discussed research findings.

The excerpts above indicate that culture can impact which identity layers are emphasized in an individual. While no general claim can be generated from these findings, there was evidence that women from high-context cultural backgrounds tend to emphasize the spiritual in combination with the familial self. That does not mean, however, that the familial self is not equally important for women with a high-context cultural background.

Conclusion

This study set out to explore how culture impacts the way expat women express and manage their identities in interaction. The second aim of the research project was to test the hypothesis that identity is a communicative process.

The findings have shown that culture can impact how people experience and consequently express and manage their identities in interaction. Moreover, the study supports the idea that identity is a communicative process.

The most obvious finding to emerge from this study was that a person's original culture can impact the way they present and manage their identities in interaction.

Code-switching to the majority language was one way through which some of the participants communicated group membership. In this respect, cultural patterns such as collectivism and polychronism were found to impact some of the participant's identities, and

---

16 And much more as compared to men from the same cultural background.

this was then evidenced in communication through the act of code-switching. Code-switching to the majority language also acted as a tool to communicate "otherness", implicitly revealing the previously addressed cultural aspects.

In the context of discussing identity gaps, there was some evidence that cultural patterns such as collectivism and individualism can impact how people experience their identities. While there is no sufficient data to support this as a general claim, strong evidence was found that the communal identity is emphasized more strongly in high-context cultures.

Also, while not exclusively addressed during the interviews by all participants, but based on long-term observations by the author, identity gaps between the personal and enacted layer, and the psychological stress that often occurs as a result (Jung & Hecht, 2004), were dominant themes.

Implications

The insights gained from this study could deepen our understanding for the cultural factors that influence the development of identity gaps. For example, increased (cultural) self-awareness by knowing through which layers one predominately experiences their identity may improve a person's intercultural communication competence This in turn could help them in the process of closing the identity gap.

As just stated, communicative competence plays a critical role in this process. Michael Hecht and his colleagues (Jung & Hecht, 2004, p. 280) therefore advocate for further studies that investigate whether "identity gaps are influenced by communication input variables, such as communication styles, communication competence, and conversational improvement strategies."

Limitations

As with every research project, this study was subject to various limitations. It could be argued that the relatively small sample size was one of them. However, while the five interviews, as well as the chosen methodology did not allow for a statistical analysis, the results did generate meaningful information that would allow the author to answer the research question.

Moreover, the scope of this study, as well as the constraints due to a global pandemic happening at the time of this research project limited a more extensive data collection. However, the author could draw from long-term observations gathered during a period of at least five years in the field prior to the official start of this project.

Lastly, the fact that all participants had a personal relationship with the author to a certain degree could be counted as a limitation. However, this rapport actually helped in addressing the research question.

Suggestion for further research

Referring back to Jung and Hecht (2004), a better understanding of how culture impacts identity can improve intercultural communication competence and consequently mitigate acculturation stress.

While research has shown that improved language skills are essential in closing identity gaps (Amado et al., 2020; Jung & Hecht, 2004, Jung & Hecht, 2008), little is known about how communicative competence affects the identity negotiation process.

Further studies on identity gaps in intercultural business communication could be valuable, given the rise in cross-cultural professional interactions.

References

Abubakr, S. N., Hassan, Z. M., & Muhedeen, B. L. (2019). Code-switching as Identity Marker: A Sociolinguistic Study of Kurdish EFL University Students. Journal of University of Human Development, 5(3), 57. https://doi.org/10.21928/juhd.v5n3y2019.pp57-64

Amado, S., Snyder, H. R., & Gutchess, A. (2020). Mind the Gap: The Relation Between Identity Gaps and Depression Symptoms in Cultural Adaptation. Frontiers in Psychology, 11, 1156. https://doi.org/10.3389/fpsyg.2020.01156

Auer, P., & Wei, L. (2008). Handbook of Multilingualism and Multilingual Communication. Walter de Gruyter. Retrieved from https://books.google.at/books?id=vx2jJ70WX2cC&printsec=frontcover&dq=Handbook+of+Multilingualism+and+Multilingual&hl=en&sa=X&ved=2ahUKEwjYvdzez_PuAhWwz4UKHRmkB00Q6AEwAHoECAMQAg#v=onepage&q=Handbook%20of%20Multilingualism%20and%20Multilingual&f=false

Baker, C. (2011). Foundations of Bilingual Education and Bilingualism. Multilingual Matters. Retrieved from https://books.google.at/books?id=HgbPBQAAQBAJ&printsec=frontcover&dq=Foundations+of+Bilingual+Education+and+Bilingualism&hl=en&sa=X&ved=2ahUKEwiM8Y3pz_PuAhUMqxoKHfNiD5YQ6AEwAHoECAAQAg#v=onepage&q=Foundations%20of%20Bilingual%20Education%20and%20Bilingualism&f=false

Bochner, S. (2003). Culture Shock Due to Contact with Unfamiliar Cultures. Online Readings in Psychology and Culture, 8(1). https://doi.org/10.9707/2307-0919.1073

Brown, G., & Yule, G. (1983). Discourse Analysis. Cambridge University Press. Retrieved from https://books.google.at/books?id=ZUnEAgAAQBAJ&printsec=frontcover&dq=Brown,+G.,+%26+Yule,+G.+(1983).+Discourse+Analysis&hl=en&sa=X&ved=2ahUKEwisrv31z_PuAhXnxoUKHY33CbYQ6AEwAHoECAMQAg#v=onepage&q=Brown%2C%20G.%2C%20%26%20Yule%2C%20G.%20(1983).%20Discourse%20Analysis&f=false

Crowe, S., Cresswell, K., Robertson, A., Huby, G., Avery, A., & Sheikh, A. (2011). The case study approach. BMC Medical Research Methodology, 11, 100. https://doi.org/10.1186/1471-2288-11-100

De Fina, A. (2007). Code-switching and the construction of ethnic identity in a community of practice. Language in Society, 36(03). https://doi.org/10.1017/S0047404507070182

Emerson, R. M., Fretz, R. I., & Shaw, L. L. (2011). Writing Ethnographic Fieldnotes (2nd ed.). Chicago, USA and London, UK: The University of Chicago Press.

Gafaranga, J. (2008). Code-switching as a Conversational Strategy. In Auer, P., & Wei, L. (Eds.), Handbook of Multilingualism and Multilingual Communication. Walter de Gruyter (pp. 279-312). Retrieved from https://books.google.at/books?id=vx2jJ70WX2cC&printsec=frontcover&dq=Handbook+of+Multilingualism+and+Multilingual&hl=en&sa=X&ved=2ahUKEwjYvdzez_PuAhWwz4UKHRmkB00Q6AEwA-HoECAMQAg#v=onepage&q=gafaranga&f=false

Gee, J. P. (2005). An Introduction to Discourse Analysis: Theory and Method. Psychology Press. Retrieved from https://books.google.at/books?id=VkmpW9xa9FwC&printsec=frontcover&dq=Gee,+J.+P.+(2005).+An+Introduction+to+Discourse+Analysis&hl=en&sa=X&ved=2ahUKEwjx0o2E0PPuAhVESxoKHfSbDS8Q6AEwAHoECAAQAg#v=onepage&q=Gee%2C%20J.%20P.%20(2005).%20An%20Introduction%20to%20Discourse%20Analysis&f=false

Gee, J. P. (2014). How to do Discourse Analysis: A Toolkit. Routledge. Retrieved from https://books.google.at/books?id=O4SrAgAAQBAJ&printsec=frontcover&dq=Gee,+J.+P.+(2014).+How+to+do+Discourse+Analysis:+A+Toolkit.+Routledge.&hl=en&sa=X&ved=2ahUKEwjLro_Nx_XuAhVV8OAKHYM6BnQQ6AEwAHoECAAQAg#v=onepage&q=Gee%2C%20J.%20P.%20(2014).%20How%20to%20do%20Discourse%20Analysis%3A%20A%20Toolkit.%20Routledge.&f=false

Gordon, C. (2014). Contextualization Cues. Center for Intercultural Dialogue. Retrieved from https://centerforinterculturaldialogue.org/2015/03/30/key-concept-57-contextualization-cues-by-cynthia-gordon/ website: https://centerforinterculturaldialogue.org/2015/03/30/key-concept-57-contextualization-cues-by-cynthia-gordon/

Gudykunst, W. B. (2003). Cross-Cultural and Intercultural Communication. SAGE. Retrieved from https://books.google.at/books?id=-5sjpr1ypmcC&printsec=frontcover&dq=Cross-Cultural+and+Intercultural+Communication.+SAGE.&hl=en&sa=X&ved=2ahUKEwi82Nb-0PXuAhVHnaQKHapkD8gQ6AEwAHoECAAQAg#v=onepage&q=Cross-Cultural%20and%20Intercultural%20Communication.%20SAGE.&f=false

Gudykunst, W. B. (2004). Bridging Differences: Effective Intergroup Communication. SAGE. Retrieved from https://books.google.at/books?id=B9LReJA44WwC&pg=PA389&dq=Gudykunst,+W.+B.+(2004).+Bridging+Differences:+Effective+Intergroup+Communication.+SAGE.&hl=en&sa=X&ved=2ahUKEwjf6aCI0fXuAhVLC-wKHW0wA_0Q6AEwAHoECAAQAg#v=onepage&q=Gudykunst%2C%20W.%20B.%20(2004).%20Bridging%20Differences%3A%20Effective%20Intergroup%20Communication.%20SAGE.&f=false

Gumperz, J. J. (1982). Discourse Strategies. Cambridge University Press. Retrieved from https://books.google.at/books?id=aUJNgHWl_koC&printsec=frontcover&dq=gumperz+discourse+strategies&hl=en&sa=X&ved=2ahUKEwi24K-AxfXuAhVx9OAKHWQ-DB0Q6AEwAHoECAEQAg#v=onepage&q=gumperz%20discourse%20strategies&f=false

Hecht, M.L., Choi, H. (2012). The Communication Theory of Identity as a Framework for Health Message Design. In H. Cho (Ed.), Health Communication Message Design: Theory and Practice. SAGE. (pp. 137-149) Retrieved from https://books.google.at/books?id=MACkkuKWEqEC&printsec=frontcover&dq=The+Communication+Theory+of+Identity+as+a+Framework+for+Health+Message+Design&hl=en&sa=X&ved=2ahUKEwj3g-PxivbuAhXyo4sKHWA6DxIQ6AEwAHoECAMQAg#v=onepage&q=entity%20as%20a%20Framework%20for%20Health%20Message%20Design&f=false

Hecht, M. L., Jackson, R. L., & Ribeau, S. A. (2003). African American Communication: Exploring Identity and Culture. Routledge. Retrieved from https://books.google.at/books?id=GQ-QAgAAQBAJ&printsec=frontcover&dq=African+American+Communication+Hecht&hl=en&sa=X&ved=2ahUKEwiO7IzlxPXuAhXcAmMBHZ1xBN4Q6AEwAHoECAAQAg#v=onepage&q=African%20American%20Communication%20Hecht&f=false

Hecht, M.L., Jung, E., Krieger, J.L., Warren, J.R. (2005). The Communication Theory of Identity: Development, Theoretical Perspective and Future Direction. In W. B. Gudykunst (Ed.), Theorizing About Intercultural Communication. SAGE. (pp. 257-280) Retrieved from https://books.google.at/books?id=E12VSljBmvAC&q=social+science+perspective#v=onepage&q=tajfel&f=false

Hofstede, G. H., & Hofstede, G. (2001). Culture's Consequences: Comparing Values, Behaviors, Institutions and Organizations Across Nations. SAGE. Retrieved from https://books.google.at/books?id=w6z18LJ_1VsC&printsec=frontcover&dq=Hofstede,+G.+H.,+%26+Hofstede,+G.+(2001).+Culture%E2%80%99s+Consequences:+Comparing+Values,+Behaviors,+Institutions+and+Organizations+Across+Nations.+SAGE.&hl=en&sa=X&ved=2ahUKEwiSqfGx0fXuAhXRzKQKHaaoASwQ6AEwAHoECAIQAg#v=onepage&q=Hofstede%2C%20G.%20H.%2C%20%26%20Hofstede%2C%20G.%20(2001).%20Culture%E2%80%99s%20Consequences%3A%20Comparing%20Values%2C%20Behaviors%2C%20Institutions%20and%20Organizations%20Across%20Nations.%20SAGE.&f=false

Hortobágyi, I. (2009). The Role of identity in intercultural communication. Bulletin of the Transilvania University of Braşov, 2(51) 257-262

Hyland, K., & Paltridge, B. (2011). Bloomsbury Companion to Discourse Analysis. A&C Black. Retrieved from https://books.google.at/books?id=X0LFXMmOD8IC&pg=PA338&dq=Hyland,+K.,+%26+Paltridge,+B.+(2011).+Bloomsbury+Companion+to+Discourse+Analysis.+A%26C+Black.&hl=en&sa=X&ved=2ahUKEwjoh9HJ0fXuAhWBGewKHdcCCyUQ6AEwAHoECAAQAg#v=onepage&q=Hyland%2C%20K.%2C%20%26%20Paltridge%2C%20B.%20(2011).%20Bloomsbury%20Companion%20to%20Discourse%20Analysis.%20A%26C%20Black.&f=false

Johnstone, B. (2018). Discourse Analysis. John Wiley & Sons. Retrieved from https://books.google.at/books?id=nNo4DwAAQBAJ&printsec=frontcover&dq=Johnstone,+B.+(2018).+Discourse+Analysis&hl=en&sa=X&ved=2ahUKEwi4hu3S0fXuAhUxPewKHctJBp4Q6AEwAHoECAAQAg#v=onepage&q=Johnstone%2C%20B.%20(2018).%20Discourse%20Analysis&f=false

Jones, G. (2005, August 22). Restoring a Global Economy, 1950–1980. Retrieved from HBS Working Knowledge website: http://hbswk.hbs.edu/item/restoring-a-global-economy-19501980

Jung, E., & Hecht, M. L. (2004). Elaborating the communication theory of identity: Identity gaps and communication outcomes. Communication Quarterly, 52(3), 265–283. https://doi.org/10.1080/01463370409370197

Jung, E., & Hecht, M. L. (2008). Identity Gaps and Level of Depression Among Korean Immigrants. Health Communication, 23(4), 313–325. https://doi.org/10.1080/10410230802229688

Kinast, E.-U., Schroll-Machl, S., & Thomas, A. (Eds.). (2010). Handbook of Intercultural Communication and Cooperation: Basics and Areas of Application (2nd ed.). Göttingen: Vandenhoeck & Ruprecht. https://doi.org/10.13109/9783666403279

Leary, M. R., & Tangney, J. P. (2011). Handbook of Self and Identity (2nd ed.) Guilford Press. Retrieved from https://books.google.at/books?id=kGK-dfHpM4gC&printsec=frontcover&dq=Leary,+M.+R.,+%26+Tangney,+J.+P.+(2011).+Handbook+of+Self+and+Identity&hl=en&sa=X&ved=2ahUKEwjtlJ6a0_XuAhUai8MKHSC-DpoQ6AEwAHoECAIQAg#v=onepage&q=Leary%2C%20M.%20R.%2C%20%26%20Tangney%2C%20J.%20P.%20(2011).%20Handbook%20of%20Self%20and%20Identity&f=false

López-Rocha, S. (2016). Intercultural communicative competence: Creating awareness and promoting skills in the language classroom. In C. Goria, O. Speicher, & S. Stollhans (Eds.), Innovative language teaching and learning at university: Enhancing participation and collaboration (pp. 105–111). Research-publishing.net. https://doi.org/10.14705/rpnet.2016.000411

Markus, H. R., & Kitayama, S. (2010). Cultures and Selves: A Cycle of Mutual Constitution. Perspectives on Psychological Science, 5(4), 420–430. https://doi.org/10.1177/1745691610375557

Martin, J. N., & Nakayama, T. K. (2010). Intercultural communication in contexts (5th ed). New York: McGraw-Hill Higher Education.

McAuliffe, M., Khadria, B., & Bauloz, C. (2019). World migration report 2020. Geneva: IOM.

Meyer, E. (2014). The Culture Map: Decoding how people think, lead and get things done across cultures. New York City, New York, USA: Public Affairs.

Mohan, V., & Tabassum, N. (2017). The Impact of Gender Stereotyping on Female Expatriates; A Conceptual Model of Research. International Journal of Family Business and Management, 1(1). Retrieved from https://symbiosisonlinepublishing.com/family-business-management/family-business-management08.php

Moll, M. (2012). The Quintessence of Intercultural Business Communication. Berlin-Heidelberg, Germany: Springer-Verlag.

Moll, M. (n.d). Intercultural Communication I, Europäische Fernhochschule Hamburg, Germany

Myers-Scotton, C. (1995). Social Motivations for Codeswitching: Evidence from Africa. Clarendon Press. Retrieved from https://books.google.at/books?id=TqD-y_IF3SwC&printsec=frontcover&dq=Myers-Scotton&hl=en&sa=X&ved=2ahUKEwiR24rk0vXuAhXjzIUKHX8sBkAQ6AEwAnoECAIQAg#v=onepage&q=Myers-Scotton&f=false

NCCC: Curricula Enhancement Module Series. (n.d.). Retrieved from https://nccc.georgetown.edu/curricula/awareness/D17.html

Phillips, N., & Hardy, C. (2002). Discourse Analysis: Investigating Processes of Social Construction. SAGE Publications. Retrieved from https://books.google.at/books?id=-3-fF5kranYC&printsec=frontcover&dq=Phillips+%26+Hardy+Discourse+Analysis&hl=en&sa=X&ved=2ahUKEwjm1tXH0vXuAhVCLBoKHUnMBxQQ6AEwAHoECAUQAg#v=onepage&q=Phillips%20%26%20Hardy%20Discourse%20Analysis&f=false

Roland, A. (1991). In Search of Self in India and Japan: Toward a Cross-cultural Psychology. Princeton University Press. Retrieved from https://books.google.at/books?id=vl5q_VGHoksC&printsec=frontcover&dq=Roland,+A.+(1991).+In+Search+of+Self+in+India+and+Japan:+Toward+a+Cross-cultural+Psychology.+Princeton+University+Press.&hl=en&sa=X&ved=2ahUKEwjHlJqw0vXuAhVOxoUKHcJY-DAcQ6AEwAHoECAEQAg#v=onepage&q=Roland%2C%20A.%20(1991).%20In%20Search%20of%20Self%20in%20India%20and%20Japan%3A%20Toward%20a%20Cross-cultural%20Psychology.%20Princeton%20University%20Press.&f=false

Scollon, R. (1996). Discourse Identity, Social Identity, and Confusion in Intercultural Communication 1.

Tannen, D. (n.d.). Discourse Analysis—What Speakers Do in Conversation | Linguistic Society of America. Retrieved from https://www.linguisticsociety.org/resource/discourse-analysis-what-speakers-do-conversation

Tatum, B. (2002). The Complexity of Identity: "Who am I?". In Adams, M., Blumenfeld, W. J., Castaneda, R., Hackman, H. W., Peters, M. L., & Zuniga, X. (Eds.), Readings for Diversity and Social Justice. (pp. 9-14) Psychology Press. Retrieved from https://books.google.at/books?id=xltVgiCSFaUC&printsec=frontcover#v=onepage&q&f=false

Ting-Toomey, S. (2012). Communicating Across Cultures (1st ed.). Guilford Press. Retrieved from https://books.google.at/books?id=ndZy_EWD0LUC&printsec=frontcover&source=gbs_ge_summary_r&cad=0#v=onepage&q&f=false

Ting-Toomey, S., & Oetzel, J. G. (2001). Managing Intercultural Conflict Effectively. SAGE. Retrieved from https://books.google.at/books?id=tUTC0FKUhBoC&printsec=frontcover&dq=Managing+Intercultural+Conflict+Effectively.+SAGE.&hl=en&sa=X&ved=2ahUKEwjIy7e8xvXuAhWnAmMBHdXxAB8Q6AEwAHoECAMQAg#v=onepage&q=Managing%20Intercultural%20Conflict%20Effectively.%20SAGE.&f=false

Tracy, K. (2001). Discourse Analysis in Communication. In Schiffrin, D., Tannen, D., & Hamilton, H. E. (Eds), The Handbook of Discourse Analysis. Oxford, UK: Blackwell Publishers Ltd.

Turner, C. (1982). Towards a cognitive redefinition of the social group'. In H. Tajfel (Ed.), Social Identity and Intergroup Relations. Cambridge University Press. (pp. 15-41) Retrieved from https://books.google.at/books?id=q0wFY3Dcu1MC&printsec=frontcover&dq=Tajfel,+H.+(1982).+Social+Identity+and+Intergroup+Relations.&hl=en&sa=X&ved=2ahUKEwjSnLqixfXuAhUoAWMBHVkRBSUQ6AEwAHoECAYQAg#v=onepage&q=Tajfel%2C%20H.%20(1982).%20Social%20Identity%20and%20Intergroup%20Relations.&f=false

Van Hout, T., Pander Maat, H., & De Preter, W. (2011). Writing from news sources: The case of Apple TV. Journal of Pragmatics, 43(7), pp. 1876–1889. https://doi.org/10.1016/j.pragma.2010.09.024

Wodak, R., Johnstone, B., & Kerswill, P. E. (2010). The SAGE Handbook of Sociolinguistics. SAGE. Retrieved from https://books.google.at/books?id=oO3C1xgzZVMC&printsec=frontcover&dq=The+SAGE+Handbook+of+Sociolinguistics.+SAGE.&hl=en&sa=X&ved=2ahUKEwijpIKzxfXuAhUV4OAKHTuxDmYQ6AEwAHoECAUQAg#v=onepage&q=The%20SAGE%20Handbook%20of%20Sociolinguistics.%20SAGE.&f=false

Wolcott, H. F. (1999). Ethnography: A Way of Seeing. Rowman Altamira. Retrieved from https://books.google.at/books?id=nqAuhKBw8x0C&printsec=frontcover&dq=Ethnography:+A+Way+of+Seeing.&hl=en&sa=X&ved=2ahUKEwiJlIi9xfXuAhWPHhQKHVo_AvkQ6AEwAHoECAEQAg#v=onepage&q=Ethnography%3A%20A%20Way%20of%20Seeing.&f=false

List of Figures

Figure 1.1: Identity layers of the CTI 245
Figure 1.2: Patterns of High context and Low context cultures 249
Figure 1.3: Impact of culture on identity 255

Figure 1.4: Code-switching: Case study example 1 259
Figure 1.5: Code-switching: Case study example 2 262

List of Tables

Table 1.1: Perspectives on identity and communication 243